'Top Trumps feuds, endless Sundays of Monopoly, crunched Subbuteo players blobbed together with Uhu – they're all here. But Berry's book is not just about toys, it's about love, families and a thousand happy childhood memories. Brilliant, life-affirming and very, very funny – if you're old enough to buy your own presents this Christmas, then put this book on your list.'
Ally Ross, The Sun

'This book cruelly reminds me of all the brilliant toys that my mum and dad wouldn't let me have, but more kindly points out their limitations. Berry is a grown man who, like so many of his generation, has failed to put away childish things – instead choosing to document them in a hilarious and heart-warming way. As someone who felt the first stirrings of my libido on a Twister mat with Stephanie Hobday in 1979, I was certainly reminded of many happy and confusing times, as well as all the Christmases where I once again failed to receive Operation, Mousetrap or Scalextric.'
Richard Herring

'As someone for whom eagle eyes and gripping hands were central to boyhood, it's nice to see I wasn't alone. This book has stirred up all kinds of nostalgic memories, some that maybe should've been left alone. I've just remembered how much it hurt when I discovered my best friend at uni had more Action Men than me.'
Al Murray

'This book rekindled that forlorn, inner longing that so many men of my age once had for something as simple as Battling Tops. Berry's amazing feat is to show us how powerfully such playthings of the past can whisk you back. I cried when I saw the photos of those Hornby railway sets, I wanted them so badly. You soon realise that toys were us.'
Harry Hill

'Berry's onto something here. A comprehensive catalogue of all that neato stuff the kid up the road had that you didn't. I was never given any of these toys, and frankly I'm still hopping mad about that. This book is part of the healing process. I only wish he'd called it Fuck you, Father Christmas.'
Charlie Brooker, The Guardian

PRESENTS YOU PESTERED YOUR PARENTS FOR

TV CREAM
TOYS

FRIDAY
BOOKS

Jacket and book design
Simon Daley (www.giraffebooks.com)

Additional material
Graham Kibble-White
Phil Norman
and David J Bodycombe, Chris Hughes, Jill Phythian, Ian Tomkinson,
Steve Williams, TJ Worthington, Adam Yates

Additional toy and game collections
Phil Hubbard (www.stuffwelove.co.uk)
Rob Stradling (www.robstradling.blogspot.com)

First published in Great Britain in 2007 by Friday Books
An imprint of The Friday Project Limited
83 Victoria Street, London SW1H 0HW

www.thefridayproject.co.uk
www.fridaybooks.co.uk

ISBN-13   978-1-905548-27-9

British Library Cataloguing in Publication Data
A catalogue record for this book is available from the British Library

Colour Reproduction by Aylesbury Studios (Bromley) Ltd
Printed in Italy by L.E.G.O. Spa
The Publisher's policy is to use paper manufactured from sustainable sources

For Joanna,
who would like her
spare room back

Just what is TV Cream anyway?

In short, it's a website. You want it shorter? Try **www.tv.cream.org**
then. Flung online in 1997 as a memorial to great TV, it has since
snowballed into an online repository of all things retro from the past
four decades – mucho ephemera, therefore, from comics to crisps,
adverts to annuals, films to fashion. Oh, and toys, naturally.

Updated woefully infrequently considering the sheer number
of people who work on it, the website does at least play host to
a couple of regular 'e-zines' and occasional definitive lists of key
pop culture touchstones (top TV themes, popular presenters,
media movers and shakers).

Its slightly sarcastic, often sweary approach has won many
admirers, most of whom have contributed to this book.

Contents

9

Acknowledgements and thanks

Web contributions Margaret Brown, Richard Davies, Chris Diamond, Chris Elligott,
Uncle Feedle, Steve Fisher, Lee Henderson, Don Hilliard, Paul Jones, Robin Lovell,
Gareth Randall, Clive Shaw and many more who didn't leave an intelligible name.

Thanks to Jim Sangster, for spiritual and physical support, drinks and quiz nights
(even if we did lose to Dick Fiddy's team). Clare Christian, Paul Carr, Heather Smith,
Clare Weber, Colette Holden and Salima Hirani for help putting the words together
(some parts unsuitable for children under 3 years). Barry Ryan and Katie Kinnaird at Free
At Last TV for screengrabbing assistance. Stefan Wrzesinski at Xtreme Information for the
advert catalogue. Plus Robert Lawrence, Rob Francis, Andrew Collins, Ian Jones, Jon
Peake, Nick Dimmock, Simon Tyers, Ally Ross, Charlie Brooker – all, one way or another,
keeping the TV Cream from going sour.

How to use this book

The entries in our catalogue of toys and games have been arranged in alphabetical order, so you can either read it in the normal way or just flick through the pages to see if we've missed your favourite. We've also cross-referenced the entries by category, as they would appear in an imaginary uber-Argos, so they sit neatly alongside those others they most closely resemble, regardless of era or importance. This should, in theory, enable you to read the book in a haphazard 'choose your own adventure' style. Judge for yourself how well we've done there.

As well as a comprehensive description of each toy and game, we've also awarded them their own score according to the following ratings:

Born The year when the toy first appeared on shop shelves. Don't hold us to the dates, though, particularly anything that was invented pre-twentieth century. You'd be surprised how many of these old toys are still in production today.

Batteries Not the type or number required but the sheer volume of batteries consumed. Thus, board games largely rate 'none' but those AA-hungry handhelds rank highly on this scale.

Players Again, not the intended number of players as depicted on the box-lids of most games, but the ideal number of players to guarantee optimum enjoyment. In many cases, solo play was more rewarding than sharing with others (or vice versa).

Breakage The likelihood and ease of either beyond-repair toy damage or one of those essential pieces getting lost. The higher the rating, the less liable we are to find one in pristine condition ever again.

Ads The effectiveness of the TV and magazine industries' efforts in boosting the 'must have' nature of each toy. Watch out for memory-jogging telly screenshots accompanying some of our entries.

Envy The sheer desirability of each toy, usually depending on whether or not we knew someone who had it (and whether or not they were willing to lend it out or swap it with us).

eBayability A rough idea of how rare the toy is nowadays on the open market. If it scores highly here and you own one, sell it immediately and buy yourself a sports car.

Overall satisfaction This one speaks for itself really – an estimation of the legendary qualities (or otherwise) of each toy in the cold, harsh light of day.

Plus, keep an eye out for mentions of what we've decided to call 'the competition'. Those were the knock-off, cash-in clones of popular toys and games usually bought for you by mistake by your well-meaning Auntie Sylvia.

Have we missed a crucial toy or game? Add your suggestions to the ongoing compendium at www.tv.cream.org

Introduction

'When I was a child, I spake as a child, I understood as a child, I thought as a child: but when I became a man, I put away childish things.'

So wrote St Paul in his Letter to the Corinthians (Chapter 13, Verse 11). Wise words from a wise man. Or so you'd think, it being the New Testament and all. It's just that, when we came to put away our own childish things, we thought 'Hang on, there's a complete *Matchbox Race And Chase* in here, and a *Big Trak* with working transport. And there's a first-edition *My Little Pony*. We could get quite a bit for that on eBay. Let's not stick 'em up in the loft just yet, eh?'[1]

Back in 2004, TV Cream – the UK's most popular and award-winning nostalgia website[2] – celebrated the top one hundred toys of yesteryear, from the tiniest 50p rubber novelty to the many bulky Bakelite candidates that vied

Subbuteo Football folk, us

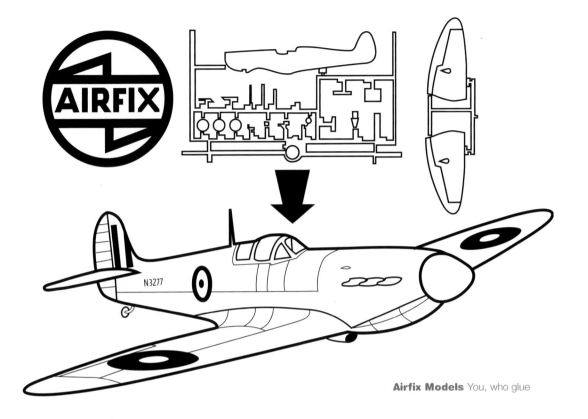

Airfix Models You, who glue

for hallowed 'main present' status at birthdays and Christmases. Or rather, we celebrated those toys that were lusted after but never actually received because – time and again – parents would mistake their offspring's fervour for overexcitement and ignore the repeated pleas, the letters to Santa or the tantrums.

You see, we used to want for things too. Before Amazon wish-lists, online ordering and 'add to basket' buttons, we relied on the catalogues: big, chunky, glossy bi-annual volumes with a dozen or so pages at the back brimming with

1 None of this is true. In fact, in common with much of this book, it's an old stand-up routine we pinched (in this case, with permission, from the very lovely Richard Herring). We're hoping that the quote from The Bible is out of copyright. Mind you, what the hell does 'spake' mean? We can't find that on our *Speak & Spell*.

2 The award was Yahoo! Find Of The Year 2003 (they found us after six years, bless 'em). What's with all this 'we' business? Well, we'll come to that in a bit. In the mean time, get used to these footnotes; the book is riddled with them. They're the paper equivalent of a director's commentary.

Armatron No limb-its

toys, games, crafts and novelties. Special wishing books just for kids: Littlewoods, Kays, Grattan, Freemans, Marshall Ward, Great Universal, Argos. They were our Internet. That was where we learned to 'browse', circling toy after toy with red felt-tip, carefully planning imaginary shopping trips but never really believing we'd go on them.

Never forget, there are entire generations for whom giant stores like Hamleys and Toys 'R' Us were unimaginable fantasies on a par with space cars, food pills and robot butlers. The rear sections of the catalogues were a 2D vision of some incredible future where thousands of toys might be gathered in one place in a tableau of pastel colours. It was a hypnotic, limbo-state where girls were subtly encouraged to take up crafts and think about a life of domesticity, while boys were pointed towards combat toys and things that could be kicked.

Then, as we grew up, we also started to explore some of the other pages (and yes, thanks, the adolescent jokes about the underwear section have already been done – in 1996, by Frank Skinner, so let's leave it there, eh?). Girls tended to graduate to jewellery and – for the poor are always with us – occasionally the clothes. As far as boys were concerned, however, it was usually the digital watches that were first to attract attention, followed shortly by the posh 'scientific' calculators. Nowadays, it's all mobile phones, ringtones and 3G video clips.[3] But what is a mobile phone if not a portable toy for grown-ups?

---

3 Gawd, how dated is that sentence going to look in two years' time? Don't get us wrong, we're not trying to be curmudgeonly or wring our hands at 'the youth of today' (although, c'mon, they really don't know they're born, do they?). There are plenty of future classic toys and games for twenty-first-century children. They'll just have to write their own nostalgia book, that's all.

Back in what we fondly call the Cream era,[4] the summer holidays were longer and hotter, sweets were cheaper and bigger, and toys were there to be played with – abused, battered... broken, even. They weren't bought as an investment, to be squirreled away in storage for collectors and completists, or auctioned off thirty years later, 'mint on card', 'brand new in box' or 'factory sealed'. The toys you'll find in this book are the ones that had us wide-eyed

Astro Wars
Loving the aliens

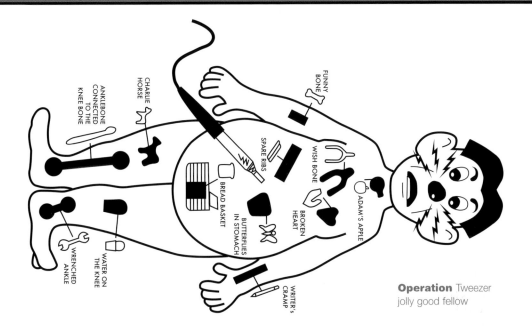

ANKLEBONE CONNECTED TO THE KNEE BONE

CHARLIE HORSE

FUNNY BONE

SPARE RIBS

WISH BONE

BREAD BASKET

BUTTERFLIES IN STOMACH

BROKEN HEART

ADAM'S APPLE

WRENCHED ANKLE

WATER ON THE KNEE

WRITER'S CRAMP

Operation Tweezer
jolly good fellow

with anticipation, tearing down the stairs at five in the morning on Christmas Day; the toys we hoped to find among a mountain of wrapped-up boxes; the toys we'd rip recklessly from the packaging and put straight to work.

What we've tried to do is capture at least some of that experience[5] but without being too earnest about it. They are only toys, after all. On the one hand, there's the catalogues and, on the other, there's cataloguing (in the most dry, joyless way imaginable). We hope the next couple of hundred pages will illuminate the difference. Along the way, there'll be some mildly interesting trivia (did you know that the original Sooty was just a mass-produced Chad Valley bear puppet?), some weak observational jokes (such as: why is it that

---

4 Your own Cream era is the period in your life that created the most vivid and enjoyable memories, the ones that conjure an indescribable yummy feeling and that don't need to be validated by Kate Thornton gurning away on some godawful TV talking heads compilation. Alternatively it's that year – any time from the '60s to the '90s – when you hit ten years old. Whichever definition suits you best... Watch out for 1977, though. That's the year Star Wars (and a flood of merchandise spin-offs) changed the toy business forever.

5 This book is a collection of shared experiences. No single person can claim them. You can't claim them. Steve Berry can't claim them. Even TV Cream itself can't claim them. They belong to us all. Just look at the list of contributors for one thing! The toy and game floor of TV Cream Towers is inhabited by a sort of gestalt creature. So, because we're all in this together, this book has been written in the first person plural (or, as our Queen would prefer, the royal 'we').

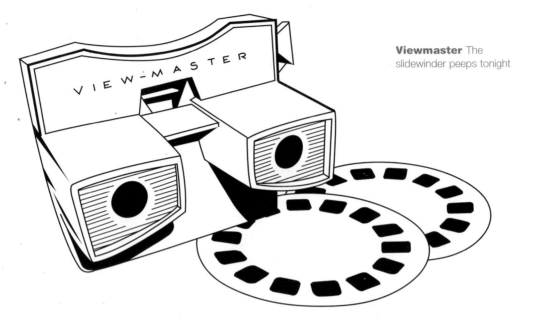

Monopoly is only made by one company?) and far too many references to Doctor Who. If that's not your cup of tea, we'll chuck in some tortuously extended metaphors, just for good measure.

Why? Because what we're trying to do is reclaim our childhoods, like so much silt from the fens. Rising from the wetlands of that original online top one hundred, this book examines in detail the seven score or more toys we most yearned for as youngsters (plus a good couple of dozen others that get a mention in passing). These are the peerless playthings of a nation's youth, the ones that encapsulate a time and place to which we can never return, no matter how many mini-desktop versions The Gadget Shop churns out. Neither a definitive history of the toy industry, nor a stat-packed collector's price guide, TV Cream Toys is the Christmas morning you should have had when you were young enough to appreciate it.

And that's it really. All you need to know to use this book. So hold firm, St Paul, as it's now time to unpack those childish things for one last circuit around the living room carpet.

The toys

'A La Cart Kitchen'
Training the housewives of tomorrow

Born	1984
Batteries	None
Players	👤
Breakage	🍷🍷🍷
Ads	▣▣▣▣▣
Envy	🏆🏆🏆🏆🏆
eBayability	🖱🖱🖱🖱
Overall satisfaction	👍👍👍👍

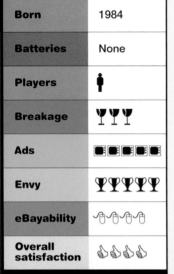

This is how it begins – with a none-too-subtle reinforcement of gender stereotypes for the *Daily Mail* readers of the future. Many are the generations of little girls that were saddled with 'mini-mum' plastic ironing boards and carpet sweepers from an early age (all the better to brain your little brother with), and many the house that was cluttered with all the paraphernalia of pretend cleaning without any real cleaning actually getting done.

Reminding us once again that a woman's place is in the home, this particular primary-coloured party-pooper was a complete kitchen set comprising oven, hob, sink and, erm, washing machine on a handy moveable cart – hence it's 'A La Cart', geddit? Quite why the more predictable inclusion of a kitchen fridge was omitted is anyone's guess.[1] However, the toy was successful in ingraining itself on the nation's collective memory primarily because of an extremely enduring TV advert. Briefly, this featured a small girl who got up unfeasibly early in order to potter around for a few hours, knocking together bits of plastic in a brisk but pointless way and eventually arriving in the parental bedroom to feed her dad cold baked beans and arctic roll from a plastic saucepan ('Wake up Daddy, breakfast's ready!'). He at least had the unshaven grace to pretend to look happy – we can only imagine how a genuine parent might've reacted.

Although this sorry display surely says something rather serious about the division of household labour in the late twentieth century, we're not quite sure exactly what (although we'd love to know the whereabouts of 'Mummy'). Besides, if that child is so keen on household chores, surely 'Daddy' can find a chimney to shove her up?

Manufacturer Bluebird continued to expand its range of authentic, though slightly strangely juxtaposed, culinary workstations on wheels with the Walford-inspired *'East End Market Stall'*,[2] one side a fruit-and-veg trader's stand, the other a burger bar. All the major food groups well-represented there, then. Conspicuous cuckoo in the nest this time was a bright-red telephone stuck in the middle. Even in those pre-mobile days, we can't envisage a market trader installing a landline on their trolley. Presumably they used it to phone in bulk orders of beans and jam roll to the cash and carry.

Bluebird's founder, Torquil Norman, retired in 1994 a multi-millionaire. He has since spent £30m turning London's Camden Roundhouse Theatre into a *Big Yellow Teapot*.

See also Mr Frosty, Petite Super International Typewriter, Girl's World

---

1 Check out the miniature branded groceries, though. Daz, Mr Kipling's cakes, Ryvita. Yum!
2 The inverted commas were actually part of the name. Not so with the *Bluebird Café Royale*, however, despite the flamboyant use of French. Brands represented in this deliberately unisex fast-food restaurant training kit included Heinz Beans, Saxa Salt and Bisto. The eggs and sausages supplied were made of plastic, much like in yer real greasy spoon.

Action Man
Military mannequin

Born	1966
Batteries	None
Players	👤👤
Breakage	🍷🍷🍷
Ads	▣▣▣▫
Envy	🏆🏆🏆
eBayability	🖱🖱🖱🖱🖱
Overall satisfaction	👍👍👍

See also *Cyborgs, ROM the Space Knight, Six Million Dollar Man, Barbie*

There's nothing wrong with boys playing with dolls!

But just in case there's the slightest chance that doing so could turn 'em a bit... y'know, make sure the dolls are butch soldier types who look good in a buzzcut and military uniform.[1] So went the thinking, we assume, when Palitoy imported America's *GI Joe* and rebranded him *Action Man* for Brit kids in the – ahem – swinging '60s.

Initially available with only painted-on hair and combat fatigues, the range was soon augmented by a whole wardrobe of snazzy outfits (including frogman, pilot, sailor, traffic cop and Red Indian)[2] and cybernetic extensions to Mr Man's physiognomy ('gripping' hands, 'real' hair, 'eagle' eyes). And, much like *Barbie*, the big fella got his own fleet of personal transports – although not for him the pink limo treatment. Our favourite was actually the fairly unsophisticated, thumb-operated backpack-copter (which enabled us to re-enact the best bit of *Thunderball*), although it must've been

---

1 Yes, there were wars, and violence, and bloodshed, and tea, and medals. But at least we were *learning* something. Military history, for one. The Paras, US Marines, SS Stormtroopers, or (dialing down the testosterone) the RNLI. *Action Man* had proper guns that actually looked like they might hurt people. Nowadays, he's either a neutered

Extreme iPod Eco-Warrior or wishy-washy *Skateboard Surf Ninja*.
2 Altogether now: 'It's fun to stay at the YMCA.' *Action Man* never ran out of outfits as long as your granny had enough green wool.
3 Palitoy's token-collecting system meant you had to send off for exclusive extras (on

cool to have owned its full-size army hospital helicopter cousin. There were, we recall, two tank varieties (a Scorpion and, erm, whatever the bigger one was called), a jeep or two, plus inflatable and outboard motor-powered dinghies.

Frankly, there wasn't anywhere our hero couldn't go, except perhaps somewhere that required him to stand on an uneven surface (a deep-pile carpet, anywhere on grass). Basic instability problems could be avoided with the application of a child's fertile imagination (which would require that members of the Grenadier Guards always adopt an insouciant, leaning-against-a-wall attitude to their sentry duties, or that the 21st Lancers conduct their parades lying down). In the '70s, more poseable joints were added to the basic model, including one around the neck that enabled Action to adopt a 'sniper' pose with one or more rifles from his impressive armoury.

Endless battles could be enacted with this almost limitless selection of plastic weaponry in a war of attrition the '80s superpowers would've boggled at (particularly given the unusual prospect of witnessing a fight between *Talking Commando Action Man* and *Captain Zargon*). Rumour has it that classic *Dr Who* adventure *The War Games* was written entirely while Patrick Troughton's young sons were pitching German paratroopers into combat with the Queen's Horse Guards.

The biggest hostilities *Action Man* encountered were, of course, brought about by his owners. Sad to say, *Action Man* abuse was rife in the Cream era. Bangers, matches, caps, magnifying glasses, fireworks – all were employed in creating 'realistic' battle scars to show off to friends or maiming him beyond recognition.

So, although we know that nearly everybody owned an *Action Man*, the important thing is that everyone we knew wanted more.[3] By virtue of the fact that the combined forces of our street could never amass a platoon of even *Dad's Army* strength, *Action Man* remains on our wish list.

offer in the '70s were a Canadian Mountie outfit or a pit-bull). Then there were the additional figures: *Tom Stone*, the first – gasp! – black *Action Man*; the *Intruder*, a muscle-bound, dwarf Liam Gallagher-alike enemy with white eyes and grabbing arms; and *Atomic Man*, with bionic limbs, plastic clicky pacemaker and a light where his left eye should've been.

Airfix Kits
Inch high club

Born	1952
Batteries	None
Players	👤
Breakage	🍷 🍷 🍷 🍷 🍷
Ads	▪️ ▪️ ▪️
Envy	🏆 🏆 🏆
eBayability	🖱️ 🖱️ 🖱️
Overall satisfaction	👍 👍

See also *Hornby Railway Set, LEGO, Flight Deck*

Rather like a box of cotton-wool buds that warns 'Do not insert into ear canal' and the punter replies incredulously: 'But what else are they for?' So it was with Airfix – loudly proclaimed to be 'display models' and not 'toys', and yet toys they so obviously were. Paint? Bah! We wanted to play with the bloody thing, not wait overnight while the Humbrol enamel dried on the still-unassembled pieces! Even the decals were an annoyance.

But, oh, there's a word. Decals.

It's hard to imagine a time when we hadn't heard of them. A time, perhaps, when we could see an RAF livery without immediately picturing one. A time before we soaked one in a bowl of warm water, slid it off its backing paper and placed it on the wing of a Spitfire or a Wellington Bomber.

For the purposes of this entry, we're limiting our examination to model planes. Because it was only the model planes that came in such a ridiculously varied range of scales and classes. Because you couldn't hang a miniature replica vintage Darracq from a piece of fishing line thumbtacked to the ceiling. Because the big ships had annoyingly fiddly tacking rigging and plastic sails. And because the planes had a truly aspirational hierarchy (which we seem to recall was based largely around the number of moving parts. Pretty much all the model cars had proper moving wheels, but it was only the bigger and badder model aircraft that included moving propellers, rotating gun-turrets and tyres, or fully opening bomb-bays and cockpits). Therefore, they win.

The decals, of course, were one of many hobby-threatening booby-traps designed to scupper your enjoyment, getting forever crinkled or folded before they could be applied properly. Here's another: polystyrene cement – which could be guaranteed to coagulate into crusty white flakes all over your fingers and tabletop without ever acting as a useful plastic adhesive.[1]

Worse still was discovering a missing part. You then had to fill out a flimsy form, send it off to Airfix and wait an interminable amount of time for the spare to arrive in the post.[2] But the biggest disappointment with any *Airfix Kit* was the huge disparity between the size of the box and the size of the finished model. We're looking at you, Hawker Harrier.

---

[1] It was also handy for adding an unwanted 'frosted' bathroom window effect to the previously clear cockpit covers.

[2] Dick Emery, comedian and then president of the Airfix Modellers Club, ran his expanded polystyrene empire in the pages of British comics. In January 1975, he rather excitingly revealed the launch of the company's new 1:12 scale construction kit of Anne Boleyn. That'll get 'em gluing, Dick!

Armatron
Programmable robotic arm

While the foreign car factories were laying off staff in favour of this toy's older brothers, kids across the land were celebrating their new-found ability to remotely move objects around the kitchen table. By twiddling around a couple of joystick levers on the base, *Armatron*'s various shoulder, wrist and elbow joints could be manoeuvred to pick up anything within it's admittedly limited reach. In theory. Anything slightly more delicate than the plastic canisters, cones and globes included (an egg, say) would break under pressure between the rubberised jaws, and so any notions of performing David Banner-style laboratory experiments were soon similarly shattered.

Although the lab-coated ginger kids on the box photos hinted otherwise, *Armatron* was actually intended as a race-against-time game of skill and coordination. Bright-orange 'energy-level' indicators on the console acted as a kind of countdown: when the gauge reached zero ('total discharge'), *Armatron* turned itself off. Although this probably conserved some of that D-cell battery life, it wasn't half annoying if you were just seconds away from tightly gripping on to your sleeping cat's tail.

Armatron was manufactured in Singapore by Tomy and imported by Radio Shack, inspiring loads of knock-off versions in the '80s.[1] A veritable miracle of engineering, it shipped with a single electric motor and a mass of nylon gears and clutches throughout the entire base and arm (as anyone who opened it up would discover). A late addition to the range was the *Mobile Armatron*, which came on caterpillar tracks (though the remote control wire was only half a metre long). Quite what this added to the game is anyone's guess.

Robotics enthusiasts delighted in 'hacking' the toy (i.e. 'tricking it out' with motion sensors or a steam-powered engine), which makes a complete one hard to track down these days. In any case, poorer kids had to make do with the manually ratchet-operated *Robot Arm*, a Terminator-esque *Robot Hand* or *Robot Claw*, each of which – though less impressive – could be secreted up the sleeve of a Parka to aid in the pretence of the owner having been transformed into some kind of futuristic human cyborg. Pop into Hamleys and you'll find a new version of these going by the name *Armatron*. But we know the truth.

Born	1982
Batteries	🔋🔋🔋🔋
Players	👤
Breakage	🍷🍷🍷
Ads	📺📺
Envy	🏆🏆🏆🏆🏆
eBayability	🖱🖱
Overall satisfaction	👍👍

1 Radio Shack eventually acquired the manufacturing rights and re-released the toy in the '90s under the new name *Super Armatron*, even though it was mechanically exactly the same.

See also *Tasco Telescope, Electronic Project, Slinky*

Backgammon
Pork-soundalike dice 'n' counters game

Born	pre-C20
Batteries	None
Players	👥
Breakage	🍷🍷
Ads	▣
Envy	🏆
eBayability	🖱
Overall satisfaction	👍👍

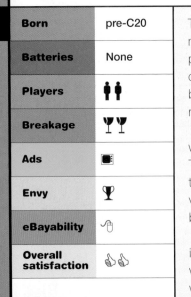

There are two reasons why this venerable strategy game leapfrogs those other most austere of board games, chess and draughts, into our list. First, its sheer perverseness. There it was – the backgammon board – always hiding on the other side of the travel draughts, stubbornly resisting comprehension. Not for backgammon the patchwork of squares. Oh no! This thing needed a whole new board with 'quadrants' and a 'bar' and everything.

Second, the whiff of maturity, the wisdom of ages. *Backgammon* carried the weight of millennia and, though we didn't know it at the time, we could sense it. The ancient Egyptians, the Byzantine emperors of Mesopotamia and now us – the great unwashed of suburbia – all staring at the pointy triangle things. At the very least, it proffered a vacant seat at the big table – a proper conversation between adult and child as the rules were explained.

Yet also it was accessible, but not too indiscriminate. Unlike the untouchable ivory chess set in your best mate's dad's study, you could get your hands dirty with the backgammon counters. Those green, snot-sleeved draughts players with their petulant 'crown me!'s kept their distance. *Backgammon* had a vocabulary of its own: bearing off, kibitzers, the gin position, double bumps and mandatory beavers... Hang on: maybe they *were* just making this up as they went along after all.

Oh, and we lied up there. There was a third reason why we wanted a backgammon of our own: the huge surge in popularity it underwent in the 1970s. Rather like snooker in the '80s and football in the '90s, backgammon suddenly became trendy. Leading players jetted from tournament to tournament, wrote bestselling books (about backgammon, obviously) and made the front pages in 'my hotel sex-romp roast hell' tabloid headlines.[1]

However, we come not to damn the game but to praise its Cream-era maker. Before Paul Heaton and his mates were a twinkle in a skiffle-humming Hull milkman's eye, the name 'House Martin' was already a stamp of quality thanks to the Hackney-based games factory. Specialising in no-nonsense, phlegmatic renderings of popular post-war games, House Martin unashamedly embossed every box with the legend 'Made in England'. No wonder they went under.

See also Othello, Connect Four, Yahtzee

1 One of Graham Greene's last novels, *The Captain and the Enemy*, is about a boy who is won from his father by a con man in a game of backgammon. Possibly one to omit from the bedtime story selection for the little ones, there.

Barbie
Whore next door[1]

Born	1959
Batteries	None
Players	👫
Breakage	🍷🍷🍷🍷
Ads	▪▪▪▪
Envy	🏆🏆🏆🏆
eBayability	🖱🖱🖱🖱🖱
Overall satisfaction	👍👍👍

See also Sindy, Rainbow Brite, Girl's World

Barbie had been knocking around since the arse-end of the '50s in one perma-tanned form or other, but we're most interested in the so-called 'aspirational' late '80s when manufacturer Mattel realised they could sell the dolls as collectors' items as well as mere playthings. Or, as the marketing speak of the day put it: to improve profitability and maintain consistent revenue streams, Mattel began a strategy of maximising core brands while simultaneously identifying new brands with core potential. Ah yes! There's the insipid corporate message at the heart of your Dream Glow Barbie.

But then she's always been one for the commercial tie-up, has Barbie. From the days of her first-run adverts during the Mickey Mouse Club to Barbie couture and those straight-to-DVD CGI-saturated movies, she's monetised every innovation, trend and fashion in search of global dominance. In fact, she'd probably use a word like 'monetise' without blushing. If she wasn't wearing so much blusher in the first place.

Fair play to the girl, though – always impossibly glamorous and immaculately turned out, Barbie has proved to be a role model to a million all-American, body-conscious Diet Coke heads. And she sure shifts some units, taking upward of three billion dollars over the counter each year.[2] What could be more upwardly mobile than that?

As Mattel's trademarked mission statement solemnly avows, Barbie is 'more than a doll'. What exactly she wants to be, though, is still unclear. Model, gymnast, fashion designer, rock star – Barbie's had a punt at every job under the sun, presumably packing each one in after a few days in floods of tears before settling down in front of Trisha with a packet of milk-chocolate digestives to 'consider her options'.[3]

Call her anything you like, but don't call her unpatriotic. There is a Barbie doll in a time capsule due to be opened in 2076 to celebrate 300 years of the American Revolution: she is dressed in a stars-and-stripes dress featuring a line of soldiers in uniform on the hem. Cut her down the middle and she'd have the letters 'U', 'S' and 'A' stencilled through her like a stick of rock. Blow her head off and the blood on the wall behind would be red, white and blue.

---

1 Just as a matter of record, we'd like to point out that no-one at TV Cream thinks that Barbie is a whore (nor, indeed, that she lives next door). We're just being flippant, based on perceived notions of the doll's proportions as being just that bit too anatomically unrealistic. Christ, we're only three words in and already there's a footnote.

2 Initial profits from Barbie allowed Mattel to become a PLC in 1960. Goodbye garage-based workshop, hello stockholder-pleasing listings on the Fortune 500.

3 In recent years, Barbie's fortunes have seesawed, as she suffered declining sales in the face of the Spice Girl-indebted Bratz dolls.

Battling Tops
Gyroscopic gladiators

Battling Tops? Why, 'tis a grand olde European folk game, sir, as famously depicted in sixteenth-century paintings by Brueghel and his ilk. However, we suspect his *Battling Tops* weren't housed in a blue-plastic arena, presumably didn't go by such wrestling-ring monikers as Super Sam, Tricky Nicky, Twirling Tim, Dizzy Dan or, erm, Smarty Smitty, and certainly were far from Ideal.

Yep! Since 1968, the company that invited you to wind up *Evel Knievel* had been dishing up more red-plastic crank-powered fun with their repackaging of an old wooden favourite. With defiantly un-medieval box art depicting various '50s-type kids and their worryingly Barry Cryer-like dad enraptured by the centrifugal tournament taking place under their noses, this was the tabletop arena game to end all tabletop arena games. Wind the spindle with string, give a yank on the starting cord and away you go!

A similar game, *Space Attack*, was an air-hockey variant on the rotating theme. Crank the red handle with all your tiny might and stop the spinning top being knocked into a trough with a plastic slider. Or, as they put it, 'Fight off the lightning alien attacks!' The 'space' theme was provided by a piss-poor 'galactic' backdrop on the field of play, with a pointless concentric red ring design overlaid. They might as well have written 'Look, it's in space, all right? Use your bloody imagination, you ungrateful little sods!' and been done with it. Ideal at least went the whole hog and – in the wake of *Star Wars* mania – launched a rebranded *Battling Spaceships* game, which also included some extra, *Monopoly*-inspired round-the-board progression.

Space Attack and *Battling Spaceships* shared one gameplay drawback – the frequency with which one of the spinning combatants would be knocked right out of the ring. Frequently the victorious top would be the one that found its way under the radiator, still merrily buzzing away on the lino long after the rest had limped to a standstill.

Although the original is still out there, produced under licence from Mattel,[1] no additional TV Cream points will be awarded for spotting that this game and its various spin-offs over the years have left us with the legacy that is *Beyblades*. Now those things really do look like you can take someone's eye out with them. They're like Chinese throwing stars. Seriously, they've even got 'blade' in the name. Why hasn't someone reported them to Trading Standards?

Born	1968
Batteries	None
Players	👤👤👤👤
Breakage	🍷🍷🍷🍷🍷
Ads	📺📺
Envy	🏆🏆🏆
eBayability	🖱🖱🖱
Overall satisfaction	👍👍

See also *Crossfire, Raving Bonkers Fighting Robots, Hungry Hippos*

Space Attack
On the rebound

---

1 You won't be astounded if we tell you that the arena of this new game is bleedin' tiny now, will you? This isn't just a case of 'the memory cheats' – we know Wagon Wheels and Creme Eggs are the same size and our hands just got bigger. But with these games, they're deliberately shrinking our childhood!

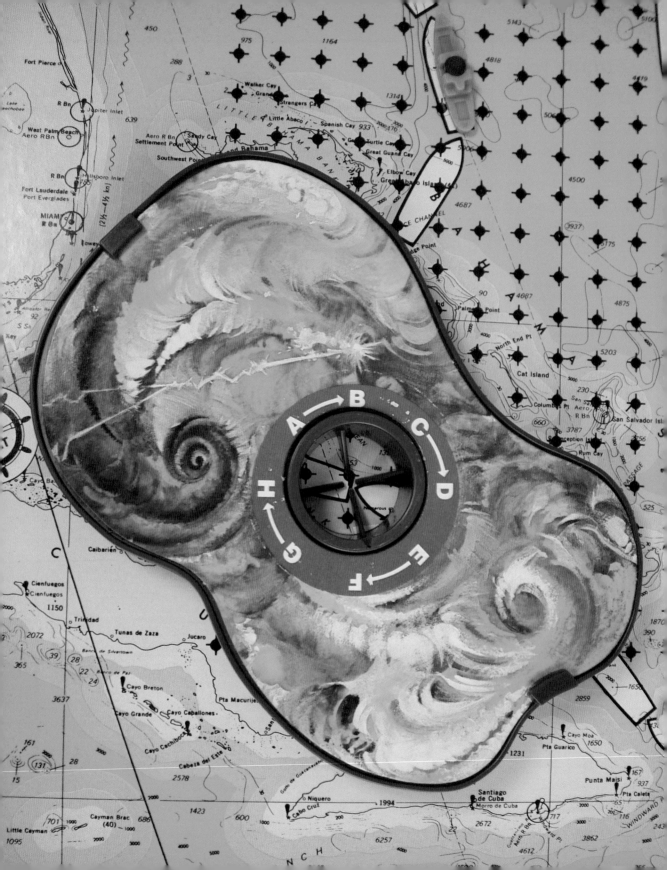

Bermuda Triangle
Makes people disappear

Way before *The X Files*, back in the mysterious 1980s, part-work magazines such as *The Unexplained* and telly shows like *The Crazy World of Arthur C. Clarke*[1] – he invented satellites, you know – cashed in on our periodic fascination for paranormal phenomena. Strange how, in cycles of almost exactly 20 years, ESP, spontaneous combustion, spoon-bending and all that bollocks inexplicably suckers in an entirely new generation. One might say that the regularity itself is almost... supernatural. Woooo!

Further back in the mists of time, in 1974 to be exact, Charles Berlitz wrote a book called *The Bermuda Triangle*. Then, in 1981 – by complete coincidence – Barry Manilow had a Top 20 hit of the same name. Spooky, huh? In the intervening years, MB had cashed in handsomely with this ships 'n' storm cloud ludo variant.

Yet even at a young age, when our experience of triangles was limited to early maths lessons, school band practice and Quality Street,[2] we spotted the one thing lacking from this game. The board was square. The cloud was – erm – acoustic-guitar-shaped (and we'd love to have been sitting in on the design meeting for that one). Even the 'shipping route' around the game was just some random meandering.

That aside (and ignoring the very fundamental imprudence in setting up a merchant-shipping operation in the middle of an area renowned for strange disappearances), it was a fun game. Move your fleet around the board, trading for bananas, oil, timber and sugar, and try to avoid the ominous, foreboding, magnetic cloud that wants to eat your ships. Simple.

Various 'spoiler' tactics could be employed (blocking your fellow players' ships from each dock), but none was more effective than bribing whoever was moving the cloud to spin it just that bit too fast, thus preventing the ominous 'click' of magnet on magnet and keeping you in the game for another go. Many *Top Trumps* and sticker collections would unaccountably vanish under the table when the *Bermuda Triangle* rolled into town.

Incidentally, theories that the strange occurrences of the real Bermuda Triangle are caused by aliens sucking boats and planes out of the sky with giant magnets have not yet been disproved. But then, as the great Arthur C. Clarke himself said, 'Your guess is as good as mine.'[3]

See also Up Periscope, Computer Battleship, Chutes Away

Born	1976
Batteries	None
Players	👤👤👤👤
Breakage	🍷🍷🍷
Ads	▪▪
Envy	🏆🏆🏆🏆
eBayability	🖱
Overall satisfaction	👍👍👍

---

1 You must remember it, surely? No? Oh, alright, it was actually called *Arthur C. Clarke's Mysterious World*, but we'd love to have seen the auld fella fetch up on *Top of the Pops* singing 'Fire'. That would've been fab!

2 The green ones. You can also buy posh chocs in triangle-shaped boxes. Toblerone doesn't count – technically, it's a prism.

3 He's the president of the H.G. Wells fan club, you know.

Big Trak
Futuristic battle tank and apple cart

Born	1979
Batteries	◖◖●●◖◖
Players	🧍
Breakage	🍷🍷
Ads	▣▣▣▣▣
Envy	🏆🏆🏆🏆🏆
eBayability	🖱🖱🖱🖱
Overall satisfaction	👍👍👍

Resembling nothing more than a vehicle from *Captain Scarlet and the Mysterons* redesigned by Clive Sinclair, *Big Trak* was controlled, as the presenters of *Tomorrow's World* breathlessly related, by that all important 'silicon chip'.[1] With just a few taps on the keypad, this fully programmable beast could be instructed to move and turn in different directions, fire up its 'photon canon' and make a couple of modish electronic noises. It was, of course, used mainly to frighten the family pet. Pretty good value for £20.

The novelty was that it was ostensibly capable of navigating a path around cumbersome household objects – assuming no-one had actually moved any of them while you were busily punching in the required sequence of movements – usually a case of trial and error. *Big Trak* worked best when its route avoided shag-pile carpet, inclines and anywhere outdoors. According to the manual, programming distance travelled was calculated in noncommittal units of 'roughly 13 inches', while the angle of rotation 'may not be enough to make the turn you want. Or it may be too much.' You want vagueness? MB Electronics delivered it in spades (which themselves were probably of wildly indeterminate size).

Used in conjunction with the *Big Trak Transporter* (yours for only another £15), *Big Trak* was rumoured to be able to ferry objects around the house – maximum load: 'about one pound'.[2] Promised innovations that never materialised were voice synthesis and additional accessories (there was a mysterious unassigned keypad button marked 'IN' on the keypad for just this purpose).

Not to be outdone, Kenner Toys came up with *Radarc*, another twenty-first-century-esque remote-controlled tank. The gimmick with *Radarc* was that, instead of being programmable, it was operated by 'muscle control' – a radio transmitter that strapped to your forearm, with buttons on the inside that made contact as you worked your hand and wrist (stop sniggering at the back!).[3]

However, with six chunky traction tyres, sticky labels 'to add exciting detail' and a camp little signature tune that played before and after every, erm, motion, *Big Trak* was much coveted and seldom seen – the dictionary definition of toy envy.

See also *Star Bird, Speak & Spell, Armatron*

---

1 A 4-bit Texas Instruments TMS1000 microcontroller running at approximately 0.2 MHz, chip fans. That's just 64 bytes of RAM to you.
2 A fabulously complicated and tortuous process for carrying out otherwise simple household tasks? Clearly this was a toy aimed at men.
3 There was also *TOBOR*, a robot from Schaper that looked like a cross between R2D2 and Darth Vader, was operated by a 'transmitter' that was nothing more than a tin clicker, and was utterly defeated by any carpeted surface.

Big Yellow Teapot
It's big and it's yellow, but there's no tea in it

Born	1981
Batteries	None
Players	👤👤
Breakage	🍷🍷🍷
Ads	▣▣▣▣
Envy	🏆🏆🏆🏆
eBayability	🖱
Overall satisfaction	👍👍👍

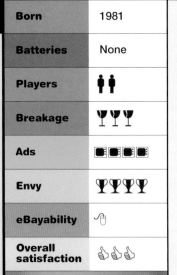

Now-defunct toy manufacturer Bluebird was founded on two very solid principles. Small girls like doll's houses. Small girls also like plastic tea sets for serving cups of invisible tea to their dollies.[1] Then someone fell into a filing cabinet at the office Christmas party and came up with the bizarre idea of crossbreeding the two. Yes, this was a doll's house, but made of yellow plastic and shaped like a huge teapot.

Why was this? No reason was ever given. The house was inhabited by small plastic peg-like people (somewhere between stunted *Playmobil* folk and *Weebles* without the wobble) with welded-together legs, all the better to slide them down the chimney or make them ride round and round in the roundabout-cum-teapot lid (the latter 20 seconds of entertainment – 'lots of fun for everyone' – also forming the most memorable moment of the accompanying ad). This delightful pied-à-terre was furnished throughout with a small quantity of monolithic red and blue teacup chairs and tables, with the further appointment of additional decor simply printed on cardboard walls (where it floated slightly above the floor in an unconvincing fashion).

A rival effort came courtesy of Palitoy, whose *Family Treehouse* obeyed the same basic design principles and yet had the added bonus of a trunk-based elevator (which presumably attracted a better class of tenant than the average council-estate teapot). Another was Matchbox's *School Boot*, adding a whiff of academia to the old 'woman who lived in a shoe' routine and thus robbing it of much appeal, although there was at least a variety of playground-themed accessories.[2] Live-in chimneys and pumpkins caught the tail end of the trend.

Basically, *Big Yellow* was a doll's house for the *Duplo* generation: those who required everything to be large, unbreakable and safe to chew, yet were still innocent enough to refrain from shoving the little plastic people down (or up) the cat for a change (or indeed, trying to create a teapot tropical monsoon by actually pouring boiling water on them).

See also *Weebles, My Little Pony, 'A La Cart Kitchen'*

1 If you were unlucky enough to be a boy and wanted one of these? No chance. You'd get boxing gloves instead and a stern talking-to from Dad.

2 Matchbox had another crack at real estate with the *Mushroom Playhouse*, a four-floor fungi flat, but Bluebird had already moved on. Their mobile *Big Red Fun Bus* continued the primary-coloured fun. Sadly, the property market collapsed before the range could be completed with the release of the adult-oriented *Big Blue Hotel*.

Binatone TV Master
Blip... blip... blip... blip...

The *Binatone TV Master* was the first computer-game experience witnessed by many Cream-era households, nestling as it did in the Argos catalogue alongside the portable black and white TVs (with which it shared a parasitic relationship). Radio Rentals would even lend you one for the night. Aeons before kids sat hypnotised in front of the latest *Grand Theft Auto* clone, sacrificing great chunks of their lives to completing the next level, this slab of circuit-based entertainment dragged us in off the streets to watch a box-shaped pixel zigzag its way across the screen. What a choking irony, therefore, that this gatekeeper of the soon-to-be-ushered-in console era attempted to mimic a selection of sports games.

Pre-SCART cable connections, the *Binatone* would have you scrabbling behind the family telly to plug in the RF aerial lead. That is, if you were lucky enough – in the days before a plasma screen in every room – to be allowed to use it in the first place. Typically, you'd be pushed to squeeze in a game of *Binatone* tennis between dinner and the start of *Nationwide* (and only then if your parents didn't want to watch the *News At 5.45*). Otherwise, play meant sacrificing valuable *Swap Shop* or *TISWAS* time – oh, how we wished for a week-long bout of chickenpox.

As for the games themselves, they were clunky interpretations of bat 'n' ball favourites such as squash or, erm, football (actually more like doubles tennis)[1] on the basic, easyJet-orange model. The beige variant promised some capacity for *Tin Can Alley*-style shooting games with a so-called 'light gun', which inevitably didn't work unless you were holding it so close to the telly you left scratches on the screen.[2] The two standard controller 'bats' were chunky boxes with *Etch-A-Sketch*-type knobs that, fantastically, could be packed away into the *Binatone*'s battery compartment for storage.

The TV Master was superseded almost immediately by brasher, more state-of-the-art TV games such as Mattel *Intellivision* and *Colecovision* and then, fatally, by the home computer. How very British. The *Binatone* logo (was it pronounced By-na-tone or Bin-a-tone?) was a lovely crown-bedecked affair that wouldn't have looked out of place on the bass drum of a '60s Merseybeat band. Those sporty games icons, however, were a constant reminder of the local leisure centre and the fact that they had a proper sit-down *Galaxians* game that you could go on when your mum was having her badminton class.

Born	1976
Batteries	◖◖◖◖◖
Players	🧍🧍
Breakage	🍷
Ads	▣▣
Envy	🏆🏆🏆
eBayability	🖱
Overall satisfaction	👍👍👍

See also ZX Spectrum, Commodore 64, Galaxy Invader 1000

---

1 The lack of 'play against the computer' option meant that a lot of *Binatone*-generation kids grew up ambidextrous.

2 If the gun broke, you could still turn the sound off and watch the silent cube 'target' bounce sss-softly off the imaginary walls of your TV set. A nice precursor (hem hem!) of the Windows screensaver, we feel. Plus, the gun itself, cable tucked neatly into your snake belt, made for an excellent *Blake's 7* ray gun.

Black Box
Atomic mass

Born	1977
Batteries	None
Players	👤👤
Breakage	🍷🍷
Ads	📺
Envy	🏆
eBayability	🖱
Overall satisfaction	👍

See also *Mastermind, Rubik's Cube, Dungeons & Dragons*

Way before Nintendo DS *Brain Training* and Carol Bloody Vorderman jumping on the Sudoku express, we already obsessed about our IQs. There was always a smart-arsed kid who'd decided to enrol into that original smug-bastards club, MENSA, and would parade his or her certificated 'intelligence quotient' of 160 or whatever around the classroom.[1] Strangely, rather than resulting in a beating for the boffin, this would actually instigate a school-wide outbreak of competitive puzzle-testing and problem-solving as each pupil sought to out-IQ his or her peers.

While the juniors struggled with such 2D conundrums as spotting the odd one out in a list of prime numbers or reorienting dice from the sides you could see, seniors graduated to proper spatial-awareness posers and brainteasers of the 'Who was two to the left of the person three to the right of the queen next to the seven of clubs?' variety. Oh yes, *The Krypton Factor* had a lot to answer for.

All of which must have alerted the really big brains at the country's centres of higher learning who – let's face it – were slouching about in the refectory waiting to appear on *University Challenge* and wishing someone would hurry up and invent computers so they could practice their FORTRAN and COBOL. Weren't they?

Well, one such affable graduate was Eric Solomon, already knee-deep in diplomas and employed in civil and structural engineering but, vitally, with a bit of atomic-research work experience under his belt. His game invention, *Black Box*,[2] required players to 'fire' X-rays into a darkened vessel in order to determine the positions of 'atoms' positioned by an opponent. Hellishly complicated rules governing the behaviour of these beams and their direction apparently revealed the hidden squares, but it was all carried out with coloured pawns and ball-bearings, of course.

Solomon's other games rejoiced in such fashionably abstract names as *Entropy, Hexagrams, Thoughtwaves* and, erm, *Billabong*. Each was clearly intended to be played with a furrowed brow and semi-religious solemnity (except, perhaps, *Billabong*, which possibly required a corked hat). Widely pirated since (particularly by jealous FORTRAN and COBOL programmers), *Black Box*'s most recognisable successor is probably the *Minesweeper* game on your work PC.

1 A hugely impressive score for a teenager – right up there with Sir Jimmy Saville and Lisa Simpson.
2 The game acquired its name not from the flight recorder of a jumbo jet but from a term used by scientists to describe an object or system that operates in an unknown way. Although can it be merely coincidence that those 'Who knows the secret of the Black Magic box?' Rowntree's choccie ads were on a lot in the '70s? They should bring those back.

Boglins
Hand-puppets from hell

You have to hand it to some big brain at Mattel: once they'd hit on the brilliant consonant-swapping simplicity of the name, the *Boglins* story must've written itself. Essentially near-relatives of the *Finger Fright* family, these fist-powered fuckers sprung seemingly full-armoured from the ground and on to toy shelves back in the late '80s. Packed into caged boxes that doubled as display cases (replete with faux bent bars and plenty of 'do not feed' warnings), *Boglin* lore borrowed quite heavily from that other mischievous monster hit of the era, *Gremlins*.

Apparently fashioned from more old retreads than an ITV Saturday-night line-up, these clammy rubber collectables initially arrived in one of three flavours (Dwork, Vlobb and Drool) and were marketed as pets with puppet pretensions. Given that the average kid had only two hands, we doubt that very many people owned all three. Simple operation (and large glow-in-the-dark eagle-eyes) made for almost instant 'alien voice' ventriloquism practice and plentiful under-the-bed ankle-biting assault tomfoolery. Woe betide the little sister who mocked a *Boglin*.

A worrying element of the *Boglin* box-top back-story (at least for sensitive souls with a penchant for thinking too much about such things) was the implication that humans had somehow descended from them and the originals had remained – until now – buried in the primordial slime. The non-biodegradable nature of *Boglin* parts means that they probably will be dug intact from the decaying sludge of human remains when the aliens finally do arrive.

Plenty of other *Boglin* subspecies were released to cash in on the success of the initial range, including *Soggy*, *Baby*, *Hairy* and *Glow Boglins*, with astonishingly swift diminishing returns. By 1990, when Matchbox launched a competitor, *Monster in My Pocket*, Mattel's lumpy swamp offspring had already decided to take the hint and, well, bog off.[1]

See also *Finger Frights, Squirmles, Slime*

Born	1987
Batteries	None
Players	👤
Breakage	🍷
Ads	▪️▪️
Envy	🏆🏆
eBayability	🖱🖱🖱
Overall satisfaction	👍

---

1 Ah, but it was good to see one turn up on *Fantasy Football*'s parody of *Toy Story*. The *Boglin* played former Northern Ireland international Ian Dowie (which isn't fair, as Dowie looks a lot more like a Vogon off the *Hitchhiker's Guide* TV series). Although dropped by Mattel, *Boglins* re-emerged in the mid '90s under the aegis of none-more-Cream-era toy company Action GT (since absorbed into the uber-family of LIMA licensee of the year 2003 and 2004, Vivid Imaginations).

Buckaroo!
Saddle-stacking balancing game

Born	1970
Batteries	None
Players	👫
Breakage	🍷🍷🍷🍷
Ads	▪️▪️▪️
Envy	🏆🏆🏆
eBayability	🖱️
Overall satisfaction	👍👍

See also Tip-It, Mousetrap, KerPlunk

Does it not now seem that in the '70s the marketing people were trying to sell to parents, not the kids? What else can explain the prevalence of TV ads throughout the decade saturated with cowboy imagery – the likes of Golden Nuggets, Texan Bars, the Milky Bar Kid... and *Buckaroo!*?

The thing is, mums and dads had most likely been children themselves in the post-WWII era and would've been brought up on Saturday matinees, John Wayne flicks and Wild West adventure serials. Somebody, somewhere decided that these were the folk who had the disposable incomes (nobody having yet invented the concept of 'pester power'). Thus, we have a decade-long obsession with everything whip-crackin', rootin', tootin' and animal abusin', pardner.

At least *Buckaroo!* was blessed with simple gameplay. Easily snapped plastic mouldings (ten-gallon hat, pitchfork, grappling hook, billycan and all that) are gently lowered in turn by players on to a 2D bucking bronco.[1] As the ad explained: 'Put on a shovel, try a pick – if the load's too heavy the mule will kick.' Words to live by, we think. Too much weight causes *Buckaroo!*'s hair-trigger to release, sending the aforementioned implements flying across the living room, under the settee, into the dog's mouth and so on.[2]

Later variations cashed in on Spielberg's *Jaws* (the eponymous game was a neat reversal of the same conceit: remove skulls, anchors, bits of boat, etc. from mouth of shark before it snaps shut) and, we presume, Cleese's *Fawlty Towers* (*Don't Tip the Waiter* employed a cardboard waiter on to whose carefully balanced tray players were required to add counters depicting pizza, cakes and sandwiches). Note the use of the exclamation mark in the title to imply excitement and/or surprise. Therein lies an unspoken suggestion that, at the climax, we might want to cry out the name of the game in a moment of catharsis and delight. This is a favourite device of toy manufacturers (see also *Sorry!* and *Stay Alive!*, although strangely not *Yahtzee*), pretentious restaurateurs (*Fish!*) and musical theatre impresarios (*Oliver!*, *Hello, Dolly!*). On a not entirely unrelated note, the phrase 'fuck right off!' works with an exclamation mark too.

1 The latest commercially available version of *Buckaroo!* is rendered in 3D as if, until the advent of CGI, children wouldn't previously have been able to cope with anything quite so real. Alongside yer bog-standard *Buckaroo!* (with a design clearly riffing on the donkey from *Shrek*), you can also buy a seasonal *Buckaroodolph!* ('the mule who doesn't like Yule').

2 If you're so inclined, you can also play a variant of the game with your drunk friends. Once they pass out, pile on as many empty cans, fag packets, ashtrays, frozen sausages and shaving-foam squirts as you can until they wake up.

Cadbury's Chocolate Machine
Obstacle to chocolate

It's bizarre that this should even make it into a children's wish list of most desired games or toys, being the very definition of the anti-toy. Ostensibly a cross between a savings bank and a chocolate-dispensing machine, it actually fails to live up to the promise of either. But that is to underestimate its novelty.

Although in reality it amounted to a deferral of pleasure, no more than a tuppenny barrier between the chocolate and your mouth, there was still something of the faintly exotic in getting hold of a load more of those mini-Dairy Milks and Bournevilles than you would ever find in a box of Roses.[1] In the days before washing-powder tablets and digital cameras, the fascination with anything miniaturised was not to be underestimated.

The classic dispenser was designed and moulded in '50s-throwback red plastic (leading us to fancifully imagine that the Fonz himself would dish out his chocolate from one) with properly embossed gold Cadbury's branding, plus it came preloaded with a dozen baby chocs.[2] In theory, a 2p piece slotted in the top would, with a twist of the hidden knob within, release a single, fully wrapped miniature that could then be enjoyed in isolation. In truth, and in part because not only was the chassis of the dispenser made of plastic but also the lock and keys, it took about ten seconds for greed to overcome the flimsy workings of this metaphorical chocolate chastity belt.

With the contents therefore devoured in their entirety (and not so easily replaced, at least not until the next Argos trip), what essentially remained was a moneybox and, given that it generally wouldn't contain more than about 14p, not a very good one at that.

Born	1974
Batteries	None
Players	👤
Breakage	🍷🍷
Ads	▣
Envy	🏆🏆🏆
eBayability	🖱
Overall satisfaction	👍

See also '*A La Cart Kitchen*', *Mr Frosty*, *Whimsies*

39

1 Oh, and Terry's Neapolitans fitted too, didn't they? Want to know what happened to Terry's, once the pride of York, now just a Dawn French-perpetuated brand extension of Kraft Foods Inc, Illinois? The corporate giant bought the 1000-worker-strong factory in 1993 and closed it down in 2005. York Fruits? Produced in Slovakia, mate. Chocolate Orange? Czekoladka pomarańczowy, more like. Where's Michael Moore when you need him, eh?

2 Chocoholics, masochists and fatties rejoice! The freely available *Chocolate Machine Money Box* from Humbrol is a fair enough modern approximation of the old Peter Pan version. And guess what? The chocolate miniatures are actually bigger than the ones that used to fit in the old machine.

Cascade
Bouncy castle for ball-bearings

Born	1972
Batteries	
Players	
Breakage	
Ads	
Envy	
eBayability	
Overall satisfaction	

See also
Crossfire,
KerPlunk,
Domino Rally

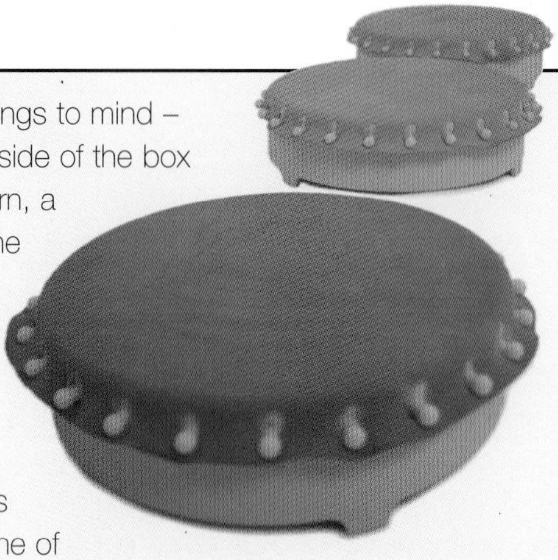

Many board games – *Othello* springs to mind – usually bear a trite slogan on the side of the box along the lines of 'A minute to learn, a lifetime to master'. Surely, then, the motto for *Cascade* was 'A lifetime to set up, a minute to play'. But what a minute it was!

Made by mini-car kings Matchbox, *Cascade* was bizarrely addictive, totally pointless and definitively uncompetitive – one of those games where eventually no-one really played by the rules, a bit like just reading out the questions from *Trivial Pursuit* without the board.

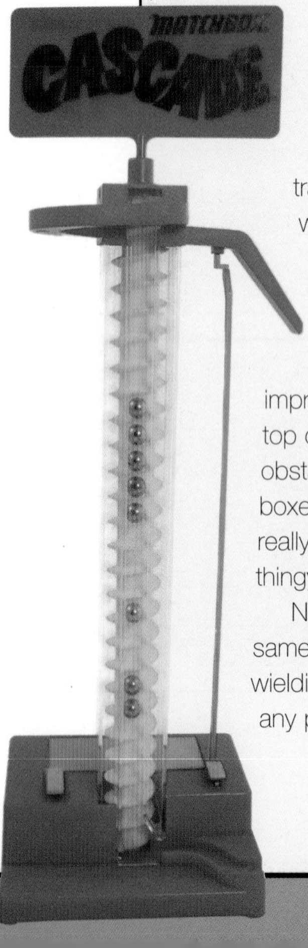

So the set-up, then: an acid-yellow plastic mat had spaces marked out for the five pieces of *Cascade* furniture. At one end there was a towering Archimedes screw that sucked up ball-bearings and launched them off a short ski-ramp. Then came the bam-bam-bam bounce across three taut red timpani thingies, before the balls hit a mini-pinball table and fell into several scoring slots. Certain balls would be returned to the screw via a three-foot track for another go around the system. At least, that's what was supposed to happen.

Of course, lest the gradient tolerance of your bedroom carpet be suboptimal, the little metal buggers would scatter to either side and roll under your bunk bed (we imagine Barnes Wallis felt similarly disheartened in that bit from *The Dam Busters*). The best improvement via improper game play was to put the launch tower on top of your wardrobe and let the balls *really* bounce. Constructing little obstacles between the trampolines, such as piled-up *Subbuteo* team boxes, would assist in efforts to test how high the ball-bearings would really go. A Mars-Staedtler rubber under the edge of each trampoline thingy helped angle them perfectly for extra distance too.

No-one had any idea what the scoring system was, but in the same way that someone can win ten grand on *Better Homes* without wielding so much as a staple gun, you could 'win' *Cascade* without any personal involvement whatsoever. And it was fun, so who cares?

Chemistry Set
Kitchen-based catalysis

Born	1920ish
Batteries	None
Players	☺
Breakage	♟♟♟♟♟
Ads	📺
Envy	♟♟♟♟
eBayability	🖱🖱
Overall satisfaction	👍👍

See also Electronic Project, Magic Rocks, Tasco Telescope

Common-or-garden chemistry set box lids always featured a boy with brown hair in the pudding-bowl style, wearing a white lab coat and peering intently at a few cubic centilitres of vaguely blue compound in a test tube. The over-serious look in his eyes said it all: 'Why won't this explode?'

Yes, the substances you'd find inside one of these were always disappointingly dull. An average set included that dependable stalwart, bloody copper sulphate,[1] followed by a rack of anonymous-looking off-white powders ('slaked' lime, tartaric acid, etc.[2]) and rubbish like iron filings and litmus paper. C'mon guys, where do you keep all the fun stuff? The red lead? Arsenic? Silver nitrate? A lame spirit burner provided the only hint of impending danger, and there were usually only enough chemicals to do about ten experiments. And one of those was 'growing a crystal out of sugar' on a string. (On a string, for crying out loud!) Heaven only knows what we were supposed to do with the mysterious 'watch glass'. Just sit and watch it, perhaps?

But at least the chemistry sets marketed by the likes of Salter and Merit made some affectation towards proper school lab learning. Dreary they may have seemed, but they didn't patronise us youngsters like the modern-day National Curriculum-approved 'yukky science'-type sets. Chemistry isn't fun, no matter how much you dress it up with 'slimy' green food colouring and 'funky' fizzy sherbet. Write *that* down. On those earlier sets you'd find abundant warnings of the 'adult supervision recommended' kind in the instructions, even though every single kid in the land threw them away. If you couldn't bang out a batch of stink bombs, then it was hardly worth the effort. The sole experiment conducted thereafter could be noted down thus: 'Just bung a bit of everything in one test tube; then heat it up to see what happens' (results: lame fizzing and stuff that glued itself to the kitchen table). As if we were hoping to drink the stuff and then transform, Dr Jekyll-style, into a horrible monster and eat our own parents. No, really... as if!

1 In the presence of water, anhydrous copper sulphate turns blue. To test for reducing sugars (aldehydes), a solution including blue copper sulphate will turn red. So there you have it: the most exciting thing you can do with copper sulphate is watch it change colour. It is the chemical-compound equivalent of a traffic light.

2 Off the top of our heads? Probably ammonium chloride, calcium hydroxide, sodium carbonate, sodium hydrogen sulphate, aluminium potassium sulphate, phenolphthalein, zinc, calcium carbonate, ammonium iron sulphate, iron sulphate and sodium thiosulphate. All that, *and* a tiny bog-brush for cleaning out test tubes!

Chic-a-boo
Monkey-faced brown-noser

If ever there was a warning about genetic experimentation, then it was Stephen Gallagher's 1982 debut horror story, *Chimera*, a prophetic tale of a half-human, half-primate creature developed by scientists for use in slave labour and organ harvesting. In the end, the titular creature went crazy-ape bonkers in the Lake District and killed everyone.

Although slightly less violent in intent, the original *Chic-a-boo* dolls might as well have been spliced together in that same laboratory. This baby-faced bear/monkey hybrid was created by Japanese boffins back in the '70s, apparently to 'bring a message to children about the beauty of love'.[1] Well, only a mother could love a face like that. Originally marketed in pairs (boy and girl – my God, they could mate!) and sold naked, it was the accompanying Hanna Barbera TV series in 1980 that brought the dolls to international attention.

Alternatively named *Futagonomonchhichi*, *Monchhichi* or, in France, *Kiki*, the popularity of *Chic-a-boo* helped launch a whole raft of accessories (mainly clothes) and merchandise for girls (mainly stationery). Most notably, the early '80s saw a huge number of knockoff 'gripping monkey/bear' pencil-toppers designed to exploit the hitherto unexplored toy potential of the bulldog clip.[2]

Perhaps in a bid to inspire empathy in preschoolers, *Chic-a-boo* constantly sought comfort – witness the opposable digit perpetually jammed in its gob. Clearly, though, the toy's appeal lay largely in its pleading expression. Taking the Disney style – those reassuringly Aryan juvenile features – and exaggerating it to a natural conclusion, *Chic-a-boo* was a blue-eyed, chubby-cheeked, button-nosed freak, the forerunner of Japanese Anime characters. What little girl could ignore that cutesy 'love me' expression, caught halfway twixt happiness and tears? (What adult fella could ignore the same on imported 'naughty schoolgirl shags betentacled space monster' Hentai cartoons?) *Chic-a-boo* was probably the first truly anthropomorphic toy to break through into a young child's wish list, although it was swiftly superseded by similarly short-lived, dough-faced progeny (*Cabbage Patch Kids*, *Pound Puppies*, *SnuggleBumms* and many, many more).

Still popular in their native Japan (latest variety: *Rasta-man Monchhichi* an' t'ing), the thumb-sucking fun carries on to this day, although you'll be hard-pushed to find a vintage example that hasn't had its brown nose rubbed clean away 'with love'. In the mean time, we wait with bated breath for Stephen Gallagher's next horror opus, *The Tiny Tears of Blood*.

Born	1975
Batteries	None
Players	👤
Breakage	🏆🏆
Ads	▪▪
Envy	🏆🏆🏆
eBayability	🐭🐭
Overall satisfaction	👍👍👍

See also *Tiny Tears, My Little Pony, Smoking Monkey*

1 *Monchhichi* was originally created by Sekiguchi Ltd after the founder spotted a doll in a market in Germany. So goes the official story. It could have been a really hairy baby. Particularly if it was East Germany.

2 The "monkey grip", as many unsuspecting kids would find out to their cost, could also mean being pincer-grabbed by the school bully just above the knee, thus trapping the nerves in a very unpleasantly ticklish way.

Chopper
Think once, think twice, think bike!

Born	1969
Batteries	None
Players	👤
Breakage	🏆🏆
Ads	▣▣▣
Envy	🏆🏆🏆🏆🏆
eBayability	🐭🐭🐭🐭
Overall satisfaction	👍👍👍👍👍

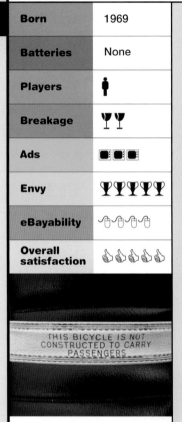

THIS BICYCLE IS NOT CONSTRUCTED TO CARRY PASSENGERS

See also Racing Bike, Spacehopper, Peter Powell Stunter Kite

Okay, we know this book is supposed to be about toys you wanted but never got, and we're prepared to concede that pretty much everyone owned a bike as a child. Indeed, given our obsession with catalogues, we'd put money down that plenty of 'em were bought at a rate of a pound a week for fifty weeks from the subs lady who came round on Wednesdays. But the 1970s opened our eyes to the potential of something new – the designer bike – and, in particular, the Raleigh Chopper.[1]

Possibly the last bike ever to adopt that penny-farthing-inspired differently-sized wheel ratio, the Chopper was (as designer Tom Karen has gone on record saying) intended to reflect the power and style of a dragster. Those 'apehanger' handlebars mimicked the customised Californian motorbikes of the '60s – think Dennis Hopper's Harley in *Easy Rider*. The overlong banana seat and spring-mounted saddle conjured up the desired 'hot rod' image. It sounds impressive but doesn't quite explain where the goolie-knackering crossbar-mounted gear shift was supposed to fit in. Nevertheless, about two million of the frigging things were sold (and there are two million adults with the healed-over grazes to prove it).

The colour of Chopper you owned would reflect your personality – if not at first, then soon enough by means of customisation with reflectors, spokey-dokeys, mirrors and lights (chunky boxes of battery-powered plastic or sleek wheel-rim-driven dynamos), bottle-carriers and panniers – and be invested with great dedication and pride (except maybe when it came to cleaning it). Mainly, though, a Chopper (like any bike) would unlock a world of adventure beyond the end of your own street; going

1 Believe it or not, the kids' bike industry in the Cream era was virtually a closed shop; Raleigh alone manufactured the Budgie, Tomahawk, Striker, Chipper, Chopper, Boxer and Grifter, so all that brand rivalry and envy kids wilfully engaged in was just a false war perpetuated by The Man. The likes of Elswick, Dawes and Falcon – the other independent British kids' bike makers of the day – have since been absorbed by bigger companies or gone to the wall.

to your mates' houses, picking up comics from the corner shop, stickleback fishing, popping wheelies, giving backies, racing – it was all for the taking.[2] Well, as long as there weren't any hills en route. Choppers were not good with incline ratios. Your legs weren't strong enough to pedal uphill and any pressure on the brake going downhill invariably sent you over the crossbar.

The advent of the BMX in the early '80s put paid to the simple pleasure of owning a bulky, rusty, aggressively designed death-trap and turned the bike trade into a genuine, even respected, sporting industry. As sales plummeted, the previously distinctive Raleigh brand saw out the era it helped to define making run-of-the-mill mountain bikes, city bikes and something now referred to as a hybrid, whatever that is.

2 What do kids have now? Tom Clancy's Splinter Cell? Shove it up your fat, sofa-bound arse. Nothing beats the thrill of riding a bike without stabilisers for the first time. For crying out loud, does anyone even bother with the cycling proficiency test any more?

Chutes Away
Discreetly named air-war leviathan

Born	1977
Batteries	None
Players	👤👤
Breakage	🍷🍷🍷
Ads	▪️▪️▪️
Envy	🏆🏆🏆🏆
eBayability	🖱️🖱️
Overall satisfaction	👍👍👍

'Chutes' be damned! This was, to all intents and purposes, Carpet Bombing For Fun, as evinced by the explosion noises made by playing kids as they dropped the 'chutes' on the revolving target, curiously painted up to look like some presumably inconspicuous fictional landmass, although it did resemble a sort of pre-continental-drift Africa, now we come to think of it.[1]

Anyway, the stout bomber – sorry, troop carrier[2] – was mounted on a robust gantry and controlled by one of those initially-exciting-looking, dial-heavy flight-deck consoles that, on closer inspection, turns out to have just two actual controls (three, if you include the off switch), the rest being useless stickers.[3] Ah well.

As the ground spun relentlessly beneath, you would position your plane fore and aft, look through the crosshairs, wait for a target to come into view, and then bombs – er, chutes – away! Get all ten in the waiting cups below and you win.

In a desperate attempt to reinforce the liberation-not-annihilation element, a lesser-known sequel game was eventually introduced – *Night Rescue Chutes Away* – although the good intentions were slightly undermined by its description as a 'target' game. The difference here? Your paratroopers could be dropped in the dark because there was a spotlight stuck under the plane.

In theory, this exciting development could have been a major USP, allowing as it did for the possibility of covert, post-curfew playtime. Unfortunately, the clockwork turntable that drove the thing made so much bloody noise, we might as well've had an actual plane in there with us.

Anyway, it was all good clean Dresden fun, brought to you by the good people of Gabriel. Gabriel?! No, us neither.

See also *Vertibird, Up Periscope, Flight Deck*

---

1 So much so that we'll put money on it that the *Chutes Away* landscape is directly responsible for the look and feel of every British safari park since the '70s. Those of a more political sensitivity could also flip the card over and draw in their own Falkland Islands-themed felt-tip topography, natch.
2 A twin-prop yellow-and-white airbus that could've just roared out of the opening titles for *Tales of the Gold Monkey*.
3 One of which was a red 'Important! Read instructions first!' label that might as well've been stuck there by your parents. Along with the ones that said 'Don't break it, it cost a lot of money!' and 'Let your brother have a go! It's for sharing!' Cuh! Talk about the nanny state – as if anyone reads the instructions first anyway.

Cluedo
After-dinner Agatha Christie

Cluedo seemed to appear out of nowhere as some murdery-mystery rival to *Monopoly*. In fact, it was devised by a solicitor's clerk from Birmingham (the home of many unsolved crimes, we're saying – the Bullring and Spaghetti Junction to name but two). Posh kids had it first, probably because it featured a 'study' and a 'drawing room', but it wasn't long before the whole street was testing their detective skills with miniature tools of death and cards that you had to keep in little wallets like After Eights.

Essentially a glorified board version of 20 Questions (just keep asking until you guess whodunit, where-they-dunit and with what) but featuring murder, it stirred the nascent serial killer in many a small child. Show us a grown-up who claims they didn't secretly want to see Mrs White bludgeoned to death with the lead pipe in the bedroom, and we'll show you a suspiciously new-looking patio out in their back yard. (Of course, this almost-amusing observation conveniently ignores the fact that the actual murder victim – Dr Black – couldn't simultaneously be one of the players. Neither could you record a verdict of suicide or accidental death. No wonder we grew up to be such a distrustful generation.)

Quite where the stereotype characters were drawn from remains unexplained, although we suspect some play on words implicit in Mrs Peacock and Col. Mustard. Popular opinion had it that one of the suspects in the French version was a Welshman called Jack Hughes (*j'accuse, geddit?*), but sadly that's just a grand old urban myth. 1986's *Super Cluedo Challenge* did introduce three new characters – Captain Brown (just nervous, we expect), Miss Peach and Mr Slate-Grey but, like new-formula Coke, it never caught on.[1]

Although it must be said that both Rev. Green and Prof. Plum weren't exactly marketed as teen heart-throbs, Miss Scarlet stirred more than just violent urges in the fellas, appearing as she did on the cards as a bright red pawn with a mane of flowing blonde hair and a saucy-yet-sophisticated smile. Thinking about it, any game that prompted a prepubescent sexual frisson from a chess piece, or educated young Crippens as to which household items could best be used to kill, should probably have come with some form of parental advisory warning. But this was in the good old pre-PC days, so we had free rein to don our imaginary balaclavas and go a-garrotting. With the length of rope. In the kitchen.[2]

Born	1948
Batteries	None
Players	👤👤👤👤
Breakage	🍷🍷🍷
Ads	▪️▪️
Envy	🏆🏆🏆
eBayability	🖱️
Overall satisfaction	👍👍

See also *Monopoly, Electronic Detective, Escape from Colditz*

1 Neither did the ratings haemorrhage of a TV show that broke through on ITV primetime in the '90s. Although they managed to churn out four series, host Chris Tarrant (later replaced by Richard Madeley) claimed it was his 'all time low... fucking bollocks... I just hated it'.
2 Another crime is the literal bludgeoning in the past decade of the *Cluedo* franchise, with the original game beaten to fit into travel, card, PC, junior and *Simpsons*-branded versions. Hasbro has also introduced a nostalgia edition (whatever that means), which comes in a wooden box. Which is where we'd have to be before you'd find us playing the animated *Cluedo DVD Game*.

Commodore 64
Breadbin-shaped family computer

Born	1982
Batteries	Mains
Players	👤
Breakage	🍷
Ads	■■■
Envy	🏆🏆🏆🏆🏆
eBayability	🖱🖱
Overall satisfaction	👍👍👍👍

The BBC Micro
Computer programming

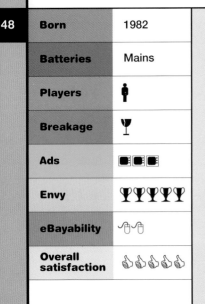

Often, the first computer to grace the family home would not be bought as a present for the kids but would be borrowed as another toy for a tinkering dad. Commodore Business Machines had already dangled their *PET*, one of the top 'take home from work for the weekend' computers, in front of inquisitive parents across the globe, but it was with the introduction of the *VIC-20* and *Commodore 64* in the very early '80s that they cornered the younger (i.e. games-obsessed) micro market.[1]

More eccentrically named than their closest competitors, Commodore computers also pretty much outclassed any in their price range. As any owner wouldn't tire of banging on about, the *C64* had much better – that is to say, more arcade-like – graphics than the *Spectrum*, thanks to something called 'sprites'.[2] Its sound chip was also more sophisticated, leading some very zingy music to accompany the on-screen action rather than the usual bleeps and boops.

On top of that, the *C64* also had a purpose-built matching cream lozenge colour-scheme tape deck or floppy disk drive, a 'proper' keyboard and that extra wodge of actually-not-very-important-in-the-event DRAM memory (a full 16K more than the 48K *Spectrum* – still some 6000 times less powerful than the average 3G mobile phone). But it did mean that a few classic programs were unique to what modern technologists would deem 'the platform': *Dig Dug*, *Gilligan's Gold* and the assault-on-Hoth-apeing *Attack of the Mutant Camels* to name but three.[3]

More than any other micro, though, the *C64* was positioned as a grown-up's office tool with all kinds of spreadsheet, word-processing and accounts applications available. All that processing power! However, once computer and accompanying colour portable telly took up residence in the spare room, so did we. Come on, it was 1982! We could close the curtains, watch the first edition of *The Tube* on Channel 4 and then play *Defender* 'til bedtime. You can catalogue your record collection later, Dad.

---

1 Atari and Apple were starting to enter the home-computer market in the States, but in the UK it was pretty much a straight fight between Commodore and Sinclair. Largely ignored pretenders to the throne included Oric, Dragon and Jupiter. They were right ones for making their products sound like something out of *The Lord of the Rings*, these

computer manufacturers, eh?
2 We could come over all technical now and go on about attribute clashes and scrolling, but our workable knowledge of *C64* BASIC begins and ends with the PEEK and POKE commands. To be honest, we don't really know what they're for either, but

Worthy, wealthy households instead chose to purchase the distinctly public service remit *BBC Model B*, which at least had a couple of Sunday-morning computer-literacy TV shows to back it up – although precious little in the way of games at first. Price wars and a failure to keep up with the increased specifications in the industry did for most of these machines in the end. Time has been kind, however, and a thriving retro scene keeps emulated versions of the *C64* and all its contemporaries alive online somewhere out there on the Internet.[4]

See also *ZX Spectrum, Binatone TV Master*

they sound funny.

3 In fact, rumour has it that the *C64* was initially developed to serve as a simple, reusable arcade cabinet engine – i.e. an upgradeable games machine – and not intended for the home market at all.

4 And in the real world. A 'plug and play' joystick-sized version of the *C64*, with thirty games included, will set you back less than £15 at Amazon. Age 5+. Bah!

Computer Battleship
Find-the-square military tactics game

Born	1977
Batteries	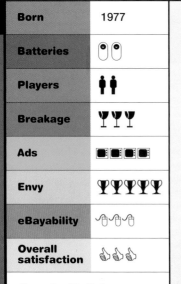
Players	
Breakage	
Ads	
Envy	
eBayability	
Overall satisfaction	

See also *Up Periscope, Chutes Away, Tank Command*

Milton Bradley (which we're still not sure wasn't the name of that comedy alien bloke off *Fast Forward*) had tried before with a plastic push-peg version of the pen-and-paper grid-based classic. But it was with the addition of flashing LEDs and whistle-boom! sound effects that they hit upon the deluxe, truly sought-after edition.

For some reason as rare as hen's teeth in your actual Christmas stocking (maybe it was overpriced – we can't remember), *Computer Battleship* was memorably marketed (although we suspect that whoever it was that came up with the 'You've sunk my battleship!' dialogue for those Oxbridgean navy-ponce-themed telly ads wasn't exactly bordering on genius), seemingly during every commercial break of our childhood.

The set-up? A plastic grid – a Siamese variation on the original analogue cases with flip-top lids – split vertically and separated into two playing areas (grid-squared maps of an unnamed ocean manufactured in the regulation James-Bond-film transparent plastic) plus assorted miniature gunships, boats, aircraft carriers, etc. Batteries, natch, were not included and at any rate would have lasted only until Boxing Day.

There were drawbacks, though. The limitations of the titular computer meant that, far from containing the imagined intricate sensors to automatically locate the position of your fleet, every single occupied square on the board had to be laboriously 'programmed' in before a game could start. For both players! The slide-rule-like apparatus had a tendency to be a bit glitchy, too, so unless every input coordinate was millimetre-perfect, your guess at C6 could easily register as D7, throwing your whole strategy out of whack. Plus, the reversal of the board meant that player one's A1 position was actually player two's K1 position, and so on, and so complicatedly forth.

But, for sheer literal bells and whistles, *Computer Battleship* couldn't be matched. MB later rechristened the game *Electronic Battleship* and, later still, it was joined by the less successful refurbished version, *Talking Battleship*.[1] Nevertheless, the original remained a popular staple of end-of-term games days – often, its owner would have to instruct potential opponents to form a queue. The enduring playability did not go unnoticed by BBC bosses, either, who adapted the game for a Richard Stilgoe-fronted children's programme, *Finders Keepers*.

---

1 In the late 1980s, there was another variant called *Blow Up Battleship*. Instead of calling your guess out loud, you would use a small set of bellows to send a jet of air to your opponent's fleet and blast away a section of ship.

Connect Four
Tic-tac-toe, four in a row

Born	1974
Batteries	None
Players	
Breakage	
Ads	
Envy	
eBayability	
Overall satisfaction	

See also Downfall,
Pocketeers, Othello

Traditionally the arena of combat wherein eldest son would beat Dad (as depicted on the front of the box) in some gaming rite of passage ('Look Dad, diagonally!'), *Connect Four* was the insanely addictive board game destined to split families asunder across the globe. Originally marketed as *The Captain's Mistress* on account of a rumour traditionally linking it with Captain Cook (he was playing it, not shagging it, so the story goes), the definitive '70s edition is part-owned by – and why are we not surprised by this? – David Bowie.

A fiendishly simple premise – it's basically noughts and crosses[1] – you'd drop coloured counters into a vertically positioned seven by six-holed board and compete to see who would be first to get four colours in a row.[2] Launched in the early 1970s by MB Games, 'the vertical strategy' game had an ace climax wherein upon winning the victor could shout 'Connect Four!' and then pull a flap out from under the board causing the stacked counters to clatter out all over the melamine surface of the kitchen table.[3] Although there were other 'vertical strategy' games available (cf. the safe-cracking style of *Downfall*), *Connect Four* had an alluring purity to it that made it seem all the more desirable. This was a thinker's game, frill-free.

Rather as in poker, you could judge the ability and personality of your opponent by the way in which they played with the 'chips'. One who stacked their counters into a tower would most likely be loath to commit, worried that making a move might cut off other opportunities. Whereas your counter-fiddler would be more liable to drop 'em into the grid like lightning, hoping to set the pace of the game and win by forcing an error in their opponent. *The Apprentice* would've been a much shorter TV series if they'd just got all the wannabe business tycoons to play a quick game of *Connect Four* on day one.

Like a family-friendly bright-blue plastic backgammon or *Go*, *Connect Four* was for your chin-rubbers and that boy genius about to take Dad out diagonally. And David Bowie. It's still heavily marketed by MB, but we're advised that current editions are rather smaller than the mid '70s definitive set (with the exception of those annoying gigantic pub versions), taking a good few inches off all aspects of the game – and a couple of decibels off that all-important victory clatter too.

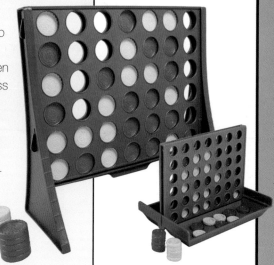

1 Some people are just never happy with three, are they, eh? Although why let your ambition stop at four? Why not *Connect Five* or *Six*? Because that would be for madmen, that's why. **2** It's way beyond the scope of this book to calculate the statistical probability of a stalemate result within all the *Connect Four* outcomes, but, let's face it, there are Nobel Prize-winning mathematical theses written on less frivolous subjects. **3** Additional strategy point of order: older brothers were wont to 'accidentally' knock the flap out and cause a counter cascade whenever they sensed they were within a whisker of defeat. No, actually, we won't 'just call it a draw', you cheating bastard.

Corgi 007 Lotus Esprit
Reinventing the wheel

Born	1977
Batteries	None
Players	👤
Breakage	🍸🍸🍷
Ads	🎞️🎞️
Envy	🏆🏆
eBayability	🖱️🖱️
Overall satisfaction	👍👍

See also *Tonka Trucks, Matsushiro Knight Rider Radio-Controlled Car, Hornby Railway Set*

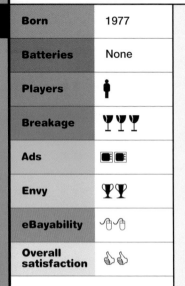

Much has been written about the British die-cast toy industry, most of it in better-researched books than this one, but here's a quick summary. Dinky were first to retool their WWII ordnance machinery, initially making scaled-down cars as background detail for Hornby trains (courtesy of a shared parent company in Meccano Ltd.). Lesney's Matchbox brand hit the shops next, famous for tinderbox packaging, various classic car series and, later, the *Superfast* and *Superking* ranges. Then Corgi, setting up shop in Swansea (hence the name) and introducing separate plastic windows for their cars – an innovation that had passed the other two businesses by.

In the end, all three collapsed under pressure from a corporate US giant (Mattel and their bleedin' *Hot Wheels*),[1] but that's a lesson history keeps teaching us over and over again. So much for facts. Most of the cars made by Dinky, Matchbox and Corgi have now ended up in dusty display cabinets, in museums and – the horror, the horror! – private collections. Was that really the point after half a century of miniature motoring? What happened to all the fun? Surely cars were made to be played with?

In fact, short of creating a traffic-jam on the lino by the patio doors, play scenarios were hard to come by. What really interested the Cream-era car buff – embryonic Clarksons all – was the toy that had an unexpected extra feature. Yer '70s' Matchbox roster read like a roll-call at the Wacky Races (*Blue Shark*, *Dodge Dragster* and *Turbo Fury* to name but three), including dune buggies that the Monkees wouldn't look out of place driving. Perennial favourite, the green hovercraft, remained and although Matchbox had experimented with *S400 Streak Racing* (plastic strips with loop-the-loops), the *Adventure 2000* set was the real eye-opener. The vehicles themselves were a mishmash of sci-fi rip-offs (including *Rocket Striker*, which looked suspiciously like Dinky's *SHADO* mobile), but you could also send off for a poster of the toys... which would come back with your name on it in big, blocky letters! Now that *was* impressive.[2]

---

1 It's as if we never learn, isn't it? Maybe, just maybe, we Brits aren't good enough at this stuff. That's something to ponder over a Starbucks latte and a Krispy Kreme donut, eh?

2 The poster (inspired by those similarly personalised 'El Cordobes' bullfighter one-sheets, we're saying – perhaps Mr Matchbox had been sunning himself on the Costa Brava in '77?) was a poisoned chalice. You could request three names to be

Corgi, meanwhile, hitherto known for modern nuts-and-bolts stuff (branded articulated lorries, Routemasters, Land Rovers – especially for the Tarzan fold-out box set), aimed for a classier market with official film tie-ins. Yes, that does mean the camp Adam West Batmobile, but let's not forget Bond. 007's *Goldfinger* Aston Martin DB5 cemented Corgi's reputation for attention to detail, with faithfully reproduced battering rams, bullet shield and that all-important ejector seat. Their *Spy Who Loved Me* Lotus was even better (but mainly 'cos the Esprit didn't actually look like any car we'd ever seen before, even when it was in the film).

Dinky, thinking on their feet, had thrown their lot in with Gerry Anderson, creating tie-ins to his younger-demographic-skewed Supermarionation shows. A shrewd move, it turned out, as the mammoth success of their *Joe 90* range in 1968 proved – they became the top-selling toys of that Christmas. *Spectrum SPVs* and *Thunderbird 2s* capitalised on the F.A.B. vibe. Even *Space 1999* got the Dinky treatment, the *Eagle Transporter* mopping up some of *T2's* leftover metallic green paint ('cos yer kids don't like 'all white' toys, right?).

Eventually, it was simplicity that did for the die-cast dinosaurs. The stoic, some might say plain, British brands simply didn't inspire excitement (where were the go-faster stripes, the flame decals or the ability to transform into a fighting robot, say?). They weren't big enough to have action figures in 'em (*MASK*) or small enough to hide in your mouth (*Micro Machines*). In fairness, Matchbox did have a desperate last attempt to liven up their standard car range by introducing the *Motorcity* packages (bumper-value multiple-car pile-ups and elaborate multistorey playsets), but it was all to no avail.

It all went tits up for Matchbox in 1982 (perhaps their equipment was requisitioned for the Falklands?), and the others soon followed in a great mess of mergers and acquisitions. The companies may be dead but the brand names live on. Never say die.

Stock cars Collectors' catalogues listed new toy ranges, such as Adventure 2000 (below) and Space 1999 (bottom).

printed, presumably to keep siblings happy, but one had to be credited under the threatening alien baddie also pictured. Two heroes, one enemy. Oh, the arguments!

Crossfire
Junior *Rollerball* for trainee snipers

Born	1971
Batteries	None
Players	👫
Breakage	🏆🏆🏆🏆
Ads	▪️▪️
Envy	🏆🏆🏆
eBayability	🖱️🖱️
Overall satisfaction	👍👍

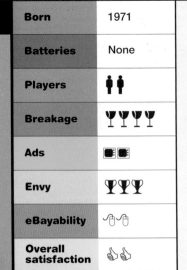

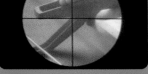

There's something about the sheer size of so many toys and games of our era: they weren't just played in the house – they took over the house. Nowadays, everything's been reissued in petite 'coffee-table' versions on sale at Firebox.com[1] Back then, you needed French windows just to get the likes of *Crossfire* indoors.

Basically a combination of pre-*Pac-Man* arcade favourite Air Hockey and a fairground rifle range, this two-player combat game required the steady aim of an SAS-trained marksman and the ruthless determination to win of an American athletics coach. The object of each round? To score goals against your opponent by firing a constant stream of steel ball-bearings – that's steel ball-bearings, folks – against a rolling puck (also steel) until it passed through his net (incidentally also made of steel). Any ball-bearings that fell into your half became your next round of ammunition (to be loaded into the top of chunky red firing pistols at either end of the long chipboard playing area).[2]

Crossfire could be a fast and furious game (to paraphrase the advertising spiel, 'The only game as exciting as its name') and, by crikey, it was certainly a noisy one. In addition to the endless chime of ricocheting steel on steel, the pistols themselves had a stiff and clunky trigger mechanism that not only discharged each ball with a loud crack but also had a tendency to jam mid-game (calling for a swift and strident blow to free the offending ammo). If nervous relatives felt the need to leave the room, who could blame them? In any case, the footprint required for both game and players to play in comfort (i.e. lying full stretch on the floor) meant that the settee had to be moved, so good riddance.

Two other important words to bring into the mix here: agonising blisters. Never mind the potential for RSI, endless chafing of fingers on a red-plastic trigger made for a certain unforeseen amount of bloodshed. The problem could be alleviated mildly by the application of a plaster or insulation tape around fingers or gun, but *Crossfire* would inevitably end up a messy game. Still, there's no such thing as hygienic warfare.

As with all ball-bearing-dependent games, some would be lost over time. Had it been possible to detach the pistols from the field of play, however, and brandish them, airgun style, in the street, we concede that they would've gone missing a hell of a lot sooner.

See also *Stop Boris, Battling Tops, Hungry Hippos*

1 Case in point: you can still buy *Crossfire* in the shops, although now it boasts a so-called 'giant playing field' of just two feet! New manufacturers FEVA are British, though, so we'll let them off.
2 Given the fundamentally two-player nature of this game, why any parent would buy this for an only child remains a mystery. An alternative *Crossfire* scenario for such unlucky kids was to create a Roman-style combat amphitheatre for woodlice by lobbing a few of them in the middle and blasting off a random bombardment of balls.

Cyborgs
Sci-fi figurines with interchangeable limbs

This early '70s Strawberry Fayre range – actually Takara Henshin originals imported from Japan by Denys Fisher – beats later incarnations developed around the same theme (including *Timanic Cyborgs* and *Micronauts*) by virtue of being constructed to a larger scale. In playability terms, that meant they could be pitched in interspecies war with *Action Man*, Dr Who and the Bionic pair.

Cleverly manufactured in a combination of clear plastic, chromed parts and die-cast metal, they were very cool-looking toys (in two flavours, Muton and Cyborg). There was, naturally, some comic-strip business on the back of the boxes setting up an interplanetary war back-story,[1] but kids just make up their own, don't they? Chief factors in their appeal: you could see their internal organs and pull them limb from limb (what kid could resist that?).

There was also the slightly scary implication, not exploited by the later brands, that we would all one day become part human, part machine, with plastic or metal replacing what once was flesh. Which, when you were a youngster conversant with the plot of the *Six Million Dollar Man* (the TV series was based on Martin Caidin's 1972 book *Cyborg*), seemed eminently plausible.[2] Forget the rubber-suited Cybermen or the monotone Borg – here's a frightening notion: when the Queen Mum had her hip replacement, she technically qualified as a Cyborg. A PR opportunity missed there, we feel.

As with the later figure collections, there was an abundance of accessories, in this case, weapons sets (various arm-replacements for Cyborg, including the *Cybo-Liquidator* – a water pistol – and the *Cybo-Eliminator*), flying discs a la the Green Goblin and the prohibitively expensive *CyboInvader* spaceship. Muton even had actual outfits to wear, known as 'subforms' and comprising Torg (a horned demon thing), X-Akron (a red roboty thing) and Amaluk (a green fishy thing). Third member of the team and Johnny-cum-lately, Android, seemed cast in a different manner, being more 'brittle' and lacking the rubber head. His chest panel popped open to reveal a four-missile launcher, which could be fired by pressing a button on his back.

Sadly, the only real-life cyborg we know of is the University Of Reading's Kevin Warwick, who seems to make a living by implanting microchips in his forearm and telling newspapers that he's turned into C3P0. This should not reflect too badly on the university's robotics department as, before this, it was most famous for building Sir Jimmy Saville's special *Fix It* chair.

See also Action Man, ROM the Space Knight, Dr Who TARDIS

Born	1976
Batteries	None
Players	👤👤
Breakage	🍷🍷🍷🍷
Ads	▪▪▪
Envy	🍷🍷🍷🍷🍷
eBayability	🖱🖱🖱🖱
Overall satisfaction	👍👍👍

1 Muton was an intergalactic space-parasite-type who'd decided that it was Earth's turn to be laid to waste. Humanity's best scientific minds got together to create the ultimate defender of the human race, Cyborg. Android was designed later as an extra 'hero' toy to gang up on poor ol' Muton. A million bullied kids sighed in recognition: two against one.

2 Bloody Hazel O'Connor and her chart-topping *Eighth Day* misanthropy didn't help matters much either. This 1980 tune wrapped quasi-religious bunkum in with 'machine becomes sentient' lyrics, while the video featured O'Connor herself going mental in a *TRON*-inspiring neon skeleton suit. Proper worrying.

Domino Rally
Chain re-ACTION!

Born	1981
Batteries	None
Players	👤
Breakage	🏆🏆🏆
Ads	▪️▪️▪️
Envy	🏆🏆🏆
eBayability	🖱️
Overall satisfaction	👍👍

See also Cascade, Mousetrap, Guess Who?

Yet another thing the Yanks did bigger and better than us. For the Cream-era child, hardly a week would pass without kids' telly showing yet another colour-saturated videotape of record-breaking domino topplers in a Milwaukee aircraft hangar. Thereon, jaundiced-looking Spielberg-alikes would spend days setting up elaborate domino displays under hot sodium lamps (usually suffering a cataclysmic setback when a stray grasshopper knocked over a 10,000-tile Flags of All Nations set-piece overnight). America, Holland, China... you name it, everyone had a crack at the record books.

Just not the UK. What hope of government funding for a would-be domino athlete, eh? You'd just about scrape together enough cash for one wooden, slidey-top box of those Bakelite buggers. The carefully positioned mosaics and pixellated patterns (albeit created by teams of Stateside nerds) may have lent the domino an exotic air it never would've acquired from years as an old man's knock-on-the-table game in murky brown pubs. Plus, with only the living room to experiment in, future British domino topplers would be lucky to get together a run of ten, never mind an entire course of dominoes sliding down chutes, setting off rocket launchers and swinging across mini-ravines.

Confidently stepping into this gap in the market came Action GT and its *Domino Rally* sets (mark 1, mark 2 and, perhaps inevitably, mark 3), featuring masses of brightly coloured tiles[1] plus all kinds of gimmicks, stunts and tricks for them to perform (loop-the-loops, elevators, steps, slides and 'sunbursts'). *Domino Rally* also had one extra-special ace up its sleeve: most of the dominoes were fastened along flat, perfectly spaced lengths, so resetting them was a quick flip of the wrist away.

However, the unique selling point of domino toppling (not much more than 'set them up, knock them down' as the box blurb reiterated) started to feel a little like too much effort after a while and, as the young player him/herself tumbled inexorably towards adolescence, the plastic set took up final residence in the loft.[2] Nowadays, if you hear someone say they fancy dominoes, you're more than likely expected to get the pizzas in.

1 The technical term is apparently not tiles but 'stones', which makes them sound very rock 'n' roll, doesn't it? Hence, we suppose, why Eric Clapton chose the pseudonym *Derek and the Dominos* to record Layla. And, erm... well, there's also Fats.

2 You can, however, book now for the annual Domino Day in Leeuwarden, the Netherlands. They need 80 volunteer domino-setters. But beware – according to their website, 'It is hard work, often on hands and knees, and requires an enormous amount of concentration and stamina.' That sounds like an altogether different kind of Dutch holiday to us.

DOMINO RALLY

Downfall
Upright counter-based safe-cracker game

This '70s entry ticks nearly all the boxes required of a board game. First off, even before the lid was lifted, you had the double-meaning implicit in the name (successfully exploited by the burglar-centric telly ads) insofar as not only did the red and yellow counters of the opposing sides 'fall down' through the vertical playing construct but also, while you were trying to win, you could have been assisting your competitor in their attempt to plot your 'downfall'.

Second, it required only minutes to understand how to play, set up and go. For the record, the counters – two sets of five, numbered and in different-coloured sets to vary the manoeuvring difficulty if required – were loaded into feeder chutes and all the combination-lock-inspired dials were set to a required start position. Then, in turn, each player made a single spin of any dial in an attempt to pass the counters through the dials and down to the waiting tray at the bottom.[1] Most satisfying was being able to navigate a full set of counters into the bottom dial for the final turn, before watching the crestfallen reaction of your opponent as they tumbled out en masse.[2]

More recent versions of the game have ditched the original board's institutional blue and grey in favour of the usual kid-friendly acid colours or, in one case, stripping out the board altogether and leaving just some key-operated tumblers floating in midair. Call that iconic? Pah!

The aforementioned mid '80s ads played on the addictive qualities of the gameplay: apparently, even housebreakers would find it impossible to resist just one more go, giving the police plenty of time to turn up and arrest them. 'You've won!' 'I think we both lost!' If only there'd been one of these set up in Tony Martin's Norfolk farmhouse, he could've avoided a lot of silly bother.

See also Connect Four, Hangman, Computer Battleship

Born	1970
Batteries	None
Players	
Breakage	
Ads	
Envy	
eBayability	
Overall satisfaction	

1 Each dial was numbered one through five and could hold the corresponding quantity of counters – except two and three, which, for some reason, were transposed. Why did they do that? No, really, it's this sort of thing that keeps us awake at night.
2 Experts created varied fiendish ways of playing in order to increase the difficulty: use one set of counters, or two; insist on all the counters finishing their route in numerical order, or reverse, or not. And so on. So just how bored of a game do you have to be to start inventing new ways of playing?

Dr Who TARDIS
Long-running children's TV series spin-off

Born	1977
Batteries	None
Players	👤👤
Breakage	🍸🍸🍸🍸
Ads	▪️▪️▪️
Envy	🏆🏆🏆🏆🏆
eBayability	🖱️🖱️🖱️🖱️🖱️
Overall satisfaction	👍👍👍

Although the 1960s had seen impressionable young viewers bombarded with all manner of Dalek merchandise, it was not until 1977 that a toy manufacturer realised that there was mileage in producing an entire range of action figures based on telly's favourite Time Lord.[1]

At this time, *Doctor Who* was of course at the height of his ull-on boots-and-boho eccentric incarnation, and the corresponding Tom Baker figure came complete with the expected wide-brimmed floppy hat, burgundy coat, scarf and non-functioning Sonic Screwdriver. However, despite being in possession of all the right accoutrements, the doll bore far more resemblance to avenging coffee-shaker Gareth Hunt.

Nonetheless, the figure was a cut above most cash-in plastic renditions, particularly useful either shoved in the fridge for the purposes of conducting an 'ice world' adventure or for the judicious addition, in 1981, of red felt-tip question marks to his shirt collar. Other figures in the range included chamois-clad savage companion Leela (complete with knife, feral hair and suspiciously prominent frontage), a Dalek, Cyberman[2] and, somewhat perplexingly, the Giant Robot.

The only real playset was the inevitable TARDIS, which came with an imaginative special feature – when Doctor Who was placed inside its doors, pressing a button on the top would cause the 'time space column' (i.e. a plastic cylinder covered in artwork that vaguely recalled the Baker-era title sequence) to rotate, and Doctor Who to 'dematerialise' into the other side. Pressing an adjacent button would cause him to return, although more astute owners fashioned a story in which Doctor Who entered the TARDIS and a Cyberman came out (or maybe this was just something we saw on *Crackerjack*).[3]

Also available around this time were a talking Dalek and K9 from Palitoy, who incessantly repeated their catchphrases with the aid of one of those little plastic records also found inside vintage talking dolls and the average 'bag-o-laffs'. If you had the right mates, you could switch them with the identically operated *Talking Commander Action Man*, which made for some interesting cries of 'Exterminate' in the trenches and the eerie sound of a deep-throated Dalek asking for volunteers 'for a special mission'.

See also *Cyborgs, War of the Daleks, Six Million Dollar Man*

1 2006 saw something of a glut of these, too, of course.
2 This 'fearful monster' was pictured looking bow-legged and as camp as a tentful of Girl Guides, naturally.
3 This adventure took place between *Revenge of the Cybermen* and *Earthshock*, continuity freaks.

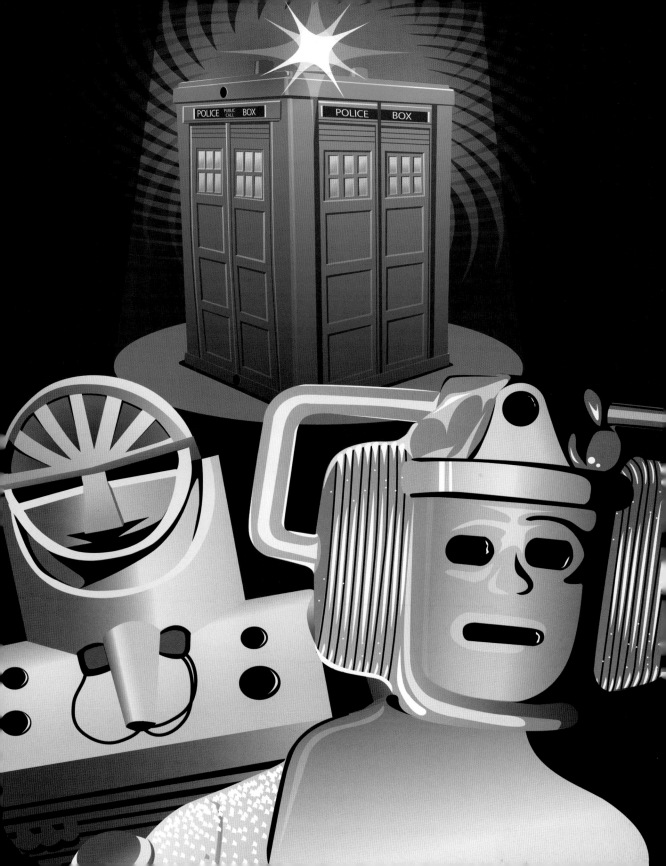

Dungeons & Dragons
'Alternative reality' adventure role-play game

Born	1974
Batteries	None
Players	👤👤👤👤👤👤
Breakage	🍸
Ads	📺
Envy	🏆🏆🏆
eBayability	🖱🖱
Overall satisfaction	👍👍👍

Amplified by the almost permanent presence of *The Hobbit* on '70s and '80s English lit. syllabuses, *Dungeons & Dragons* offered those who were unpopular in the playground some solace in an imaginary Tolkien-esque world they could control.

Manufactured in Basic and Expert flavours by US company TSR, and based on an original premise by Chicago-born college dropout E. Gary Gygax, *Dungeons & Dragons* sets mixed mediæval Britain with magical folklore and monsters to create a fantasy magpie's nest in which an unlimited number of pretend, non-cardiovascular but meticulously detailed battles and adventures could take place. Despite, or perhaps due to, a target audience primarily comprising those for whom competitive sport was a no-go, the later creation of *Advanced Dungeons & Dragons* betrayed the inherent 'survival of the brainiest' appeal to the asthmatic, astigmatised or Asperger's.[1]

How to play? Extensive rule books (but no board) and fiendishly complicated challenges (requiring the appointment of a Dungeon Master to preside over events) made it difficult to get to grips with, but *D&D* soon established itself as a sort of lunchtime school-club subculture in much the same way as chess, astronomy and orchestra rehearsals (largely due to it being legitimised by an allocation of early-lunch tickets). A typical game exposition: 'Your attempt to cast a spell on the Orc fails and he strikes a blow with his axe. You lose three stamina points.' With much talk of druids, clerics and the *Call of Cthulhu*, players would most likely take elements of the fantasy beyond the game itself, growing up to drink real ale and join Marillion-aping folk pub bands labouring under monikers like Moon Runelight and Arcadian Pentangle.

The game could also be expanded into a hobby with trips to Games Workshop to purchase Citadel Miniatures (an assortment of pewter figurines to collect and paint) and magazines such as *White Dwarf*. The '80s cartoon series of the same name was a collaboration between TSR and Marvel comics and starred Donny Most (Ralph Malph from *Happy Days*) as Eric the Cavalier. For the less dedicated role-player, the *Fighting Fantasy* books by Ian Livingstone and Steve Jackson were a portable alternative. For the totally disinterested, there were at least the multicoloured resin dice with an unexpectedly large number of sides (our favourite was the tangerine dodecahedron).[2]

See also Trivial Pursuit, Black Box, ZX Spectrum

---

1 It's the age-old question, isn't it: do the nerds make the game, or does the game make the nerds?

2 Even now, most role-playing games on computer or console are based on the dice-throwing model that *D&D* set up, from *Rogue*, *Nethack*, *ADOM* and the like to the recent *Diablo* and *Neverwinter Nights*. All the odds are generated via random integer selection, which unfortunately takes out the fun of throwing the flamboyantly shaped dice, but it's still your d10 initialization and d20 to hit, or d8 to damage and d6 to dodge and d4 to see whether you noticed the boulder breaking your legs and whatnot. Only, it's much quicker.

Electronic Detective
Computerised *Cluedo*

This late '70s effort from Ideal is getting lumped in with its lesser-known American cousin, Parker Bros' *Stop Thief* on the basis that nobody ever asked Father Christmas for two electronic crime-solving games in one lifetime. Except maybe Morse, the cheerless bastard.

Starting with the premise that a single console full of 'suspect data' could mimic a police computer holding details of over 130,000 committed murders (and we're presuming that's with the institutionalised racism programmed out),[1] players took it in turns to ask questions of the *Electronic Detective*. Roughly translated, that meant keying in stuff like 1,3,A,1,0,1,6 ('I was on the West Side, uptown, at an art show with two suspects called Jeremy and Sadie'). The computer responded in typical-for-the-time LED fashion and one of 20 suspects (cards) would be selected for you to interrogate. Make an incorrect accusation based on your deductions (kept on your private data sheet) and you would find yourself 'shot' (signified by an electronic farty noise). Blimey! That's quite some punishment. Never mind a demotion back to uniform, electronic justice is swift and harsh.

Stop Thief, by contrast, veered too much towards the frighteningly realistic in its presentation. Like a sinister treasure hunt, it was a case of finding the correct square on a board that contained the missing felon. 'The thief is out there! Can you stop him? Use the handheld scanner to collect clues! Buy tips from the squealing slags on the streets! Break down doors and burst into tenement flats! Nail the little toe-rag! Kick him while he's down! Go on, kick him in the head!'[2]

Gentler, board-game-based sleuthing was never as attractive as the electronic variety, so manufacturers drafted in various TV names to spice up the action. Kojak, Columbo and Jessica Fletcher all welcomed a junior murderer or two to the dining-room table over the years. In the States, *Electronic Detective* combined circuit board and celebrity by featuring Don Adams (of spy sitcom *Get Smart*) on the box. Why we couldn't have had Van Der Valk or Callan is yet another unsolved mystery.

Note, however, that in both of these games the computer is the one responsible for setting up the crimes. Which, if we know our Guy Ritchie films well, meant that the microchip itself was Mr Big. Indeed, pull out a few diodes and transistors with the tape-recorder turned off and *Electronic Detective* was known to squeal like a piggy.

Born	1979
Batteries	🔋🔋🔋🔋🔋🔋
Players	👤👤👤👤
Breakage	🍷🍷
Ads	▪️▪️
Envy	🏆🏆🏆🏆
eBayability	🖱️🖱️
Overall satisfaction	👍👍

See also *Cluedo, Computer Battleship, Hangman*

---

1 The names given to the various suspects seem to indicate otherwise, though. What are Pepe Perez, Ling Tong and Mickey O'Malley if not cultural stereotypes of the first water?

2 We might be exaggerating the box blurb a bit here but in those 'Get yer trousers on – you're nicked', *Sweeney*-fied times, life on the streets was tough.

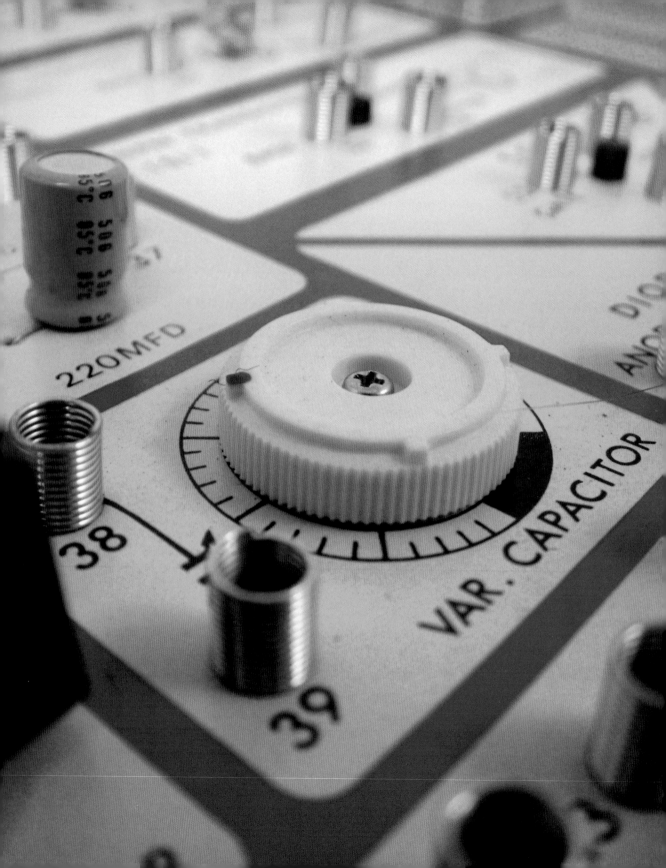

Electronic Project
Solder-free fun for the junior boffin

200 in 1! *150 in 1*! The not-very-catchy *65 in 1*! And *50 in 1*! Yes, it's that oscillator-obsessed cousin to the generic chemistry set, *Electronic Project* (a product from the on-its-sleeve-for-nerdiness named Science Fair), a big wooden box full of circuits, cables and dials that boasted anything from 50 to 200 possible projects for you to build, depending on how much cash Mum and Dad were willing to shell out.

In the *150 in 1* kit, for example, there was mucho fun to be had from a seven-segment LED display and an advanced integrated circuit, all of which could be burned out to spectacular effect by overloading the wiring with too much voltage. *65 in 1* promised to unlock the secrets of the Sonic Fish Caller, Plant Growth Stimulator and a decidedly *Stylophone*-looking electronic organ. When you factor in some of Science Fair's other products, such as the build-your-own *Solar Power Lab*, the *Psychostrobe* and – better than either – the *Lie Detector Kit*[1] (sporting a box depicting an under-pressure dad surrounded by his suspicious family), then surely some wholesome *Weird Science*-type experimentation was but a crocodile-clip away?

Sadly, no. As the blurb on Salter Science's *Introduction to Electronics* lid hinted ('Make a radio, police siren, Morse code and more!'), most of the experiments were pretty samey... and sound-wavey.[2] Plus, there wasn't even a soldering iron in it. How infuriatingly safety-conscious!

It takes a special kind of enthusiasm to get excited by transistors, resistors and capacitors that connect with pre-cut wires and already-assembled spring coils. We'll put good money down that those same kids' hobbies later included CB radio and the early home computers. Naturally, what every other child in the land was hoping to build was some kind of infrared CCTV-style early-warning system for their bedroom.[3] A near-impossible task given the raw materials, which were only ever intended to make a series of enthralling light-controlled logic gates.

Born	1978
Batteries	
Players	
Breakage	
Ads	
Envy	
eBayability	
Overall satisfaction	

See also *Chemistry Set, Stylophone, Walkie-Talkies*

---

1 'Play 'truth' games, measure 'kissability'. The *fun* kit for parties. Pocket size!' Now that's a sales pitch.
2 Although there were opportunities for experimentation even here. Some *50 in 1* kits contained an FM transmitter, which, though legal in America, was completely illegal in the UK. By running a long wire from a back bedroom window down to the clothes-line pole it was possible to broadcast Radio TV Cream to the end of the road, most likely screwing up everyone's TV reception in the process. One episode of *Coronation Street* is a small price to pay for freedom of speech, though, isn't it?
3 Girls were understandably protective of their privacy as they entered adolescence, what with 'the curse' and all that. The boys were usually trying to work out a way to watch that borrowed *Electric Blue* video without being caught.

Escalado
Heavy betting

Born	1928
Batteries	None
Players	👤👤👤👤👤
Breakage	🍷🍷
Ads	▣
Envy	🏆🏆
eBayability	🖱🖱
Overall satisfaction	👍👍

See also *Monopoly, Test Match, Subbuteo*

Several attempts have been made to capture, in game format, the excitement of horse-racing (although for our money the buzz begins and ends with a Ladbrokes payout). Chad Valley, redoubtable makers of toy guitars, humming tops and drum kits for several generations of British youth, was there first. As the cod-Spanish name suggests (*escalado* literally means 'climbed'), this game was ancient even by the Cream era – it dated from the 1920s in fact.[1]

Anyone who's ever been to a fairground will be familiar with those frantic roll-a-ball horse-racing games, and, in truth, much the same level of excitement could be generated at tabletop height. Depending on the size – and income – of your family, this personal Aintree could come with five, eight or twelve (probably highly poisonous lead) model horses and would vary in imitation furlong length. The rules were simple: pick your jockey, stick a bet on at the bookies and put the horses under starter's orders.

The problem with this enterprise, of course, was how to replicate the element of chance and surprise fundamental to the thrill of the turf. The answer: by exploiting the random power of the wobble. By turning an old-fashioned crank at one end of the track, the green felt racecourse vibrated, resulting in much erratic movement of the mid-gallop-frozen runners. Some made for the finish line. Some didn't budge. Some fell over. Nearly all fell over, in fact. But – hey! – that's racing.

There was a token system of betting, but small-change-laden children certainly weren't above acting like grown-up men of the world and suggesting they make things 'a little more interesting'. Thus were many kids additionally introduced to the notion that 'the house always wins'. For a while, The Valley tried to extend the brand with variants, including greyhound and speedboat – speedboat? – editions, but only the original lasted through the decades, with little changing save for a reduction in the toxicity of the model horses to tender young intestines.[2] For those of us too young even to go on fruit machines, *Escalado* was a tentative toe in the glamorous waters of that mysterious world beyond the blacked-out windows of William Hill.

---

1 Much like Chad Valley itself. Although the parent company had been going for nearly 100 years, the toy maker's famous – if rather prosaic – name didn't appear until the business moved to Harbourne in Birmingham, next to the river Chad. Nothing to do with those wartime wall-topping 'Wot no chips?' cartoons, sadly.

2 Until 2002, when it was discontinued. Nowadays, you can invite friends round for a Saturday booze-fest in front of one of those 'race-night' DVDs. The only shortcomings of these are: a finite number of race outcomes; some long-winded complicated rules; and they last so long, you'll end up missing *The X Factor* results show.

Escape from Colditz
Teutonic incarceration fun for two or more

Born	1973
Batteries	None
Players	👤👤👤👤👤👤
Breakage	🍷🍷🍷
Ads	▣ ▣
Envy	🏆🏆🏆
eBayability	🖱🖱
Overall satisfaction	👍

See also Tank Command, Dungeons & Dragons, Sorry!

At TV Cream, much of what we know about the Second World War we learned from Saturday matinees on BBC2. We know that Kenneth More lost his legs crashing a plane while trying to impress a girl. We know that Richard Todd blew up the Ruhr Dam with bouncing bombs and once had a dog called Nigger (until his name was cut by politically correct censors). Oh, and we know that John Mills escaped from Colditz during a 'Hot Mum-style amateur dramatics revue by climbing down a rope made of blankets.

In the '70s, hostilities were resumed by the BBC, who dominated the Sunday-night drama slot with various Allied resistance serials – chief among them another superlative retelling of the Colditz story. Like the British Lion film, it was also based on the writings of Major Pat Reid MBE MC, an actual escapee of Leipzig's most famous stronghold.

Which brings us neatly to *Escape from Colditz*, one of surprisingly few Nazi board games that made it on to our childhood wish list. It was devised by Reid and published by Parker Bros and promised more fun than a week in the cooler with just your baseball and glove for company.[1]

Thankfully, no familiarity with Kraut-distracting Ents Corp stage business was required, but that's just as well as it was otherwise a hellishly complicated move-counters-along-the-squares-and-collect-objects-and-cards board game (in the vein of *Monopoly* and many others). The difference here was that one team had to play the part of the baddies with strict instructions to block off escape routes, 'discover' tunnels and, by landing on players' counters, banish them to solitary confinement. As a goodie (in charge of a team of POWs), your sworn duty was to escape (and, as we recall, cause much bally trouble for the Bosch in the process). There was no option to just keep your nose clean, do your time and sit out the war in relative comfort. Seemingly the odds were in favour of the three teams of escapees but, although there were few guards, there were even fewer legitimate ways to evade them.[2] Frankly, we think it was foolish of the SS to allow us free run of their so-called top-security prison in the first place but we imagine, like so many German waiters, zey ver only taking orders.

---

1 Later reissues were published by Gibson games. Strangely, both versions initially featured a bloomin' great swastika on the front of the box, although this eventually disappeared in favour of various generic renderings of the Nazi eagle.

2 A big complaint about the game was its realism – escape was as rare as *die Schaukelpferdscheisse*. You could spend hours slowly making your way around the castle only for the Jerries to call an 'Appell' and have every piece returned to the yard in the middle of the board.

Etch-A-Sketch
The big-knobs drawing-on-a-screen game

Developed in the late 1950s by Frenchman Paul Chasse,[1] the *Etch-A-Sketch* was first marketed as *L'Ecran Magique* (*The Magic Screen*). The toy hit the big time at the 1959 International Toy Fair held in – surely the world capital of all recreational fun – Nuremburg. Here it was snapped up by the Ohio Toy company and given the 'Etch... A... Sketch!' moniker that would later lend itself to a bafflingly catchy jingle.[2]

Was it really 'magique', though? Readers who wish to preserve their disbelief in its suspended state should look away now.

No, of course it wasn't, you fools! It was a machine! Essentially a box full of industrial-grade crap (aluminium flakes, if you're going to be fussy), *Etch-A-Sketch* worked thanks to an internal stylus moved around by twiddling two pleasingly robust knobs. The stylus scraped the film of flakes off the inside of the screen, ergo a line appeared. In short, it was a bit like scraping your car windscreen – if what motivated you to scrape your car windscreen was the opportunity to produce a simple line drawing of a house with blocky smoke coming out of the chimney. Once you'd looked at the finished picture for a bit, you'd simply shake the whole thing about (that's the *Etch-A-Sketch*, not your car), thereby flinging the aluminium crap back on to the inside of the screen and obliterating your work.

In appearance, the red-clad *Etch-A-Sketch* was a *Tron*-esque vision of the future, an actual plasma slab you could sit on your lap and create *Hitchhiker's Guide to the Galaxy*-style animations with. As a seemingly miraculous device it was much coveted, but in truth its appeal was limited, really lending itself only to drawings of steps, mazes and circuit diagrams.[3] Mind you, that lad off the '80s *QED* doc – Stephen Wiltshire, the one who could draw the London skyline from memory – he'd have been ruddy fantastic on it we reckon.

Somewhat poetically, with *Etch-A-Sketch* there was no going back – no regrets, no anxieties. Like a life lived end to end, each drawing comprised the many movements of a single, unbroken line. The only way out was to erase the lot. Does that say something conceptual about the essentially transient nature of art? We dunno. Ask Charles Saatchi. In fact, we'll bet a tenner that at some time he's shelled out way over the odds for an *Etch-A-Sketch* drawing, the art-obsessed idiot.

Born	1960
Batteries	None
Players	🧍
Breakage	🍷 🍷
Ads	▪️▪️▪️
Envy	🏆🏆🏆🏆
eBayability	🖱️
Overall satisfaction	👍👍👍

See also *Magna Doodle, Spirograph, Binatone TV Master*

1 The prototype was actually invented by engineer Arthur Granjean but, as he was working for Chasse's garage at the time, he lost out on the patent rights to his boss.
2 The box additionally claimed that *Etch-A-Sketch* was 'the magic screen that's fun for all the family'. Er, in what way exactly? We don't recall our parents ever writing shopping lists on it instead of a notepad.
3 Some versions of *Etch-A-Sketch* shipped with plastic-maze or join-the-dots grids to lay over the screen and, we suppose, play a game with. Bingo! An instant ten more minutes of fun. Ohio Art tried flogging 'hot pink' and 'cool blue' varieties, but they never caught on.

Evel Knievel
Wind-up right-wing stunt man

By the time Evel Knievel – Bob to his friends – crashed his bike after clearing 13 double-decker buses at Wembley Stadium, his international fame was already on the wane. He'd already failed prior jump attempts over the fountains at Caesar's Palace, Las Vegas (a suitable venue for one so keen to gamble with his life), a baker's dozen Pepsi-sponsored delivery trucks and the overblown prog stunt that was Snake River Canyon.

To the rescue, Ideal Toys of New York, just one of many companies to license Evel's image for fun and profit. Who was to know that small bendy effigies of this mid-western bike-shop owner in his stars-and-stripes jumpsuit would revitalise the toy industry and make a small fortune for their real-life daredevil inspiration? Well, to Cream-era kids, he was a god, staring death over the handlebars almost as often as any *Chopper*-owning child on their way to the corner shop for the latest *Whizzer and Chips*.

Powered by a wind-up gyro 'energiser', each Knievel toy vehicle was more ridiculous than its predecessor. The *Stunt Cycle* was most popular for recreating the *World of Sport*-glimpsed exploits in your own backyard. Grazed knuckles were a small price to pay[1] for the opportunity of sending Evel careening over a ramp (if indeed he ever made it that far). Then there was the similarly revved *Crash and Stunt Car*, whose appeal was limited insofar as the figure, safely ensconced inside, couldn't fall off and twist his supple limbs in the wrong direction.

Other toys included the *Dragster*, the *Trail Bike*, the *Scramble Van* and the *Super Jet Cycle* (a daft sci-fi bike with pod thrusters that spewed out sparks like a cheap, plastic ray-gun). At the more esoteric end of the scale, there were the playsets (*Stunt Stadium*, *Stunt World* and the just plain weird *Escape from Skull Canyon*, which included a werewolf, green boulders and skull-adorned trees for Evel to jump over). No-one we knew ever owned these.

Allegations of wife-beating and then imprisonment for actually beating up the biographer who made the allegations did for Knievel's hero status. Movie stinker *Viva Knievel* added insult to injury. The Lear Jets, the fleet of luxury cars, the homes in Florida, Montana and Las Vegas – they all went the way of Evel's career (i.e. down the shitter), but true followers clung to the belief that, when God created man, he created Adam and Evel.

Born	1973
Batteries	None
Players	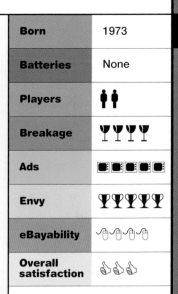
Breakage	
Ads	
Envy	
eBayability	
Overall satisfaction	

See also Ricochet Racers, Scalextric, Matsushiro Knight Rider Radio-Controlled Car

1 The crank handle on Evel's energiser was just that bit too close to the floor. But like the man's own broken collarbones, these injuries were a badge of honour.

Finger Frights
As if fingers weren't frightening enough

Born	1976
Batteries	None
Players	🧍
Breakage	🍷🍷
Ads	▪️▪️▪️
Envy	🏆🏆🏆🏆
eBayability	🖱️
Overall satisfaction	👍👍👍

See also *Boglins, Smoking Monkey, Squirmles*

Looking like a vulcanised Gonzo or some other freak cast-off from the Henson workshop, *Finger Frights* promised 'hours of joy for a girl or boy', or so cried the nicotine-stained street trader who sold them out of a suitcase in the city centre. (The same scruffy fella later made a living peddling Gordon the Gopher squeaky hand puppets, only to return the following year with exactly the same stock dyed pink and touted as Mr Blobby.[1])

Inexpensively fashioned in crude, coloured latex, these digit-targeted mini-monsters had distinctive, staring white eyes and wobbling rubber arms, raised, *Curse of the Mummy* style, in predatory fashion. Their appeal lay not in the perpetually snarling expression (for who was ever frightened of a *Finger Fright*?) but in their ubiquity and variety. At the very least there were red, blue, gold, green, purple and white *Frights*, crammed into big boxes of novelties (pile 'em high and sell 'em cheap!) in toy shops and newsagents across the land, alongside jumping spiders, chunky stacking felt-tips, gonks and those party-blower things for which no one ever came up with a name.

And yet it was impossible to own enough.[2] Kids leaving birthday parties would be seen ferreting around in their goody bags for a prized rubber fiend. Entire bull trading floors were established in primary-school quads. Like pigeons, *Finger Frights* were vermin. (Also like pigeons, it was quite easy for them to lose a limb through excessive gnawing or sheer violent accident.) But these were vermin of the playground and pencil case: wherever you stood or sat, you always knew you were less than two metres from one.[3] Now that actually *was* frightening.

[1] Oh, and 'Lighters – three for a pound!' was another familiar cry – the legacy of Thatcher's Britain. A massive increase in duty on matches in the March 1981 budget basically killed the UK production of 'England's Glory'. Manufactured in Gloucester for over 100 years and then at Bryant & May's factory in Liverpool, they are now imported from Sweden.

[2] Get more than ten at once, and you'd be hard pushed for protuberances to stick 'em on and in very serious danger of giving passing old ladies their own personal fright.

[3] Finger Frights popped up in the most unlikely of places. They made cameo appearances as the 'Dancing Boogiemen' on Bally's Scared Stiff and Elvira pinball machines (a couple of the rubber rogues were fitted to metal slingshots so that they'd jiggle in time with the music).

Fisher-Price Activity Centre
Industriousness for the under-fives

Fisher-Price – the name is not a quaint reference to the toys' budget demographic but actually two of the founders of the company (for some reason the third, Helen Schelle, slipped through the cracks[1]) – is responsible for the formative sensory experiences of four or more generations of toddlers. From pull-along talking telephones and dogs to clockwork music boxes and record players, the New York preschool colossus had products in every pram and playroom. Forget designer babies and genetic screening – for nearly 80 years kids have been imprinted with an indelible 'f-p' logo at the earliest possible age. Friendly letters they may be, but indelible all the same.

Now, of course we weren't covetous of these chunky, cheery toys at the time – good God, we could barely wipe our own arses! But who was it, do you think, that looked down at the cross-legged eight year-olds busy with the 23-piece toolkit, shape-sorter or play family garage and thought 'Hmm... this lot are a bit lazy, all told – we could do with starting them a bit younger'? Whoever it was, we'll bet our state pension they're the same people who are now campaigning to raise the retirement age.

Accordingly, the *Fisher-Price Activity Centre* arrived in toy shops – a collection of moving wheels, dials, dingers and squeaks with enough sound effects to recreate the opening bars of Pink Floyd's *Money*. Suddenly we felt like we had missed out after all. Now there were tots in the cradle clocking in for a full day's button-pushing toil literally without getting up off their backs,[2] while we suffered the indignity of short trousers and real-world primary school.

In the interests of research, however, we now present those so-called 'activities' in full (and what consequences they led to in adulthood). The unit consisted of a mirror (pandering to narcissistic tendencies), a hare-and-tortoise slider (for budding inveterate gamblers), a pump-action test-your-strength-style bell (for would-be fairground strongmen) and at least three different types of spinning disc (training the local radio DJs of the future). Surely the most telling activity, however, was the telephone dial of despair. With its purposeless rotation, lack of numbers or people to call, it surely fuelled the fear of living (and dying) friendless that is our great modern-day tragedy. Seriously, we can think of no other justification for the popularity of MySpace.

Born	1973
Batteries	None
Players	👤
Breakage	🏆
Ads	▣
Envy	🏆🏆
eBayability	🖱🖱
Overall satisfaction	👍👍

See also Sticklebricks, Fuzzy Felt, Weebles

---

1 Possibly because Schelle-Fisher-Price would've sounded like a seafood trader but more likely down to good old-fashioned, home-style American chauvinism. However, we'd go so far as to suggest that, as well as a brand name, 'Fisher-Price' has now achieved the status of adjective (meaning 'childish, simplistic, cut-price', as in 'The TV Cream gang clearly fancy themselves as comic writers whereas in actual fact they're about as witty as a bunch of Fisher-Price Freddie Starrs').

2 You don't think that sounds like work? Back in 2004, Oxford-based 'power of play' centre, the Social Issue Research Group, conducted extensive comprehension and interaction tests on focus groups comprising children less than six months old! To their tiny, undeveloped minds, that's the scale equivalent of five years in a Korean sweat-shop. Probably. Which toy giant commissioned and funded this research? Oh, we think you know...

Flight Deck
The original flight sim

Born	1973
Batteries	None
Players	👤
Breakage	🍷🍷🍷🍷🍷
Ads	⬛⬛⬛⬛⬛
Envy	🏆🏆🏆🏆🏆
eBayability	🖱🖱🖱
Overall satisfaction	👍👍👍

Some toys are born great, some toys achieve greatness and some toys have greatness thrust upon them. These were the toys that no one ever saw in real life or owned (even though they definitely knew a kid up the street who said his cousin had one[1]), least of all actually played with.

High up on the list of such toys, and once possibly glimpsed pretty high on the shelves of WHSmiths too, was *Flight Deck* (rechristened a few years later, after a couple of small modifications, as *Super Flight Deck* in implicit acknowledgement – we reckon – of just how legendary the toy had become). We, in turn, could justifiably be accused of going 'plane daft' over the whole thing.

'All the thrills and excitement of landing a jet fighter on an aircraft carrier!' screamed the box. And – hell's teeth – didn't we just want a small taste of that action? Note the following checklist of factors in the game's favour. Were your parents required to knock through a ground-floor wall just to create a space big enough to set it up? Check. Was a degree in light engineering necessary to understand the combined complexity of the various cables, pulleys, levers and counterweights required to create the flight path? Check. Was the fully realised cockpit and joystick as close to a real-life jet any youngster could hope to get? Check, check and check again.

The drawbacks were many and all too evident. The time required to set the thing up hugely outweighed the amount of time it actually took to play it. For such an expensive toy, there was an awful lot of it that was just bits of cardboard and string.[2] Tangles, cock-ups and breakages were commonplace.

However, despite all this, for our money *Flight Deck* stumbles on only one point. Why go to all the effort of inspiring kids to turn their living room into a reasonable replica of the Ark Royal, only to manufacture the little fighter itself (an F4 Phantom at 1/72 scale, fact fans) in dull grey or – worse still – yellow (when any fule kno that the Red Arrows, flying Foland Gnats, were the definitive popular aeronauts of the era)? Attention to detail. It's not much to ask, is it?

See also *Airfix Kits, Vertibird, Peter Powell Stunter Kite*

1 Here's the weirdest bit of toy trivia you'll read this year. Stephen Skinner, guitarist with Orange Juice (of *Rip it Up* fame), used to own a *Flight Deck*.
2 Inability to afford this toy was no obstacle to setting up a scratch-built version of one's own. We've heard many tales of improvised *Flight Decks* constructed out of wool, fishing wire, broom handles, borrowed Airfix planes and bedroom-window latches. Although each story inevitable ended in disaster, such dedication is proof enough of the thrall in which it kept us.

Fuzzy Felt
Reusable cloth collage kit

This early learning toy was the delight of many an infant-school kid, mainly due to its simplicity, a highly tactile nature and the opportunity to make rude pictures when teachers weren't looking. Available in a variety of themes, allowing depictions of any everyday scene from 'farmyard' to 'ballet', the typical *Fuzzy Felt* set comprised a piece of card (about 10" by 6") with a dark, coloured Velcro-esque material glued to it and a collection of brightly coloured felt shapes (children, birds, trees) to attach to this background.

The significant word here, of course, is 'shape', as the *Fuzzy Felt* pieces of the Cream era were simply silhouettes, lacking distinctive features or detail. This lent the resulting montages a melancholic air, as though of a world trapped in permanent shadow. Indeed, there was something rather poignant about felt in itself, neglected by the fashion industry in favour of more glamorous cousins such as linen and satin and yet named synaesthetically ('having been touched', 'having had feelings') but most resolutely in the past tense.

A child with *Fuzzy Felt* (and it was a hotly contested item during 'activity time', of that we can vouch) could spend hours fingering the soft fabric pieces and create their own panoramic Swan Lake or (less well-regarded) Sunny Field. The most prized shapes were the more individual, identifiable ones, such as the monkey from the *Fuzzy Felt Jungle* set, although this naturally meant they were more limited in their uses. A monkey remained a monkey whichever way you positioned it, although there was a surreal pleasure in introducing an incongruous farmyard monkey from time to time.

God-fearing Christians could happily send their offspring out for a dose of Sunday school indoctrination, however, without fear of betrayal by the *Fuzzy Felt*. Although not endorsed by the church as such, the Bible Stories set included such blessed additional shapes as camels, halos, shepherds and the Three Kings of Orient Are.

The most versatile (and, therefore, most often lost or stolen) piece in any *Fuzzy Felt* set was the common crescent moon shape, not least because it could be used as a makeshift willy on *Fuzzy Felt* animals. (Joseph's donkey never looked quite so anatomically correct in the Nativity plays.) Despite this susceptibility to the base intent of toddlers, *Fuzzy Felt* was one of the most pleasant and gentle of toys of the past, but no less popular for that. The most amazing thing is that it sold so well for so long,[1] when it amounted to nothing more than a bunch of cheap off-cuts.

Born	1950
Batteries	None
Players	👤👤
Breakage	🍷
Ads	📺📺
Envy	🏆🏆
eBayability	🖱
Overall satisfaction	👍👍👍

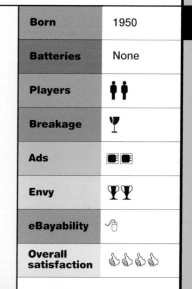

See also *Sticklebricks, Remus Play-Kits, Play Doh Monster Shop*

---

1 Someone's still making it (Toy Brokers, they're called), but it's just not the same. They've sullied the brand for *Fuzzy Felt* purists by introducing 'character' versions (*Noddy, Thomas the Tank Engine, My Little Pony*), and some of the pieces have even got detailed faces. Most blasphemously, the monkey piece is nowhere to be found.

Galaxy Invader 1000
Joystick-waggling high jinks

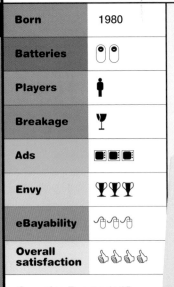

Born	1980
Batteries	
Players	
Breakage	
Ads	
Envy	
eBayability	
Overall satisfaction	

See also *Tomytronic 3D, Palitoy Cue Ball, Game and Watch*

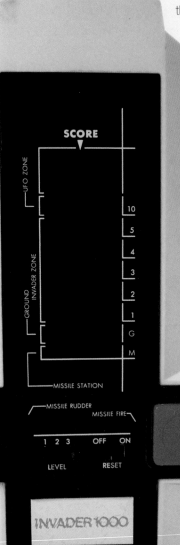

SCORE

UFO ZONE

GROUND INVADER ZONE

10
5
4
3
2
1
G
M

MISSILE STATION

MISSILE RUDDER

MISSILE FIRE

1 2 3   OFF   ON

LEVEL   RESET

INVADER 1000

To modern generations for whom even *Tetris* is ancient history, the original tabletop arcade classics must look like steam-powered fossils. But for the Cream-era kid, these chunky, miniature, self-contained games were naught short of a miracle. We won't bore you with a history of video games – there are whole encyclopaedias out there that can do that job for us – but we will summarise the important developments in the technology, thus: it all got a lot smaller.

Time was when you needed a bagful of 10p coins and a lot of patience to get half-decent on arcade games. All the big players – Taito's *Space Invaders*, Atari's *Asteroids*, Namco's *Pac-Man*, Williams' *Defender* – were pocket-money gobblers to a man, but all were designed for adult-height cathode-ray-tube display in dusty old cabinets. The invention of VFD (vacuum fluorescent display) meant pin-sharp graphics could be recreated at a fraction of the size. With a few transparent filters stuck over the top, different parts of the screen could show different colours. And with that, the market for cheap *Space Invaders* clones cracked wide open.

The flood began with *Invaders from Space* (we'd like to think that the name was the result of a poorly administered Japanese translation), a bulky white unit that sported a huge 'target' screen decoration, only a tiny part of which

1 Those *Firefox F-7* level-completing tunes in full: the theme from *Thunderbirds*,

Wagner's *Ride of the Valkyries*, *TIE Fighter Attack* from *Star Wars*, *Vultan's Theme* from *Flash Gordon* and the *Light Cavalry Overture* by Franz Suppé (oh,

actually constituted the display. Possibly the best-remembered variation, however, was *Astro Wars*, which had the added excitement of a 'docking' bonus round and featured a painful joystick operated by the thumb and early use of the magnified display ('cos the VFD graphics were so expensive they had to make 'em small). The unit's score – like so many of these things – went up to only 9999 but did change to 'good' when the bonus round was completed successfully.

The daddy, however, was CGL's *Galaxy Invader*, which had a horrible flimsy fire button and another blister-inducing thin joystick, but sported a revolutionary phallic shape that meant that it was the only product that could slide easily into the fashionable-at-the-time cream-brown Army and Navy satchel (with 'The Jam' etched in biro on the flap). Consequently, it was one of the first electronic games of any kind to get confiscated at school.

Some honourable mention must go to Grandstand's *Firefox F-7*, which stood out among its peers for two reasons. First, it featured a crazy 3D screen; second, it appeared to be an attempt at cashing in on the latest (and crappiest ever) Clint Eastwood film. It didn't in any way capture the thrills of piloting a gadget-filled supersonic jet fighter; nor did it make you feel like a granite-jawed hero, but it looked – and sounded – bloody great.[1] At the same time, we can't let *Munchman* go unpunished: if you're going to license a Pac-Man game in the UK (complete with a brilliant yellow Pac-Man-shaped case), call the damned thing *Pac-Man*.

The strain on the pocket soon told, however, with the cost of all those Ever Ready Gold Seal batteries (£1.05, Argos cat. no. 980/1444) mounting up. It wasn't long before investment was made in an AC/DC adaptor (£4.99, Argos cat. no. 982/1149)[2] – meaning the fluorescent fun could carry on indefinitely, albeit now only within range of a socket.

Clone wars Just your typical early '80s tabletop mountain

you know... the one that goes tum-ti-tum-ti-tum-ti-tum, tum-ti-tum-ti-tum-tum... no, hang on, that's *The Archers*).

2 Yes, these are genuine '80s Argos codes. We checked.

Game and Watch
Liquid crystal thrills

Born	1980
Batteries	🔋🔋
Players	🧍
Breakage	🏆
Ads	🎞️🎞️🎞️
Envy	🏆🏆🏆
eBayability	🖱️🖱️🖱️
Overall satisfaction	👍👍👍

See also *Tomytronic 3D, ZX Spectrum, Commodore 64*

If the inventor of the Casio handheld game didn't retire a multimillionaire at the end of the '80s to a luxury mansion in the Bahamas, then there is no justice in the world. For what was this toy but a perfectly weighted and targeted marketing triumph? A small, portable game that could masquerade when required as a calculator, meaning kids could persuade parents and teachers alike that it was a legitimate scholastic tool ('But Dad, don't you want me to know how to do logarithms?'). Casio's handheld games – *Boxing*, *Baseball*, *Soccer* – were the logical next step for a company that had exhausted the potential of the 50m water-resistant chronograph with built-in *Space Invaders*. It was time to take the watch off the wrist and lay it on the table.

It was a brilliant plan. It couldn't fail. However, Casio screwed up one tiny detail. Their first wave of games looked and behaved like calculators. So, though that could easily do the trick when it came to foxing your algebra prof, why would anyone want to play a game in that narrow screen across the top? By the time Casio had regrouped with a second batch of dedicated handheld games, another company had swooped in to the classroom and was preparing to teach them a lesson: Nintendo *Game and Watch*.

That's game *and* watch, by the way. Game. And. Watch. Seriously, who did Nintendo think they were fooling? 99 percent game and 1 percent watch, their credit-card-sized consoles lay flat on a desk and could be customised to appeal to almost any demographic (ersatz *Donkey Kong* for hardened arcadaholics, *Snoopy Tennis* for girly girls). With simple-to-grasp gameplay, even the class Joey could be a high-score king in minutes.

Unfortunately, the in-built LCD screens were so easily cracked that replacements had to be shipped in almost weekly. (Nintendo 1, pocket money 0, there.) The boredom-novelty churn was also managed carefully and an ever-increasing variety of games was released into the market (double-screen games, widescreen games, colour displays) until the bubble finally burst with the arrival of home entertainment systems and the fully controllable 'characters' that populated the games thereon.

As the '80s retreated, the first *Game Boy* hit the shops. The once and future king of handhelds, this was created by the same team as *Game and Watch* and shared a noble lineage. Instead of containing just a single game, the *Game Boy* had a vast library at its disposal (although everyone just seemed to use it for playing *Tetris*).

Twenty years on, and the descendents of the humble *Game and Watch* live on. Ironically, we've since produced a generation of kids who can download infinitely superior Java games on to their mobile phones but who can't actually tell the time.

Girl's World
Disembodied head in a box

Another one of those somewhat macabre girls' toys[1] destined to lie around the house and strike fear into the hearts of visiting relatives who didn't have their glasses on. You've seen that bit at the end of *Se7en*, haven't you? That's the sort of thing we mean. Oh, sorry, have we just spoiled it?

Basically the life-sized severed head of an unattractive shop dummy, *Girl's World* served two potential purposes: number one, you could do its hair; number two, you could do its makeup. But oh, the grown-up glamour that it encapsulated! Needless to say, the brunette bonce was rather disappointing in action.[2] Putting rollers in plastic hair produces a curl with a half-life of approximately 0.36 seconds, and while some of the hair could magically 'grow' by cranking a Frankenstein-esque bolt in the side of the neck, the rest of the hair didn't grow, so either she had a huge ponytail on top of her head or she didn't: your choice.

Meanwhile, the eyeshadows (green and blue crayons) and lipsticks (choose from reddy-pink or pinky-red) were actually thick smears of oily grease that were, we would find out later, nigh on impossible to remove from your mum's best cushions and had the ominous words 'Warning: contains lanolin' printed on every pot.[3] *Girl's World* was a handy training course in makeup design for girls who planned on growing up to have PVC skin (i.e. anyone you might see in *Heat* these days). In fact, after a few sessions, the slap really began to take its toll and Miss World would start to look rather battered. This was in the days before ethical cosmetics and 'Against Animal Testing', so we don't doubt that several bunny rabbits suffered to give up these particular hair and beauty secrets.

Later came *Super Girl's World*, which had rotating, rolling eyeballs (tilt the head to change her iris colour – amber, green, blue or brown) and freaky, streaky hair dyes. Or was that Girls Aloud?

See also *Tiny Tears, Barbie, Sindy*

---

1 We say 'girls' but surely Vidal Sassoon and Nicky Clarke had one of these as a child? Mind you, just look at those first names. Their parents were probably hoping for girls, weren't they?

2 No word on the blonde, though. Debates raged among preteen lads about which of the two was more of a goer, until they were frightened off by a top-former with precocious breasts.

3 Lanolin? Wool fat – or, if you prefer, sheep wax.

Born	1978
Batteries	None
Players	👤
Breakage	🍷🍷🍷🍷
Ads	▪️▪️▪️▪️
Envy	🏆🏆🏆🏆🏆
eBayability	🖱️🖱️
Overall satisfaction	👍👍👍

Guess Who?
What's My Line? without Jilly Cooper

Born	1979
Batteries	None
Players	👤👤
Breakage	🍷🍷
Ads	📺📺
Envy	🏆🏆
eBayability	🖱
Overall satisfaction	👍👍

See also *Hangman, Downfall, Connect Four*

This is the reason nobody can ever take a police photo-fit seriously. MB's *Guess Who?* attempted to test children's powers of observation via some of the strangest-looking people you'll ever see.

The twin boards featured a rogues' gallery of 40 faces attached via bits of plastic. As one of two players, you'd pick a random face card and place it in the slot in front of you. You'd then take it in turns to ask yes-or-no questions to deduce which person your opposite number had picked. With each answer, you pushed down those not applicable, so eventually you would be left with just one person still staring at you, and say 'Is this person David?' or whoever, which would win you the game. Er, if you were right, of course.

Obviously, each face had to have an easily definable aspect, hence a huge number of hats, glasses and – on far too many people – very ruddy cheeks. Clearly the pics were based on a community of folk who lived in a cold northern town sometime between the wars. (The modern game includes a rather larger ethnic mix than was the case in the original version, which was more or less entirely white.[1])

Particularly satisfying was discovering a killer question ('Is this person female?'), narrowing the choices right down and allowing you to work your way across the board slamming down face after face.[2] As with all games, you could always find a new way to play it that wasn't in the rules – occasionally you wouldn't bother with the cards, instead picking your favourite drawing on the board. This was badly flawed as absolutely everyone would always pick Philip, thanks to his uncanny resemblance to Kenny Everett.

After each game, you could turn the board upside down, so every face would stand up again and you'd be ready for another round straight away, but after a few plays this would lead to a bit of a gap while you picked all the bits of plastic off the floor where they'd fallen out.

The TV advert ('Guess who? His eyes are blue, now that's a clue!') was notable for the fact that the boy playing the game was clearly cheating by asking all his questions in one go: 'Does he wear glasses? Has he got a hat? It's gotta be Jack.' Of course he was going to win by doing that!

1 Can you fuel kids' early prejudices of racial stereotypes with the latest retail edition of *Guess Who??* Or should you let 'em watch *Little Britain* instead? Seriously, though, it's astonishing to note that even as late as 1987, there was nary a black face to be found on the *Guess Who?* playing board. 1987! The year of acid house!

2 We reckon the *Heat* generation would love a celebrity version of *Guess Who?*. 'Has she had botox?' 'Is he a closet homosexual?' 'Has a dead body ever been found in his swimming pool?'

Hangman
There's a noose on the loose

'Kids these days are sharp,' people have always said. 'You can't fool 'em. They know all the angles. Smarter than most adults, in fact.' This didn't apply, necessarily, to the kids who were – ahem – roped in and quizzed by the marketing department of Milton Bradley on the day *Hangman* was conceived. What point, we have to ask ourselves, was there in paying for a plastic version of a game you could easily do with two pencils and a bit of paper?

Perhaps it was just us, because they sold in many and varied forms – *Squares*, *Computer Battleship* (which, to be fair, was a veritable symphony of light and sound), any number of noughts-and-crosses variants and *Hangman*. The Imperial-era version (circa '78) featured Vincent Price on the box,[1] leaning on the gibbet and preparing to mete out justice in a faux Old Wild West town (probably just off the East Lancs Road in reality). 'Cos frankly, since all that Ruth Ellis nonsense, us Brits really didn't go in for death by gallows unless it came in primary-coloured plastic with a Wyatt Earp type on the lid.

TV advertised, therefore, by a pair of senile bank-tellers who thwarted a robber's activities by becoming engrossed in its singular charms, *Hangman* consisted of two *Battleship*-style hidey-behindy units, each of which contained a range of plastic tiles with letters on. With these, you could either create an impromptu mini-variation of *Domino Rally* by lining 'em up and knocking 'em over or, more boringly, slot into the spaces in the word as they were guessed. The progress of the hangee was advanced by successive pre-drawn pictures on a dial, thus foiling the other pleasure of prepubescent wits – the endowment of the luckless individual with large primary sexual characteristics. Even more boringly, this MB version didn't have the decency to incorporate a clockwork choking noise or anything when you won. We'll take imagination over plastic any day.

Born	1976
Batteries	None
Players	👫
Breakage	🍷
Ads	▣▣▣▢
Envy	🏆
eBayability	🖱
Overall satisfaction	👍👍

See also *Stay Alive!, Guess Who?, Scrabble*

1 Cream-era toy history is littered with celebrity endorsements like this. Mike Reid's *Pop Quiz* (which he helped devise), Jeremy Beadle's *Practical Jokes* and a million and one telly spin-off board games (*Dad's Army, Neighbours, Bread*).

Haunted House
Paranormal plastic fun

Born	1970
Batteries	None
Players	👤👤👤👤
Breakage	🍷🍷🍷
Ads	📺📺
Envy	🏆🏆
eBayability	🖱🖱
Overall satisfaction	👍👍👍

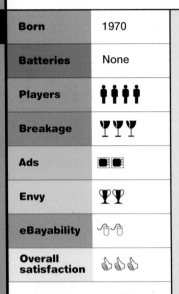

Haunted House, like *Mousetrap* before it, was one of those stalwart Cream-era board games with extra bits to assemble before play. The ads depicted spooky goings-on as stage-school kids gathered round the board inside an actual haunted house. Although the jingle insisted 'When you go to the *Haunted House* for tea, you never know quite what you'll see,' the reality was, as always, slightly less exciting.

Wannabe *Rentaghost*-busters had to take a conventional follow-the-path route around the board, which itself was split into four quarters. Each of these represented a room in the house,[1] with a large 'haunted mansion' structure at the centre creating a complex system of hidden tunnels – one entrance in the chimney at the top and several exits around the sides. Occasionally during your trip around the board, you'd be asked to pick up a card from the horror-themed pile. The game came with a glow-in-the-dark 'Whammy Ball' skull and, usually, the cards ordered you to toss the skull into the chimney to let it find its own way out of the house. If your counter (a plastic silhouette in the 'boys and girls come out to play' style[2]) happened to be in front of an exit, the skull would come crashing out and knock your child over. This sent you back to the start or inflicted some other horrible penalty, such as being turned into a plastic mouse.

If you survived the onslaught of the skull, on you went, following the footprint-shaped spaces, avoiding the danger areas, around the house until you arrived at the foot of the stairs. The winner was the first to climb these and close the lid on the coffin at the house apex, thus banishing the banshees forever. *Haunted House* featured the enigmatic Ghoulish Gerty as a notional head of the house,[3] with the skull card reading 'Ghoulish Gerty drops it down the chimney' ('it' became a marble after you lost the skull). And they never explained how to read the board after you turned the lights off for full-on glow-in-the-dark action.

See also *War of the Daleks, Mousetrap, Escape from Colditz*

Wanda the Wicked casts a spell

Glenda the Good breaks the spell

1 Broom Room, Witchin' Kitchen, Spell Cell and Bat's Ballroom. The trouble with any cardboard assembly-reliant game, of course, was that the various tabs and slots would get chewed up and mangled every time they were jammed together by juvenile hands.
2 MB's more robust reversion of the game for the '80s, *Ghost Castle*, replaced these with cardboard cartoon kids from the Scooby Doo school of scared-looking supporting characters. By far the best title the game ever got was in Sweden, however, where it luxuriated in the name *Spökslottet*.
3 The others were Wicked Wanda and Glenda the Good. The US version of the game was marketed as the somewhat sitcommy *Which Witch?*

He-Man and the Masters of the Universe
Bicep-rippling battlers with moral message

There's an almost infinite number of reasons why we should hate He-Man and his Assorted Toy-Flogging Swashbuckling Masters of the Cartoon Universe. For a start, he'd have been wedgied into the middle of next week if he'd turned up at our school disco with that pudding-bowl haircut, 'Power of Grayskull' or no. Plus, he hung around with such a bunch of cockmunchers (floating conjuring incompetent Orko, sappy love interest capture-monkey Teela and moustachioed PE teacher Man-at-Arms – real name Duncan) that he was in serious danger of looking a dweeb by association.

However, we'll quite happily go on record as saying that Mattel's He-Man toy range was excellent, simply because we've never seen a company throw itself quite so wholeheartedly into merchandising a toy in our tiny lives. Seriously, no stone was left unturned.[1] The range comprised the biggest and barmiest selection of figures, accessories and playsets the '80s ever saw, each constructed to the same, chunky, child-hand-sized scale (at five and a quarter inches of pleasingly tactile plastic, they were completely incompatible with the likes of *Action Man* or *Star Wars* figures).

Masters of the Universe was arguably also the first cross-gender toy range. Despite all the macho posturing, there were plenty of slender-thighed lady figures for sis to kick ass with and – in 1984 – an entire range of *She-Ra* toys. Blessed with long brushable hair and a selection of fashions, She-Ra fought with 'honour' rather than 'power' as heiress to the throne of Etheria. (She was, naturally, He-Man's twin sister.)

Mattel was so single-minded in its determination to revolutionise the action figure oeuvre that not even the puny TV series could stop it.[2] Around 1986, the toy giant gave up its dependence on the cartoon and started inventing its own range of villains, The Evil Horde. The *He-Man* figure alone was reissued in at least six different versions (the original, then *Battle-Armor* [sic], *Thunder Punch*, *Flying Fists*, *Laser Power* and Clark-Kent-style alter ego, *Prince Adam*). In addition to the toys, there were also *He-Man* comics, *View-Master* reels, walkie-talkies, videos, party horns, beakers, bedspreads, jigsaws and puzzles.

Lest we forget, *He-Man* also begat *Thundercats* and *Transformers* and, we'd be happy to claim, WWF. However, the abiding irony is that, in a cartoon that featured violence at its very core (there were more battle-axes this side of a Les Dawson monologue), He-Man had the gall to turn up at the end of each episode and deliver a lecture, the moral extraction of which can be summed up as 'don't be a tit'.

Born	1981
Batteries	None
Players	👫
Breakage	🍷🍷🍷
Ads	🎞🎞🎞🎞
Envy	🍷🍷🍷
eBayability	🖱🖱
Overall satisfaction	👍👍

See also *Action Man, Stretch Armstrong, Transformers*

1 Mattel *Masters of the Universe Stones Collection* came in three designs: Prince Adam pebbles, Battlecat boulders and She-Ra rocks. (Yeah, dude! She totally does.)
2 The TV ads had always eschewed the animated exploits of He-Man's cartoon cousins in favour of two Sylvia Young kiddiewinks battling it out in jump-cut conflict over the Castle Grayskull playset: 'You'll never win!' 'Oh yes I will!' Etc. For some reason, ads like these always deemed it necessary to feature a lot of gravel.

Hornby Railway Set
God's wonderful replica

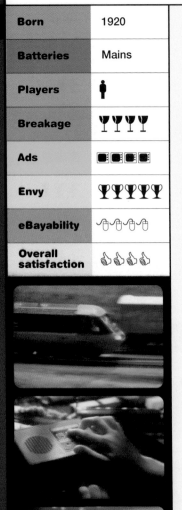

Born	1920
Batteries	Mains
Players	👤
Breakage	🍷🍷🍷🍷
Ads	▪▪▪▪
Envy	🏆🏆🏆🏆🏆
eBayability	🖱🖱🖱🖱
Overall satisfaction	👍👍👍

Building on the post-First World War success of his construction kits, Meccano Ltd's boss Frank Hornby turned his attention to toy trains. Powered by clockwork, these detailed mini-locos initially ran on zero gauge rails but, by 1938, electric power and the familiar double 'o' (or Dublo) sets were available.

Fast-forward forty years and we'd truly entered the 'age of the train' (or so British Rail would have us believe). The Inter-City 125 became a popular and familiar sight speeding through the nation's countryside (and one of BR's few true success stories to boot). Even casual observers could not fail to be impressed by slick adverts, reduced commuter journey times and the promise of even more advanced passenger trains (futuristic, tilting APTs, TGVs and ETRs).[1] There was even talk of a rail tunnel being built under the English Channel to link us directly to France!

In the meantime, Meccano trains had changed hands a few times and now traded under the recognisable name Hornby Railways, but the allure of the 1/32 scale caboose and coaches continued unabated. Hornby had cannily spotted the appeal to adult model-makers and collectors alike and was now marketing as much to grown-ups as to children. The Digital Command Controller added microchip signal technology to the Hornby range of rolling stock, recognising that most of their products were now being assembled in loft-sized dioramas of huge complexity by hobbyist dads.[2]

In 1993, the Railways Act saw Tory privatisation of British Rail, effectively splintering it into 25 smaller companies. Model railway enthusiasts found they had a whole plethora of new and diverse liveries to collect. However, as history has shown, this was bad news for real-life trains (particularly in terms of their safety record, as the Southall, Ladbroke Grove, Hatfield and Potters Bar accidents all bear witness). Hornby, perhaps in acknowledgement of the poor public image of modern rail, turned its attention to the nostalgic steam era.[3]

Always a peculiarly British interest (the Americans were far too in love with their cars to dedicate time to trains), an avid Hornby railway setter's ultimate career goal was either full-time trainspotting or RMT membership. Pleasingly, each was perfectly achievable with the right contacts, total dedication and an awful lot of time off work.

See also *Corgi 007 Lotus Esprit, Tonka Trucks, Airfix Kits*

1 The TGV (*Train à Grand Vitesse*) was a huge success in its native France, as was the ETR (*Elettro Treno*) in Italy. The UK's effort was rather more ill-fated, quelle fucking surprise.
2 Pop svengali Pete Waterman is probably the most famous aficionado of model railways, but who can forget that ad starring Colin 'Take Hart' Bennett, stuck up in the attic while his son runs around trying to – ahem – track down that important missing carriage? 'Thanks Ben.'
3 A special mention must also be given to Hornby 3DS, a weird monorail-cum-spaceship thing (from the future!).

Hungry Hippos
Greed is good

That's *Hungry Hippos* – not, you'll note, *Hungry Hungry Hippos*. Why? Because that's what we called it in Britain, so that's what it stays. You can leave all that Americanised, homogeneous 'brand realignment' at the door. Especially when it means changing the name just 'cos the advert jingle was so bloody catchy.[1] They did it with Snickers, Starburst and Oil of Olay, but those Yanks can keep their hands off our indigestion-proof ungulates. For a generation or more, the name remained *Hungry Hippos* – well, technically *The Hungry Hippos Game*, but one 'hungry' is enough, thank you very much.

Billed, typically, as 'a fast and furious' game, it might have been better described as 'ten minutes of slam, slam, slam, then back in the box'. The stars of H2G, as no one calls it, were the four grasping hippopotami – Henry, Happy, Homer and Harry – whose upper jaws you took command of. (The scientific name for those is *maxillae* – at least it is in carnivores, such as humans. Now don't say you haven't learned something today.) An RSI-inducing lever mechanic powered the marble-munching feeding frenzy, the object of which was to capture more of the potentially baby-choking balls than your opponents.

Much less a game than a great big din, the combination of plastic marbles (surely not a recognised staple of the river horse's predominantly vegetarian diet) and clattering hippo heads caused such a cacophony in the average household that parental curfews were swiftly applied. Later editions were more flimsy than the big-box original, although one or more of the pastel gobblers would ultimately capitulate under too much punishment whatever the size. The comparably sedate *Grabbin' Dragons* (modus operandi: hooking rings with a mythical creature's tail) was much less popular, which would seem to indicate that kids either prefer to really hammer their toys or they really, really dig hippos.[2]

Psychologists could probably make much of a child's selection of hippo – girls could be relied upon to pick the pink one (presumably 'cos it reminded them of George from *Rainbow*); boys, the blue – but frankly we can't. But if you see a Cream-era child wandering past those grey mud-wallowing things in the zoo without even a flicker of recognition, we think you now know why.

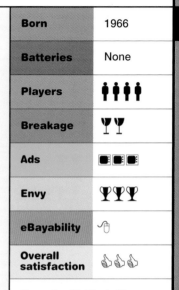

Born	1966
Batteries	None
Players	👤👤👤👤
Breakage	🍷🍷
Ads	📺📺📺
Envy	🏆🏆🏆
eBayability	🖱
Overall satisfaction	👍👍👍

See also KerPlunk, Stay Alive!, Buckaroo!

---

1 Full of lies, mind you – 'it's a race, it's a chase'. No it wasn't: those fuckers were glued down. The tune is respected in advertising circles, however. It's even been covered by, erm, Anal Cunt.
2 Homer Hippo's *Simpsons*' namesake probably put it best when he said '...and now we play the waiting game... the waiting game sucks! Let's play *Hungry Hungry Hippos.*'

Johnny Seven
Multipurpose rifle

Born	1964
Batteries	None
Players	👤
Breakage	🍷🍷🍷🍷🍷
Ads	📺📺
Envy	🏆🏆🏆🏆🏆
eBayability	🖱🖱🖱🖱🖱
Overall satisfaction	👍👍👍

See also *Tin Can Alley, Sonic Ear, Lone Star Spudmatic Gun*

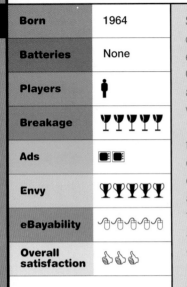

Some of the toys that didn't make it in to our Christmas stockings were ruled out (by parents, naturally) on the basis that, like designer sunglasses, their excessive cost always seemed inversely proportional to their possible uses. Of course, a toy would always score highly on both a parent's and a kid's appreciation index if it was adaptable enough to be played with in different ways and in different circumstances.[1]

In the case of *Johnny Seven* and the many lower-budget copies that followed in its wake, it was simply the fact that it had enough adjustable component parts that kept us interested. Much desired in the late '60s and early '70s, this multipart-assembly rifle-cum-rocket-launcher wasn't exactly armed-forces-issue accurate but, by ignoring the realities of ballistic hardware, the *Seven* could pack in more widgets, attachments and add-ons than your average Dyson, thus making it equally serviceable in a variety of imaginary conflict scenarios (hence the 'Seven') and ensuring its lasting popularity.[2]

The fact that it could fire real (plastic) rounds of bullets didn't hurt much either (unless you were on the receiving end of a particularly close-range shot). Even unloaded, its pull-back ratchet trigger could simulate the dakka-dakka-dakka sound of a rapid-fire tommy gun with pleasing simplicity. For lying-belly-down-in-the-long-grass fans, there was one of those bipods to rest the barrel on, plus it also came with a big enough assortment of cartridges and magazines to turn even John Rambo polysyllabic with jealousy.[3]

The toy was notably reissued in the '80s with the less inexplicably TV21-sounding name of *System 7*. This time the gun was blue and came with secret compartments, spinning disks and a parachuting 'message egg'. Anti-gun campaigners like Drew Barrymore would no doubt approve of the weapon's more politically correct projectiles in lieu of bullets and grenades (although perhaps less so the alternative consignment of dog shit that could be loaded into the descending egg).

In short, a must-have. In the ever-escalating arms race of playing fields and army games, bringing out the *Johnny Seven* had the hostile impact of an ICBM.

Talk about shock and awe!

---

1 A classic example here is the *True Lies*-inspiring double life of military-combat-versus-domestic-bliss that characterised the relationship between *Action Man* and *Sindy*, depending on whose turn it was to play with them. Remember that scene in *E.T.* when Elliot comes home from school to find that Gertie has dressed his alien pal in a frock and lipstick? That was the level of horror boys would experience at seeing *Action Man* taking tea in a younger sister's *Sindy* kitchen. Similarly, girls would cry real tears when *Sindy* was being interrogated and/or brutally tortured by the Gestapo.

2 Of course, in an actual war between *Johnny Seven* and a Dyson, the latter would win hands down. Those plastic bullets were no match for the vacuum power of a single-bagged upright, never mind an eight-cylinder cyclone.
3 Grenade missile and launcher, detachable automatic pistol, anti-tank and anti-bunker rockets, armour-piercing shell. The gun's full name was *Johnny Seven O.M.A.* ('one-man army') and was manufactured by Topper, who also came up with the *Secret Sam* spy attaché case. What was it with these guys and boys' names?

Junk Yard
Elastic-powered pinball substitute

Born	1975
Batteries	None
Players	👤
Breakage	🍷🍷
Ads	📺
Envy	🏆
eBayability	🖱
Overall satisfaction	👍

See also *Pocketeers, Binatone TV Master, Screwball Scramble*

In order to understand the appeal of this game, it's probably worth a brief refresher on junk yards as they have appeared in popular culture (also including tips, scrap-metal merchants, etc.).

The quintessential telly junk yard was the one in which Dr Who landed his police box back in the very first episode of the series. Or there was *Steptoe & Son*'s rag-and-bonemen's yard, largely home to Hercules the horse, and not really seen in all its glory until the series' big screen outings. In movies, a junk-yard setting often cropped up when there was foul play at hand (and especially if a gangster or spy needed offing in one of those car-crushers). Think *Goldfinger*, *Pulp Fiction* or *Superman III*, plus innumerable Derek Jarman 'state of Albion' classics and nearly every Children's Film Foundation effort. Junk yards were everywhere.[1]

Thus it was surely during an afternoon's skive off work in 1975 that an employee of the Ideal Toy Corp. found himself, popcorn on knee, enjoying The Who's seminal rock opera romp *Tommy*. At the heart of the film, the titular hero follows his own reflection through a mirror into a junk yard, where he finds a pinball table. Hang on... Pinball? Junk yard? Eureka! It might just work!

We reckon, however, even that deaf, dumb and blind kid would've had a bit of trouble with the resultant toy, crazy flipper fingers or no. As an analogue answer to proper lights and bumpers pinball, the central conceit of *Junk Yard* was seemingly purloined from those open-to-reveal saucy birthday cards of yore. That is to say, half of the illustration on each of the various scoring tags was hidden from view. Each tag fastened to the frame with an elastic band, tautly hooked under a plastic firing range (used to best effect with a window pane which, once you'd scored a direct hit with the stainless-steel ball, leapt up to expose the broken glass beneath). Even the drawings themselves were, on the face of it, half-inched (in this case from *Top Cat*, being the typical cartoon-inspired scrapheap fodder – old boot, fish-bone skeleton, knackered tyre, and so on).

Sadly, like its film and TV counterparts, this *Junk Yard* was always destined to add a bit of background colour rather than feature centrally. By the late '70s, any and all rubber-band-powered toys found themselves heading to that great jumble sale in the sky, replaced in our favour by their all-electric descendants. Ooh, weren't we fickle?

1 There's even one of those anonymous downtown L.A. hard rawk bands called Junkyard. They are, rather aptly, rubbish.

KerPlunk
Don't lose your marbles!

This indomitable favourite from Ideal brought a plastic revolution to games, with strange new shapes and Day-Glo colours liberating us from the boxy, beige and Racing Green world of the boring old British board game. Over-perspexed, over-played and over here – truly the Americans had landed.

Yes, as all children knew, plastic was ace, and *KerPlunk* was the trailblazer. Resembling the central console column of a 1950s Soviet TARDIS,[1] the fully assembled rig – base tray, two clear plastic beakers, a load of good old-fashioned have-your-eye-out pointy 'straws' stuck through the middle, and the marbles nesting on top – towered above its low-level rivals with a lurid, Vegas-style promise of raucous gravity-derived antics to put their bookish, dice-rolling shenanigans to shame. Initially, it was great – unashamed, no-brainer, straw-pulling anticipation. Would the marbles fall? Not yet. No, not yet, either. Nor, indeed, quite yet. Hmm. What's for tea, I wonder? Then, allofasudden – *KerPlunk!* Or, more accurately, rat-atat-atat-atat! (For all the onomatopoeic potential of the brand name, unless that tray was three feet deep with water and each marble the weight of a bag of sugar, the ending was always a clattering anticlimax.)

However, it's impossible to convey to today's young generation with their Harry Potter iPods and polyphonic Robosapiens the sense of joy that used to be gleaned from what was, essentially, some balls falling a distance of roughly eight inches, so it's fortunate none of them will be reading this. But we just know, don't we? *KerPlunk* was the bee's knees.[2] Scholastic post-script: the intermittent tap-tap-tap of marble on plastic must have worked like Chinese water torture on teachers, at least round our way, because the last day of term bring-in-a-game rule was, soon after the likes of this (and the placcy-scattering *Buckaroo!*) appeared, hastily amended to bring-in-a-quiet-game, thus introducing many a child to the despotic tendencies of the harassed authority figure.

See also Tip-It, Buckaroo!, Downfall

Born	1967
Batteries	None
Players	👤👤👤👤
Breakage	🍷🍷
Ads	▪️▪️▪️
Envy	🏆🏆🏆
eBayability	🖱️
Overall satisfaction	👍👍

---

1 Other things that people sometimes think are *KerPlunk*: Edward Scissorhands' cocktail shaker; a magpie's nest near a knitting-needle factory; Green Day's second album.

2 That said, we do know that 2005 brought with it the release of Mattel's *Electronic Super KerPlunk Mega Edition*. Which, as far as we're concerned, sounds like the title of the best unreleased Fall single we've never heard.

LEGO
Building-brick enemy of the vacuum cleaner

Born	1949
Batteries	None
Players	👤👤
Breakage	🍷🍷🍷
Ads	⬛⬛⬛⬛
Envy	🏆🏆🏆🏆
eBayability	🖱🖱🖱🖱
Overall satisfaction	👍👍👍

For sheer too-excited-to-eat-breakfast thrills, you couldn't beat tumbling down the stairs of a birthday morning to find a bloody big rattly box of *Technic LEGO* waiting for you. You'd just have to pray it wasn't a school day. The hours would just fly by as you knelt, elbow deep, in the most advanced children's construction set ever, replete with working piston engines, pneumatic hoists, chunky steerable rubber wheels and – if you were lucky – a working motor. By evening, you'd be driving around a custom dune-buggy fork-lift truck some seven feet in length. Or so it seemed.

Because that was the dream. The reality was a little different. By and large, *LEGO* came in intentionally rationed boxed sets of various sizes, each with ostensibly just the one goal – construct whatever was photographed on the lid. Like a scene from *Charlie and the Chocolate Factory*, you'd be thinking yourself lucky if you got a small set once a year. Perhaps just enough to assemble a simple house, car or plane. Or, if you were dreadfully poor, a short wall.

As time went on, you'd be able to add a few of the larger, more flexible models

1 *LEGO* is a Danish invention, from 'play well' (*leg godt*). Denmark is very close to Sweden, the home of IKEA. By jingo, those Scandinavians like their self-assembly leaflets, don't they?
2 Our best guess – a cross between a bike and a monocle – has been described by *LEGO*'s UK PR dept as 'wrong'.

(a *LEGOLAND* petrol station or – at the height of *Star Wars* fever – one of the cool spaceships with transparent cockpits, satellite dishes and little astronaut figures) and slavishly follow the illustrated building instructions,[1] at least the first time you put them together. Thereafter, you could start to exercise the full force of your own creativity, making a space car, say, or... erm, a petrol house. Then there were the vocational sets, or the castles, the forts, the pirate ships. There were even some specialist sets designated only 'for experienced *LEGO* builders' of 12 years and older. Experienced? Already our *LEGO* CV looked threadbare.

Two houses along, of course, would be the Verucca Salt type with a huge bin full of *LEGO* bricks of endless shapes and sizes, which she would use to make houses for her dollies. For crying out loud! What about the electric transformer-equipped sets? How exactly were we supposed to be embraced by the *LEGO SYSTEM*? What the hell was a *BIONICLE*?[2]

Of course, we're showing our age. Kids these days can build and program robots with *LEGO MINDSTORMS*[3] or create and buy their very own personalised models online at the *LEGO Factory*[4] (although that does rather seem to be missing the point of *LEGO*). The vintage stuff we were used to now shifts on eBay by the hundredweight, alongside those lovingly preserved boxed sets that look clunky by today's standards (but heck, it's *LEGO* – how else is it going to look?).

See also *Sticklebricks, Airfix Kits, Zoids*

LEGO sets Once more around the block

---

3 Snakes alive! They're going to take over the earth! And we thought *Big Trak* was advanced!

4 Some adults are still feeling the pain of a *LEGO*-less childhood, out of which there are two roads to recovery. Take the kids to LEGOLAND Windsor or spend

six months building life-sized *LEGO* models of dogs and people just to get on the local evening news and proclaim yourself the Lord of *LEGO*. Sorry, did we say two roads?

Little Professor
Ruddy-faced maths spod

Born	1976
Batteries	
Players	
Breakage	
Ads	
Envy	
eBayability	
Overall satisfaction	

Dallas – the home of cowboys, oil wells and early integrated circuits as produced by Texas Instruments. Originally founded in seismography (to wheedle out those reticent little underground reservoirs of oil), TI moved into electronics in the '50s. A couple of decades later, the *Speak & Spell* was born (and the rest is history), though it was preceded by its less talkative cousin, the *Little Professor*.

Essentially a rebranding of the company's TI-1000 calculator[1] with a bit more hoo-hah going on around the semiconductors, the *Little Professor* boasted the features of an owlish caricature boffin (thus informing an entire generation of kids what to expect from scientists, maths whizzes and academics) sporting a bushy 'tache, glasses and mortar-board look that sat well with Bash Street teachers and graduating students the world over. *Little Professor* was that most bizarre of maths 'learning aids',[2] an uncalculator. Its object? To teach you to do addition, division, etc. in your head. And that's fun how, exactly?

In any case, TI should've found themselves in trouble with the International Committee for Children's Toy Colour Codes (that's the TW3C), if it wasn't actually just something we made up, as *Little Professor*'s basic yellow colour scheme didn't conform to the recognised TI arithmetic blue of *Speak & Maths*. But then, Playskool went and screwed that up anyway – using yellow and orange for their speccy show-off 'computer friend' *Maximus* and blue for *Major Morgan the Electronic Organ*. Music? Blue? What shape of insanity is this?

Where TV numbers supremo Johnny Ball had showed us how to learn maths by stealth (always disguising anything of educative value in a joke, sketch or trick), Li'l Prof did nothing but set sums of increasingly improbable complexity. Get an answer wrong and you would be greeted by the red LED message 'EEE'. Which is just odd. By the time the slimline version arrived,[3] we'd moved on to actual computers. *Little Professor*, it has to be said, remained sadly no more than the sum of its parts.

See also *Speak & Spell, Electronic Detective, Game and Watch*

---

1 The first iteration of *Little Professor* didn't actually work as a real calculator – no hilarious 'SHELLOIL' or 'BOOBLESS' upside-down writing antics there then.

2 The early version betrayed its Confederate State origins by shipping with a booklet that used the singular 'fun with math facts'.

3 Note, however, that the chunky plastic case remained – presumably, so that TI didn't have to retool the packaging equipment.

Lone Star Spudmatic Gun
Ammo domini

If we're brutally honest here, it was less about the guns (although anything gun-shaped was better than your fingers or a stick) and more about the bang you got for your buck. The standard, cheapest spud gun, the *Lone Star Spudmatic*, in die-cast black metal and card-mounted in the local newsagents, would undoubtedly be an early pocket-money purchase rather a Christmas present request, but it wasn't to be the last gunpowder-powered firearm in a youngster's arsenal.

The main drawback of the spud gun was its inability to fire more than a single round, a small red paper square torn from a roll of caps (or, given its four-in-one status, 1cc of water, a cork pellet or a bit of potato). Colt 45-style repeater guns such as the *Lone Star Big Six* would allow the entire roll to be loaded for rapid-fire action, especially useful for re-enactments of the final scene of *Butch Cassidy and the Sundance Kid*. But the resulting string of shattered, smoking brown paper (and the satisfying smell of burnt sulphur) was inauthentic.

Salvation came in the shape of plastic caps, six or more impregnated tubes in a circular arrangement, looking not unlike something ripped off the top of a bottle of pop but which could be slotted into the right kind of gun barrel just like – okay, almost like – a real revolver. Plastic caps also came in flat-packed squares of 60 or so for use with cap rockets, each of which could be individually fitted with a single cap to the nose before embarking on an explosive and short-lived Hindenberg-esque flight.[1] Finally, the first-year school trip to Boulogne would invariably re-ignite a child's interest in detonation and unleash the epidemic acquisition of Acme-style bangers (and, as if to reinforce the painful move towards adulthood further, rites-of-passage purchases of nudie playing cards and, erm, flick-combs).

But we'll never forget the least-treasured but oft-requested purchase (and we never got them, so they remain on our spiritual wish-list): snappers – those paper 'trick-noise-maker' crackers that looked like sperm. There always seemed to be more in a box than there actually was, possibly due to the unnecessary extra packing of sawdust and gritty residue in there. Sensibly, they only really worked outdoors and, crucially, you couldn't terrify pensioners with them for the six months either side of Bonfire Night ('cos they just weren't loud enough). *Plus ça change*.

Born	1936
Batteries	None
Players	
Breakage	
Ads	
Envy	
eBayability	
Overall satisfaction	

See also *Johnny Seven, Tin Can Alley, Walkie-Talkies*

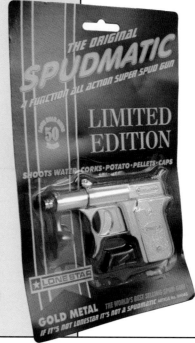

1 Cap bombs were more of an exercise in frustration anyway. You really needed an urban environment to guarantee proper incendiary conditions. Paving flags were the best surface, road tarmac being far too irregular to achieve an explosion every time (plus there was the additional disadvantage of cars squashing your flimsy plastic torpedo in the process).

Magic Robot
Quiz game with artificial intelligence

'Ask the robot questions,' said the box. 'He always gives the right answer.' We must say we were intrigued from the start. The robot in question was under two inches high, made of solid metal and stood in a strange knee-bent posture that made him look to be in desperate need of a toilet.[1]

In his hands he held a long metal pole. He could be fitted into one of two holes inside the box, while around him sheets with one circle of printed questions and one circle of printed answers were placed. The first stage was to place the robot in the 'questions' hole and point his pointy stick at the challenge of your choice, such as 'What is the capital of France?'[2]

Then you could, in theory, try to 'beat the robot' by answering the question yourself but – let's face it – most of us skipped straight to stage three: watching the robot Do His Thing. You simply placed him on the 'answers' hole (strangely enough, it was a mirror), and – whoa! – he spun around of his own accord and – bingo! – his stick would be pointing at the correct response. Bloody hell! He's only a piece of metal – how could he *know*?!

Socks were well and truly knocked off. The only downside was that there weren't all that many questions per box, so after a couple of rainy afternoons, you would be reduced to seeking amusement from illegally swapping around the question and answer discs. 'What is the capital of France?' 'The banana.' Ho ho. But, for a while at least, this was a toy with a genuine wow factor, at least for anyone aged seven or under. Retrospect may tell us that it was all done with magnets, but hey, get Derren Brown to go one on one with this geezer live on Channel 4 and we'll be there.

Born	1950
Batteries	None
Players	👤👤
Breakage	🏆🏆
Ads	▪️
Envy	🏆🏆🏆
eBayability	🖱🖱
Overall satisfaction	👍👍👍

See also *Magnetic Wheel, Trivial Pursuit, Little Professor*

The Great Marvello
Less *Magic Robot*, more Eamonn Android

1 The version manufactured by Merit was actually a Marvin the Paranoid Android lookalike in plastic with a metal base but, heck, the memory cheats. A carbon-copy competitor from Bell toys was the unfortunately racist *Dr Magini*. One might most kindly say he resembled that Zoltar Speaks wishing machine from the film *Big*. In actual fact, he'd clearly been designed – we can say fairly confidently – as a plastic black-a-moor. We've also seen a Dr Who version called *The Dalek Oracle* (and it's sink-plungingly

obvious how that one works, no?) plus – most bafflingly of all – *Eamonn Andrews Presents the Great Marvello*. Quite what on earth the former *This is Your Life* host was doing endorsing a knock-off *Magic Robot* game is anyone's guess.
2 The questions, boasted Merit, were authorised by the *Children's Encyclopaedia*. No, we don't recall this being the definitive source of childhood knowledge either. If they'd been authorised by the McWhirters off *Record Breakers*, we might be talking.

Magic Rocks
Grow-your-own underwater crystal 'garden'

Born	1940
Batteries	None
Players	👤
Breakage	🍷🍷🍷
Ads	📺
Envy	🏆🏆🏆🏆
eBayability	🖱🖱
Overall satisfaction	👍👍

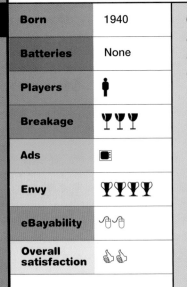

One of those things an overtime-weary lab researcher possibly stumbled across by accident in some multinational petrochemical conglomerate (see also *Silly Putty* and *Slime*). The basic premise rested on the implicit (and flawed) expectation that any child would be interested in watching small multicoloured stalagmites form as if by 'magic' over a period of hours or, indeed, days inside a large liquid-filled glass bowl (or, more realistically in the Cream-era child's household, an empty Nescafe jar). As if that in itself were somehow edifying or educational.

At best, there was something intriguing in the packaging, which required that the 'rocks' be kept separate from the powdered 'solution' with which they would react once submerged,[1] and hinted at potentially explosive results should they ever come into contact while dry. At worst, there was the implicit (and thwarted) expectation that the crystals would somehow form a sprawling and yet microscopic metropolis in the fashion of Superman's ice-dome city hideaway from the films. But for *Sea-Monkeys*, you see? (Later versions tried to spice up the landscape with additional plastic models, including *Orca Killer Whale* and the *Titanic*. No, really.)

Originally marketed as *Magic Isle Undersea Garden* (and, therefore, understandably often mixed up with 'oriental' paper-flower gardens and the like),[2] growing a full set of the bloody things was a trial in itself. The instructions demanded that the solution be emptied out and your jar rinsed and refilled at least three times to clear out any residue. Inevitably, this meant broken, brittle spires and tears before bedtime.

If the stalagmites survived, then there was also the question of what to do once the rocks had finished getting it on. It being the '70s, you might hazard a guess that *Magic Rocks* had some 'far-out' application as ornament around the lava lamps and fibre-optics, but you'd be wrong. As we recall, they lasted a couple of days on a window ledge before the whole corroded mess was binned and the jam-jar sequestered for use in a tadpole hunt. *Magic Rocks* were an ephemeral joy but... well, that's geology for you.

See also Sea-Monkeys, Chemistry Set, Shrinky Dinks

---

1 That's sodium silicate, if you're interested, science fans. In liquid form, it's a potent acid and stains clothes like a bastard. The rocks themselves were actually just water-soluble metallic salts that had been dyed and dried out. The chemical reaction between the two created a kind of gelatine, which rose up through the liquid to form deposits in a speleothemic structure. Sorry if reading this takes the 'magic' out of *Magic Rocks*, but we've all got to grow up some time.

2 Salter Science introduced a 'fun with crystals' kit that produced similar results. Variations on the same theme are still available at cheap Chrimbo-pressie outlets today.

Magna Doodle
Back to the drawing board

The official yarn we've been spun about this toy's genesis is that four Japanese engineers from the Pilot Pen company were trying to solve the problem of creating a dustless chalkboard. Oh yeah? It's called a pen and paper, lads. Or is that just too simple for you? Such a story is obviously an elaborate smokescreen for Pilot Pen's real motivation, which can be neatly summed up in the phrase 'Let's get one up on those *Etch-A-Sketch* bastards.'[1]

Nowt more than a magnetic doodling pad (now, how do they think of those brand names, eh?) or, more accurately, a honeycombed magnetophoretic display lattice, *Magna Doodle* shared a lot in common with its chunky red cousin. That is to say, there was a load of metallic crap in there, and you could draw and erase repeatedly at will. But where the newer box excelled was in the introduction of the magnetic stylus pen, which lent it one important advantage: freehand drawing. No more zigzagging across the screen to fill in an important detail. Now you could quite literally dot the 'i's and cross the 't's (and dot the little 'j's and cross the capital 'Q's – let's go mad!). At long last, freedom from the tyranny of toy-making pedagogues lay in your hand.[2]

One thing *Magna Doodle* couldn't do, though, was let you colour in your pictures. The tyranny of the torpid ferrous particle remained. But, bursting out of this murky dark grey on grey world, we should also mention Tomy's rich kids' toy, *Lights Alive*. We're not even pretending to know how this one worked – suffice to say you could get stuck in about it with a variety of handheld shapes and produce a multicoloured *Family Fortunes* board of pixellated artwork.

The box it came in included some great 'serving suggestions' for the toy, ranging from drawing a big twinkling elephant to playing noughts and crosses – futuristically! Alas, after writing your own name on it and then possibly some mild sweary words ('SNOG!'), *Lights Alive*'s appeal would dim quickly. And worse than that, it was supposed to be 'educational' too.

Ultimately, both these toys fell out of favour with kids for precisely the same reason they were popular with parents: if these were your drawing implements of choice,[3] how on earth were you supposed to make a right old scrawly mess of the living room walls?

Born	1974
Batteries	None
Players	👤
Breakage	🍷🍷🍷
Ads	⬛⬛⬛
Envy	🏆🏆🏆🏆
eBayability	🖱🖱
Overall satisfaction	👍👍👍

See also Etch-A-Sketch, *Remus Play-Kits, Spirograph*

---

1 Eventually, though, the plucky *Magna Doodle* brand was licensed by the Ohio Art Company, the makers of *Etch-A-Sketch* and now the new guardians. Oh dear, it's like Apple giving in to Microsoft, isn't it? Yes, that bad. The new owners have even 'Mini Coopered' the *Doodle*'s design and given it the ability to write in red and blue.

2 Except they did tie on that pen with a bit of string, to stop you wandering off with it, didn't they? Mind you, all the more handy for playing 'post-office' with.
3 Check out the endless repeats of *Friends* on telly and you may spot a *Magna Doodle* fastened to the inside of Joey and Chandler's front door.

Magnetic Wheel
Stringless yoyo

Born	1953
Batteries	None
Players	👤
Breakage	🍷
Ads	📺
Envy	🏆
eBayability	🖱
Overall satisfaction	👍👍👍

Gyroscope Top brass

For donkey's years, man has striven to create perpetual motion; it is a search that has taxed the minds of our most illustrious scientific names. Leonardo Da Vinci had a crack, as did Bernoulli and Congreve. M.C. Escher's paintings were full of it – endless processions of impossibly downhill-flowing streams and miraculously out-of-whack perspectives – but they were illusions. Sooner or later, the harsh realities of gravity, friction and inertia killed off any inventor's dream of creating the perfect free-energy machine.

But, by jove, when boffins in the States stuck a plastic wheel on to a thick wire track and rolled it round with their hands, they came as close as anyone in history before or since. First produced by Maggie Magnetic Inc. of New York (until then specialising in the sort of magnets you stuck on your fridge), the magnetic wheel was instantly iconic, extremely kinetic and utterly addictive.[1]

True, there is an apparent debt to that perennial look-and-learn favourite the gyroscope, at least in the 'seems-to-defy-gravity' department[2] if not a little stylistically. However, that addition of a J-shaped loop handle and magnetised axle tips allowed for mesmerising back-and-forth motion and wrist-based speed control. Those nifty holes in the plastic wheel made for a satisfyingly hypnotic whirring too – although Maggie were quick to spot a gap in the market and released coloured, spinning-top-style 'whee-let' covers. In fact, the company later developed a range of magnetic wheel games (perhaps sensing the limited lifespan of their simple to-ing and fro-ing toy), including a propagandist satellite space race and the Moebius strip-inspired *Twister Spinning Mystery Wheel*.[3]

It was the innovative original, however, that stood the test of time, from humble '50s beginnings, right through the Cream era, to the present day. Surprisingly, it never really caught on as an executive toy, but the manufacturers will not rest. They've even brought out light-up versions (which rather defeats the object, we feel – really, what's the point if the damn thing's battery-operated? It's not much use as a torch). As long as kids have still got hands and a couple of spare quid burning a hole in their pockets, these magnetised spinning wheels will keep on flying out of the shops. And that, in a way, is a kind of perpetual motion, isn't it?

See also *Newton's Cradle, Slinky, Battling Tops*

1 Although the Americans typically kept trying to brand it up, dude (once out of patent, the toy was endlessly remarketed as *Whee-Lo*, *Gyro Wheel*, *Wizmo* and any other name you care to mention), we Brits stuck with the call-a-spade-a-spade designation – 'magnetic wheel'. In periods of sudden and florid fancy, an extra word was added to give it the full-on name – 'magnetic walking wheel'.
2 The technical term for this is precession – the ability to balance a gyroscope on a line perpendicular to the ground – and it's all to do with Newton's first law of motion. In fact, you can, theoretically, demonstrate all three of those bad boys with the magnetic wheel, but this isn't an encyclopaedia. Go and look it up. Sheesh! No wonder teachers loved this toy.
3 Escher, too, did a few Moebius strip pics in his time. That one with the ants, for example.

Mastermind
Codebreaking pegathon

It was always a slow Sunday at Grandma's if the *Mastermind* had to come out. Invented by an Israeli postmaster (but then, aren't they all?), the 1973 Game of the Year was more famous for its box than the contents. Sporting the mantra 'Easy to learn. Easy to play. But not so easy to win', the cover of the later, iconic editions featured a wise old sage and his white-dressed assistant. Little did we know the sage in question was a Leicester hairdresser called Bill Woodward.[1] Quite what this Bond villain-in-waiting ('I've been expecting you... for a shampoo and set at 3pm') had to do with the contents of the box was never adequately explained, although we do know that Bill was asked to pose 'logically, as if thinking of something very cunning', so maybe that's it. The Chinese lady was presumably just a bit of racist 'inscrutable Orientals' schtick on behalf of the photographer.

Now, we're taking it for granted that you all know the game – black pegs for right piece, wrong place and white pegs for right piece, right place (or was it the other way around?); advancing up the wood-effect board/box trying to work out the combination hidden behind your opponent's shield; calculating the finite statistical probabilities of a four-colour code sequence.[2] Gosh, didn't it even *sound* fun!? No? Well, Omar Sharif and Joan Collins disagreed with you and happily went on the *Mastermind* promotional trail in the '70s. Despite this touch of Hollywood glamour, the game itself was often the last thing we wanted to play during a wet dinner hour (yet we still wanted to own it – kids aren't half contrary little fuckers, eh?). Rogue pegs would be floating around the classroom games boxes for years.

Far too many spin-off versions abounded – *Mini Mastermind*, *Travel Mastermind*, *Number Mastermind*, *Word Mastermind* (with yellow letter-shaped pegs) and a bastard-hard version with extra sets of colours. Confusion reigns to this day between the board game and the no-relation TV show, so when a (actually rather good) board game of the BBC quiz was released it had to be called *MasterQuiz*. Likewise, a lamer, unofficial Spears Games effort became *Magnus Magnusson's The QuizMaster*. Ultimately, it was box-top Bill who won out. Although his payment for that original photo session was a meagre one-off fee, he's been able to sign himself as 'Mr Mastermind' ever since.

Born	1971
Batteries	None
Players	👫
Breakage	🍷🍷🍷🍷
Ads	🎞️🎞️🎞️🎞️
Envy	🏆🏆🏆
eBayability	🖱️🖱️
Overall satisfaction	👍👍

See also *Cluedo, Computer Battleship, Electronic Detective*

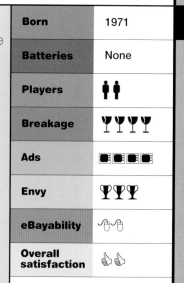

---

1 Manufacturers Invicta reunited Bill with original box star Cecilia Fung to celebrate the game's thirtieth anniversary. Bill revealed that during the original shoot he was required to pose with a cat on his lap, but the photos were abandoned when the moggy did what Frank Spencer referred to as 'a whoopsie' on his trousers.

2 Later *ZX Spectrum* games included lengthy booklets of *Mastermind*-recalling colour- codes as a method of 'security', to stop the slew of tape-to-tape pirate copies. Players were occasionally asked to type in a random combination (254: red, blue, cyan, green) to continue. In the days before scanning or photocopying, the only way to duplicate these codes was in longhand during school breaks. It doesn't relate much to this toy, but is an evocative reminiscence nevertheless.

Matsushiro Knight Rider Radio-Controlled Car
Adrenalin on rubber wheels

Born	1982
Batteries	▯▯▯▯▯▯▯
Players	🧍
Breakage	🍷 🍷 🍷
Ads	▣ ▣ ▣
Envy	🏆🏆🏆🏆
eBayability	🖱🖱
Overall satisfaction	👍👍

Let it be known that the law of remote-controlled toys of any sort adhered to these ancient commandments.

First, any remote control that connected to its parent vehicle by means of a wire was an abomination and could never bring sunshine to a child's face.

Second, the greatness of the remote control was proportional to its size. Lo, small forward-or-reverse-turn-only remotes that operated the base of, say, those inflatable robot butlers were deemed rubbish after a few hours of buffeting into the skirting boards. Additionally, the flimsy metal-wire aerial on both vehicle and control were later to be used simply to flog friends and siblings across the back of the knees. Only double-thumb joystick controllers – they're called 'servos', Grandad – like the animatronics experts used on *Making of...* documentaries were acceptable.

Third, massive radio-controlled boats with battery-powered outboard motors had to remain at the funfair where they belonged (or in sitcoms, as painstakingly built in a shed or garage by grown-up electronics enthusiasts and smashed up during their maiden voyage by a real boat at the episode's climax).

Fourth, the toy was never to be used to replicate in miniature the mundane tasks of normal cars, such as loading up with shopping at Fine Fare or the school run. Thus, ramps were built out of plywood or a pile of old annuals and driven over at high speed. Jumps over kerbs, wheelies, skids and rolls were attempted at every opportunity.

Fifth, where replicas of rally and racing cars were good in the eyes of the Christmas Day owner, they were as nought when compared with an accurate scale version of the General Lee, KITT (a black Pontiac Firebird with proper sweeping scanner light in the bonnet, mind[1]) or the Ford Gran Torino that Starsky

---

1 You want to see God working in mysterious ways? Effortless after-school cool could be accrued by wheeling out the miniature crime-busting Trans Am from the well-loved but repetitive '80s Hasselhoff starrer. Scores of scallies would duff each other up to 'get to be the one who does the voice'. Typical scenes then re-enacted included the air-ram-assisted jump over a ravine, the *Italian Job*-like rear ramp entry into Devon's truck and the bit where some dumb comedy

KNIGHT RIDER

See also Scalextric, TCR, Corgi 007 Lotus Esprit

and Hutch used to drive (but not Herbie, thanks). Sixth, a Tamiya Blackfoot was the monster of all radio-controlled trucks. But, unfortunately, that one was strictly for grown-ups. Bugger.

Seventh, come to think of it, a remote-controlled helicopter would've been the dog's bollocks, actually. So mote it be.

henchmen broke into the car and got spooked by the fact it could talk and drive around of its own accord. Although *Knight Rider* was an excellent series, it must've been tough for anyone sharing screen time with such a shiny, pimped-up babe magnet. But, to his credit, KITT never once complained.

Meccano
Miniature metal modelling kit

Born	1901
Batteries	None
Players	🧍
Breakage	🍷🍷🍷🍷🍷
Ads	▪️▪️▪️▪️
Envy	🏆🏆🏆🏆
eBayability	🖱🖱
Overall satisfaction	👍👍

See also *LEGO, Sticklebricks, Hornby Railway Set*

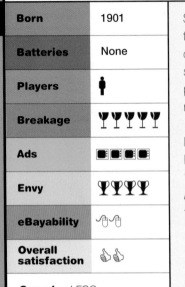

Sadly, the original recyclable construction kit fell into decline long before the end of the Cream era. The version you can buy these days, although cosmetically similar, is heavily customised to make just the one model per set (the one on the box lid). Long gone are the one-size-fits-all red and green perforated metal strips that comprised the – ahem – nuts and bolts of our nascent engineering careers.

Invented at the turn of the century by later-synonymous-with-model-railways Frank Hornby, *Meccano* revolutionised the toy industry. The name, possibly better suited to a gruff, Scottish detective, was reportedly a contraction of 'mechanics' and 'know', although Hornby first marketed it as *Mechanics Made Easy*. The company's Binns Road factory in Liverpool[1] churned out tonnes of the tiny tin plates until its closure in 1980.[2]

A boy's toy if ever there was one, each box came with a full set of spanners, screwdrivers and other hard stuff – there was no room for *LEGO*-style 'we're making a dolly's house today' exceptions here. It was robust dockyard container cranes, plate rollers and traction engines all the way. Plus, *Meccano* had a whiff of the vocational about it. It was only a short step from building your own toy skyscraper to eating a packed lunch on a fifty-third-floor beam of the yet-to-be-completed London Gherkin. (For goodness' sake, please don't take a short step from there...)

Later *Meccano* sets were more flexible – literally – but they always offered a couple of additional, extra-curricular uses. Two long strips bolted together into a cross made for a razor-sharp (and often rusty) pirate's sword, as many a sliced knee bore witness to. Then there was the extendable grabbing pincer arm in tribute to Inspector Gadget. More recently, smart-arse conceptual sculptor Chris Burden used *Meccano* to fleece the saw-you-coming-mate bosses of Newcastle's Baltic Museum out of a hundred grand for a replica of the Tyne Bridge. Reports that the artist's next installation involves taking a million-pound shipment of coals to the city are unsubstantiated.

---

1 It was also Liverpool, incidentally, where the playground nickname '*Meccano* mouth' for anyone with braces was coined. The kindly folk of the north, there.
2 As well as producing *Meccano*, Dinky toys and Hornby train sets, the factory performed a vital social function in the city, arranging works outings, sports teams and the Miss *Meccano* beauty pageant. Betcha don't get that at Computacenter.

Mercury Maze
Discontinued plastic labyrinth

Of all the defunct toys and games in this book, this is the one we can guarantee they'll never bring back. The kids'-plaything equivalent of a CFC-coolant fridge or a leaded-petrol engine, the *Mercury Maze* was so-called because it contained a measured blob of everyone's favourite poisonous liquid metal.

As with pretty much every maze puzzle since the dawn of time, the object was to steer your sphere along the correct path to the centre of the board, whereupon it would fall through a hole and return to the start at the outside again. The unique selling point here, of course, was the increased difficulty posed by mercury's predisposition for splitting in two and heading off in different directions. Essentially, the game was a boiling-down of man's age-old struggle to maintain a steady hand while compensating for the surface tension and viscosity of a base element, although they didn't think to write that on the box.

In the catalogues of the day, they used to stock these in the same section as the desk-based *Newton's Cradle*, magnetic sculptures and so on, which added the *Mercury Maze* an air of laissez-faire sophistication that was perhaps undeserved of a potentially lethal toy. Of the few varieties we recall, the most memorable was the hexagon-shaped maze, manufactured in regulation matt-black plastic with the very minimum of extraneous markings and a transparent cover.[1] It rolled off the (presumably very heavily insured) production line of Loncraine Broxton, a London-based puzzle company that also specialised in the water-based *Aquabatics* games.

The *Mercury Maze* was highly sought after away from the office, too. Outside of the last-day-of-term classroom, the only place these rare creatures could be found was in the toy department of British Home Stores, where it became quickly apparent that if the game was held upside down the mercury would collect in the lid and reform into one blob, so the maze itself could be bypassed. We are sure that this, as much as the toxic qualities of the game, served to ensure its short-livedness in the affections of the nation's youth,[2] although we're similarly surprised it wasn't revived in the mid '90s to cash in on the then-groundbreaking *Terminator 2* film, which it clearly influenced.

Born	1978
Batteries	None
Players	🧍
Breakage	🍷
Ads	▣▣
Envy	🏆🏆🏆
eBayability	🖱🖱
Overall satisfaction	👍👍

See also *Newton's Cradle, Pocketeers, Screwball Scramble*

---

1 It's too far back for us to remember, but perhaps the combination of both minimalist and chrome styling was the mark of an 'upwardly mobile executive' back in the '70s in the same way that Red Bull and Rohypnol are now.
2 After more rigid toy health and safety regulations did for the *Mercury Maze* in the '80s,

Peter Broxton experimented with replacement substances, including oil, yet none quite had the dramatic appeal of the quicksilver original. The jaggedy, ball-bearing-heavy *Crazy Maze* just didn't do the business.

Merlin
Handheld six-in-one games machine

Born	1978
Batteries	🔋🔋🔋🔋🔋🔋
Players	🧍
Breakage	🍷🍷
Ads	🎞️🎞️
Envy	🏆🏆🏆🏆🏆
eBayability	🖱️🖱️
Overall satisfaction	👍👍👍👍

See also Simon, Game and Watch, Palitoy Cue Ball

The forerunner of every mobile phone's basic 'game' package, Palitoy's Merlin was slightly too late into the market to be a serious competitor for the more-colourful Simon, but it did have the distinct advantage of having more than one game in its arsenal.[1]

Looking not unlike those early brick-style cell-phones, aside from its distinctive, indestructible red Bakelite-like casing, and boasting 'lights' (LED-backlit touch-sensitive buttons), 'a powerful computer brain' (translation: a basic ROM chip) and 'a vocabulary of 20 different sounds' (12 of which were wasted from the get-go on an ascending chromatic scale for the music composer), Merlin could 'challenge you to beat him at six fascinating games of strategy, memory and skill' (and, yes, this is just us regurgitating the blurb on the box here).

The six 'games'? Well, let's flip the little fella over and read the cover of his battery compartment. We've got: Three in a Row (that's noughts and crosses, or tic tac toe, as the Americans would have us refer to it), Music Machine (an incipient rendering of the Nokia Composer), Echo or Follow Me (that's yer Simon game, right there), Blackjack 13 (the best one, though really just a version of 21 based on a top score of, erm, 13), Magic Square (pressing an LED inverts the 'on/off' status of all the adjoining buttons, until the pattern is found to leave all eight outside LEDs in 'on' mode, like a sort of binary Rubik's Cube) and Secret Number (an electronic version of Mastermind, with a combination or number sequence to crack).

Where Merlin also scored above Simon was in his personality. For a start, he didn't keep telling you what to do. Although named after the wizard of Arthurian legend (and not to be confused with the similarly named early 1980s US TV show Mister Merlin – the 'Working in a garage ain't exactly Camelot' one, you may recall), he was decidedly snippier. A later, bluer incarnation seemed to be channelling The Karate Kid, going by the name Master Super Merlin (and featuring a mind-blowing nine games on the same LED grid).

In the aftermath of '70s sci-fi mania, it's not surprising to consider that a combination of 20 different farts and bleeps could convey an impression that this really was an electronic 'buddy'. The downside? The required six AA batteries wouldn't last you more than a week. And it didn't send text messages.

---

1 MB hit back with Microvision, another elongated slab of portable plastic but, crucially, featuring a proper LCD screen. It shipped with the popular Blockbuster bat 'n' brick game but if you ever wanted to play something different, you needed to acquire a new cartridge. Perhaps not so unrealistic for a rich Manhattan socialite, this was a major setback for the Penarth schoolboy (un)lucky enough to be the only gamer in the village.

Monopoly
Go straight to hell... do not pass go...

The quintessential feature of 'find out how the board game was invented' educational dramatisations, the likes of which you'd see on bundles of kids shows. We first encountered it on the Jeremy Beadle-helmed *Eureka*,[1] a Beeb show where real people re-enacted the origins of inventions over a bleached-out background limbo of white Chromakey.[2] Similarly, *Monopoly*'s appeal lay largely in the 3D renderings of houses, hotels and beautiful pewter playing pieces set against a flat board of Old London Town, or Pennsylvania, or wherever.

'Cos it certainly didn't lay in the playing of the bloody game, the length of which was on average anything between one and five hours – or so it seemed to a youngster for whom time is most precious (and who inevitably got knocked out early on). Never mind 'supertax' – entire currencies could rise and fall during a marathon session of *Monopoly*. There is a family in Birmingham rumoured to have started their current game on the Boxing Day before decimalisation. Rather like *Risk* and *Game of Life*, *Monopoly* was in that bracket of board game where the players' enthusiasm waned long before the declaration of an official winner.

Not that it matters, but *Monopoly*'s arcane rules were rarely followed in any case. (Really, did anyone ever auction a property instead of buying it?) What lessons was it trying to teach us? That life is basically just a case of plodding around in circles, with the odd highlight here and there? That beauty contests could be a primary source of income? What a Community Chest looked like? We still don't know.[3]

But this perennial pro-capitalist pastime lives on in an ever-expanding version sprawl (including Gay, *Star Wars* and Wales-Cymru flavours). Nowadays you can even order a personalised, custom-built edition from Hasbro (for a fee), containing locations you specify yourself (favourite pubs, the place you lost your virginity, that sort of thing). We're tempted to write in for one with alternative rules that demand the establishment of an artistic commune on Whitechapel[4] that trades in organic wheat, hemp and class C drugs. Except they tried that in Cuba, and Castro burned the lot. Fact.

Born	1903
Batteries	None
Players	👤👤👤👤👤👤
Breakage	🍷🍷
Ads	▣
Envy	🏆🏆🏆🏆
eBayability	🖱
Overall satisfaction	👍👍👍

See also Scrabble, Trivial Pursuit, Dungeons & Dragons

1 Featuring Mike Savage, ham-Yanking it up as Charles B. Darrow while marker-penning the famous (now trademarked) game board on his wife's best tablecloth.
2 This was all the rage in the '80s, wasn't it? See also *The Kenny Everett Television Show*'s Marceau pastiche, Maurice Mimer, Toni Basil's video for *Hey Mickey* and the entire *Dr Who* story *Warrior's Gate*. The Beeb used to call it CSO (colour separation overlay) 'cos of production union BECTU's aversion to brand names. That's why *Blue Peter* always used sticky tape (not Sellotape) when making houses for your dressing-up dolls (*Sindy*, *Barbie*) or action figures (*Action Man*).
3 It did get a mention in an episode of *Porridge* once: during a game, Fletcher calls for a 'Diana Dors card... (Community Chest)'. Funny, but it doesn't help. Is there a single classic sitcom that doesn't feature a *Monopoly* game at least once?
4 And this may not be *Monopoly*'s fault, but what is it with Londoners selectively adding the definite article to street names? 'The Strand', 'The Old Kent Road', and so on? How come it's not 'The Whitehall' or 'The Leicester Square'? The cockmunchers.

Mousetrap
Average board game, genius contraption

Born	1963
Batteries	None
Players	👤👤
Breakage	🍷🍷🍷🍷
Ads	▣▣▣▣
Envy	🏆🏆🏆
eBayability	🖱🖱
Overall satisfaction	👍👍

See also Sorry!, Buckaroo!, Monopoly

Probably the original 'board game plus', Ideal's epochal *Mousetrap* led the charge to leaven the drab 2D world of the dice 'n' counters board game with a plasticky, vertical dimension – the well-loved trap of the title. In its prime, *Mousetrap* (or *The Murder Of Gonzago*, to give it its proper name[1]) received prominent TV advertising courtesy of double-billing with *KerPlunk* or *Buckaroo!*, wherein a skittish Jon Pertwee advised us to 'turn the handle, down the chute, kick the bucket, take a dive... and mousetrap!' – an adequate description of the mechanics of play, we think you'll agree.

The trap itself was inspired directly by the satirical cartoons of Rube Goldberg, whose *Inventions!* illustrations were intended as an ironic comment on the overcomplicated quality of boom-time America. A point that was rather lost on the frantic kids angling to crank another mouse into oblivion.

You see, we'd always fondly hoped that the inspiration for the device came from the old Chuck Jones Warner Brothers cartoons, in particular that recurring motif where a character (usually Sylvester) rigs up a ridiculously complicated trap consisting of ropes, pulleys, safes, fridges, irons, electric fans blowing model boats, roller skates with pool cues tied to them, upended tubs of water, etc. etc. – all setting off one another in a long line. It made for great viewing, but Jones and co. were always careful to leave out the doubtless long, tedious hours spent hammering, sawing and constructing the trap in the first place.

Ideal attempted, bravely, to incorporate this into the game itself, with pieces (the diver, the barrel, the drawbridge, the boot, the marble, et al.) going up one by one as mousey counters moved round the board. As with the likes of *KerPlunk* and *Buckaroo!*, this turned the actual game itself into one protracted, suspense-filled build-up to the 'money shot' when the trap went off,[2] which it did with a perhaps surprising, if not massive, success-to-failure rate, at least until one of the crucial bits went missing down the sofa. In which case (due to the shameful absence of a Spare Drawbridge Hotline), you were sunk.

Still produced today (now by Hasbro subsidiary, MB Games), the tabletop *Mousetrap* has also inspired a couple of giant versions. Early '90s' Saturday-morning kids' show *MotorMouth* featured a short-lived *Mousetrap* quiz game and a TV studio-sized set for kids to run around in. More recently, bonkers US artist Mark Perez erected a life-sized sculpture at the Burning Man festival in Nevada. The feckin' eejit. Our in-no-way-scientific reckoning puts the ratio of completed games of *Mousetrap* to occasions when you just built the thing and set it off, counters be damned, at about one to eight.

---

1 That's a joke for Shakespeare fans.
2 Three things that could prematurely set off the mousetrap: your dad walked in and flopped down on the settee; an earthquake (especially that one on Boxing Day 1979); an actual mouse.

Mr Frosty
Snowman-shaped flavoured icecapades

Out of any of the toys and games in our wish list, this was probably the one that was most consistently denied us in our youth. Paradoxically, *Mr Frosty* is neither a toy nor a game. It's just a thing we wanted, although it was very much situated somewhere within the last 40 or so pages of Freemans, so it counts. The parental argument against buying one went something like this: it'll join that collection of stuff you only use once and then leave in the back of the cupboard forever. This, of course, was completely correct (as anyone who's ever owned a *Soda Stream* or *Breville Snack & Sandwich Maker* will be able to corroborate).

But, while acknowledging that one indisputable truth, don't forget that we're talking about a time when the closest thing to a frozen drink came in a clear plastic tube that gave your fingers frostbite. A Slush Puppy, or anything approaching it in those days, was a luxury. So to own something that promised to recreate the 'crushed-ice soft drink' experience in your own kitchen seemed like a crazed futuristic fantasy.

And fantasy it was. For what was *Mr Frosty* if naught but a plastic machine for breaking ice cubes into bits?[1] Essentially, the best he could hope to deliver from the flue at the base of his polar innards was something akin to a Lilliputian 'sno-cone' (the American non-slushy sort). We had no name for this in the UK; thus was the 'ice crunchie' born. *Percy Penguin*, claimed the blurb on the box, was there to provide a fruity flavour ('Thank you, Percy!') – for which read 'squirt some powder-derived cordial over the top'.[2]

However, these were not fatal drawbacks by any stretch of the imagination. The potential parties you already had planned in your head cast you as bartender in your road's coolest crushed-ice soft-drinks nightclub. *Mr Frosty*, of course, was resident in the chill-out room.[3]

See also *'A La Cart Kitchen', Shaker Maker, Cadbury's Chocolate Machine*

Born	1978
Batteries	None
Players	👫
Breakage	🍷 🍷 🍷
Ads	▣ ▣ ▣ ▣ ▣
Envy	🏆 🏆 🏆 🏆
eBayability	🖱 🖱
Overall satisfaction	👍 👍 👍

1 We make no bones about this, the original *Mr Frosty* barely managed to turn out a tablespoonful of grated ice per ice cube. Plus, the cardiovascular strain involved in operating the turning handle would've taxed a grown adult. See those World's Strongest Men? Raised on *Mr Frosty*, they were.

2 Three small packets of Outrageous Orange, Loopy Lemon and Cheery Cherry were included. Think they sound a little volatile? Wait 'til the kids had their fill of pure sugar and tartrazine – then you'll know the meaning of the word. *Frosty*'s cousin, *Mr Fruity* – a tree-shaped toy full of sherbet drinks and E numbers – fell out of favour even sooner.

3 *Mr Frosty* has recently undergone what people on daytime telly call 'a makeover'. Gone are the days of a rudimentary snowman-shaped toy: the current retail version has something of the *Ghostbusters* Staypuft Marshmallow Man about him. Or that artificially white ice-cream they sell in the States. Perhaps he should be called Mr Softee? Crucially, that difficult-to-crank handle now forms part of a very chi-chi red, white and blue bobble hat. He is, however, still suspiciously unwilling to divulge his first name. Still preserving that air of mystery for ver laydeez, eh, *Frosty*?

My Little Pony
Small plastic horse that belongs to you

Born	1982
Batteries	None
Players	👤👤
Breakage	🍸
Ads	◾◾◾◾
Envy	🏆🏆🏆🏆
eBayability	🖱🖱
Overall satisfaction	👍👍

See also Chic-a-boo, Strawberry Shortcake, Whimsies

While the males of the species were busy trying to cover every available surface in their bedroom with the massed ranks of *Zoids* and *Transformers*, what was it that girls were supposed to be doing? The answer, of course, is playing horses, albeit it in the most nauseatingly candy-coloured fashion possible. Behold, *My Little Pony*, ('all skinny and bony' to quote the popular playground chant), Hasbro's stable of equine collectables.[1]

Every *My Little Pony* came in a different pastel shade, with a different jaunty tilt of the head[2] and a different but always relentlessly perky name (par for the course were the saccharine-sweet Blossom, Tootsie, Bubbles and, most oddly, the pornstar name-alike Cherries Jubilee). Perhaps to prove that little girls can be nag-happy consumers too, the idea was simply to acquire as many as you possibly could but, unlike *Transformers*, these didn't even *do* anything. Nope! Not a thing. They were moulded solid, so you couldn't even move their bulgy plastic limbs.

All right, so you could comb their manes and tails, but the charm tended to wear thin after an older brother tried to give one of them dreadlocks and got the whole thing irreparably tangled. Perhaps sensing this in-built audience irritation factor, Hasbro started to churn out range after range of slightly different '*Ponies* to exponentially expand the collection. Why not try a unicorn, a seahorse or a Pegasus this time? Or what about a *Baby Pony* ('Hmm, where did those come from, Mummy?')? Or how about a *Mountain Boy Pony* – its masculinity in no doubt due to a set of mighty hooves and a delightfully macho name like Lightning or Fireball?

Stretching the brand to bank-breaking point were several potential locations for horse-play – the *Gymkhana* set (make it jump over things!), the *Grooming Parlour* (give it a hairdo!) and the ultimate *Dream Castle* (make it live out its days in a glorious heap of twiddly purple plastic!). Contrary to the standard joke at the time, *My Little Knacker's Yard* and *My Little Glue Factory* were never available. Shame, that.

In 1991, after a mandatory cartoon series and big-screen outing (the Kubrick-helmed *Foal Metal Jacket*), Hasbro put the range out to pasture. Even so, Blackpool's Golden Mile continued to – ha! – mount an illuminated *My Little Pony* tableau for – ha-ha! – donkey's years afterwards and, since 2003, the toys have returned to delight a new generation of feckless fetlock lovers. We're still waiting for those long-promised alternative 'adult' ponies, however; Night-Mare, Bareback Mountain and Osama Dobbin-Laden.

---

1 Hasbro weren't the first, in fact. In the States, hard-plastic *My Pretty Ponies* were on the shelves a full year before their vinyl successors. The object was much the same, however – preening, tail-twitching fun for girls – and once the barn door was left open...

2 Ooh, it's that coquettish 'vision of shy loveliness' look patented by Sarah Greene and Princess Di. With added Droog-heavy eyelash makeup, naturally.

Newton's Cradle
Balls

There can't be many executive toys that were thought up by TV continuity announcers. Whither Paul 'first on Four' Coia's eight-ball decision maker, for example? Or Colin 'Granadaland' Weston's magnetic art sculptures? They don't exist, of course, and quite rightly so because the notion of someone designing a desk-bound plaything while cueing up that night's witty introductory spiel for *Coronation Street* is, frankly, ridiculous.[1] Okay, these guys probably had a lot of time on their hands but, still… You'd probably do a crossword or read the *TV Times*, right? What you wouldn't do is sit down and think 'Ooh, today I'll invent an iconic toy that demonstrates the principles behind one of the laws of motion.' Would you?

Enter, stage left, Simon Prebble, jobbing soap and rep actor, radio newsreader and, in 1967, designer of a classic swinging-pendulum gizmo that would soon become very popular with American businessmen and Bond villains. Okay, so technically Prebble didn't invent it. That honour goes to Sir Isaac Newton himself but, as we understand it, he spent his final years dodging an albino monk assassin from *Opus Dei*,[2] so we have to credit our telly announcer friend with silverin' up those balls and stringing 'em on a frame some two and a half centuries later.

Harrods initially took on the task of flogging the toy but, without a huge marketing force behind it, sales were rather lacking in – ahem – momentum.[3] Enter, stage right, actor, sculptor and future film director (*Brimstone and Treacle*, *Wimbledon*) Richard Loncraine who, together with business partner Peter Broxton, reworked *Newton's Cradle* into an easily mass-produced stainless-steel version. Suddenly, the nation's CEOs were entranced by the back-and-forth motion of clacking chrome spheres and raced out to buy one. Meanwhile, kids at home were treated to an educational spin (well, more of a swing, naturally) courtesy of a John Noakes demo on *Blue Peter*: the programme featured the toy no fewer than three times in 1969.

Soon enough the shops (and desktops) were packed full of superfluous ornaments based on other scientific principles: the amazing drinking/ducking glass bird thing, 3D pin art, and that bloody mug with the photo of Einstein sticking his tongue out on it. Yes, Mr Big Shot Boss, we see you have a sense of humour. Now stop playing with your balls and get some work done.

Born	1967
Batteries	None
Players	👤
Breakage	🍷🍷
Ads	📺
Envy	🏆🏆
eBayability	🖱
Overall satisfaction	👍👍

See also *Mercury Maze, Magnetic Wheel, Rubik's Cube*

---

1 It's probably worth admitting that we haven't checked our facts here, so if you know different, please do forgive us.

2 Congratulations! You have found the obligatory spurious reference to *The Da Vinci Code*, added in a desperate bid to improve sales of the *TV Cream Toys* book at airports.

3 Prebble sold the original (wooden frame, Araldite balls) out of the back of a yellow van. We're fighting the urge to say *Only Fools and Horses* here. He also reckons – and we have no reason to disbelieve him – that *Newton's Cradle* inadvertently sparked another popular craze of the '70s, the famously banned-from-school toy, *Clackers*.

Operation
Play-at-home surgical fun without the gore

Operation was an early and surprisingly durable example of that rare thing – a natural crossover between the worlds of board game, electronic game[1] and delicate medical procedure. A pair of metal tweezers was the chief implement, used to remove comically named plastic body parts (among them Wish Bone, Funny Bone and Butterflies in Stomach)[2] from the prostrate form of a cartoonish man who looked not entirely unlike a well-groomed and marginally less uninteresting Fred Flintstone.[3]

If a player committed the cardinal error of touching the 'sides' during the operating procedure, a buzzer sounded and the huge red bulb standing in for the cartoon man's nose lit up. So far, so serial circuit physics lesson yawnsome. In fact, we're simplifying. The game had ever-more complex rules and levels of play, including various hospital occupation cards (doctor, specialist, consultant paediatrician, cardiothoracic surgeon, anaesthesiologist, to name but a few that might as well have been included for all we ever understood) and a remuneration policy that presumably informed the career choices of your modern-day private-healthcare staff.[4]

For a Cream-era kid, though, there were two small but crucial flaws in this otherwise perfectly intricate undertaking: first, the deliberately fiddly Charlie Horse would inevitably become wedged in its oddly shaped slot (a situation that was not exactly helped by the tendency of the flimsy plastic-and-card board to become worryingly and complicatingly concave after a couple of weeks' use); second, and more significantly, the wires connecting the tweezers to the board would eventually develop a break and be rendered – aha-ha-ha – inoperable. The question of what you were supposed to do if and when the bulb blew was also never really addressed.

On top of this, younger siblings were wont to find the game inexplicably frightening. See also the somewhat sturdier relative, *Purple People Eater*, a huge rubber contraption like a melting Davros mask and actually quite repulsive to the touch, from the mouth of which players were supposed to retrieve small red plastic troll figures without triggering an electronic 'monster' noise. At least this latter game was promoted by a *TISWAS*-straddling telly ad utilising an astute rewrite of the ancient novelty rock 'n' roll number of the same name. All we got for *Operation* was that posh mum saying 'Can I have a go?'

Born	1965
Batteries	🔋🔋
Players	👤👤👤👤
Breakage	🍷🍷🍷🍷
Ads	▪▪▪
Envy	🏆🏆
eBayability	🖱
Overall satisfaction	👍

See also Perfection, Tip-It, Buckaroo!

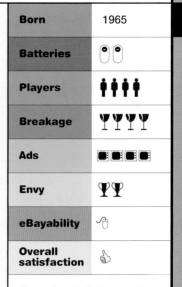

Purple People Eater
Sure looks strange

---

1 An 'electric' fun game, as '80s versions of the game would have it.
2 It is perhaps the existence of Wrenched Ankle, Bread Basket and Charlie Horse – unfamiliarly-named parts of the body – that gives away the game's Yank origins.
3 At least on the box he did, alongside a smoking doctor (the fag and cigarette holder has long since been airbrushed out of the original 1965 illustration) and what looked like a five-year old nurse.
4 We quote the spoilt advert kid: 'I did it! That's £500 for me!' Wannabe dentists had their own, similar game, which was by all accounts about as much fun as pulling teeth.

Othello
Strategy game 'from the mysterious East'

Born	1973
Batteries	None
Players	👫
Breakage	🍷
Ads	📺
Envy	🏆
eBayability	🖱
Overall satisfaction	👍👍👍

See also *Backgammon, Yahtzee, Connect Four*

Some thought went into the design of this, the best-selling British board game of 1977. Everything about it oozed deluxe Black-Forest-gateau sophistication. The lush green baize hinted at high-stakes casino gambling or billiards in the drawing room with brandy and cigars. The silent contemplation required of each player marked it out as an above-averagely cerebral game. *Othello* was not for the weak-minded. Even the counters themselves, cleverly fashioned in twin sides of black and white, symbolised the Yin Yang relationship of good and evil, day and night, master and servant. Well, that, or the bloke who invented the thing was eating liquorice allsorts at the time.[1]

Essentially a modern-day take on *Reversi*,[2] *Othello* would most likely be whipped out for a quick game among the Christmas Day dining-table detritus of cheeseboard and crackers. A classic grab-the-most game – outflank your opponent's disks and they become yours, at least until he does the same to you – where *Othello* scored highly was in its turn-on-a-sixpence twist that allowed a clever player to plan ahead and outwit a novice with a single move. Like chess, then, but done and dusted before the Bond film began. Also like chess, unfortunately, people took it far, far too seriously (holding annual world championships and programming computers to beat grand masters, that sort of thing[3]).

Ultimately, it remained a limited game. For all the pocket, magnetic and travel editions, *Othello* never broke beyond the bounds of the two-player experience. No 3D multiplayer version of this on the holodeck of the Enterprise. Plus, as the photo of a grape-munching lady's hands on the box might have forewarned (such refinement, such elegance!), parents would nab the game for some past-bedtime grown-up fun. Indeed, it was the delightful simplicity (remember, 'a moment to learn, a lifetime to master') that adults could grasp. What else can explain the laughter we'd hear from downstairs when Mum suggested getting the *Othello* out to play with after *Match Of The Day*? (Well, possibly the fact that the phrase 'the ol' fella' sounds quite similar, but we've tried to blank that from our memory.)

---

1 It was officially 'rediscovered for a new generation' by Goro Hasegawa, who popularised the game in Japan. The liquorice thing is just a guess.
2 The rules are so similar but ever-so-subtly different that they have caused more and bloodier arguments between board-game fans than any other in history. Rumour has it that Shakespeare's play *Othello* is just a dramatised version of such a disagreement:

Iago believed that you should have a pool of 64 disks from which each player picked, whereas Othello himself felt strongly that they should be divided equally between players at the start. Cassio just wished people would hurry up and invent the digital watch.
3 The '70s and '80s versions shipped with an invitation to join Britain's National Othello Federation. How many joined, do you think?

Palitoy Cue Ball
Electronic mini-snooker

Pre-*Game and Watch*, the cutting edge of electronic gameplaying (never 'gaming', please) was led by 'only from' Tomy, who loved to package an array of red LEDs with a little joystick and two buttons in various guises. The variety of things you could get away with representing with little flashing lights was, of course, extremely limited, and only two categories really made the grade in these formative years – space battles (light on dark – perfect) and sport (balls – they're round, you see?).

Among the latter were a variety of golf games that were never much cop and a big old yellow thing called *The Big Game*, a Keegan-endorsed football two-player from that bastion of rehashing other people's consoles under different names, Grandstand.[1] But *Palitoy Cue Ball*, riding high on the first wave of snooker mania, really cleaned up.

Now you too could rub metaphorical shoulders with Ray Reardon and Terry Griffiths, albeit in a jerky, red-on-black version of their domain, where the delicate 'tok' of cue on ball was replaced by a guttural electronic grunt and the laws of physics were, to say the least, variable.

Intriguing, diverting, loveable, desirable? All of the above. In any sane sense playable? No. Blinking lights may have just about sufficed to convey the brutal basics of sports like soccer and tennis, albeit without any of the subtlety that makes them interesting. Apply the same principles to one that is nothing *but* subtlety, and they go in off the black in short order.

However, the main disappointment with the game was the ratio of the game-unit footprint (promisingly massive) to size of actual playing area (dismayingly minute). It was like buying a snooker table and finding it encased in its own life-size beige-plastic Crucible Theatre.

The days when computer games would actually live up to the haywire anticipatory imagination of a child were still a long way in the future, but there was a sort of satisfying, simple sturdiness to these games, especially the way they still carried on sort of half-working when you'd got really bored and prised them apart with a screwdriver. Try doing that with a DVD-ROM!

As for those of you watching in black-and-red, if you're wondering where the red ball is, it's between the red and the red.

Born	1980
Batteries	●●●●○○
Players	🧍
Breakage	🍷
Ads	▪️
Envy	🏆🏆
eBayability	🖱️🖱️
Overall satisfaction	👍

See also *Merlin, Tomytronic 3D, Crossfire, Galaxy Invader 1000*

1 They were all living out of each others' pockets! Grandstand distributed handhelds by Tomy, Epoch and Entex. CGL imported Tomy, Gekken and Nintendo. The many websites devoted to tabletop and handheld console games tell us that Grandstand and CGL were not, as you might expect, offshoots of those huge Japanese corporations but in fact trading names for two very humdrum-sounding UK businesses – the Adam Leisure Group PLC (based in Harrogate) and Dennis Baylin Trading Ltd (based in London). CGL was even ultimately subsumed into Sir Alan Sugar's Amstrad. Gah! Another illusion shattered.

Paul Daniels TV Magic Tricks
Magic mark-up

Born	1979
Batteries	None
Players	👤
Breakage	🍷 🍷 🍷
Ads	▣ ▣ ▣
Envy	🏆 🏆 🏆 🏆 🏆
eBayability	🖱 🖱 🖱
Overall satisfaction	👍 👍 👍 👍

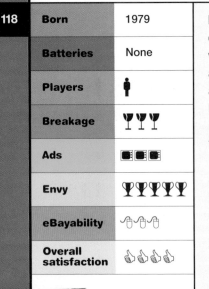

See also
Remus Play-Kits, Squirmles, Magic rocks

It is the evangelical duty of every TV Cream staffer to remind people that, once upon a time, Paul Daniels was a popular, entertaining magician whose programmes would be watched and enjoyed by millions of families all over the country. Now, of course, thanks to doggedly persistent rumours about some compromising photos of Debbie McGee, and that bloody Louis Theroux documentary, the man's just about tolerated as an eccentric (if slightly suspicious-acting) millionaire funding his wife's doomed ambition to be a ballerina.

'Twas not ever thus. In our youth, and back in the day when he was still wearing the wig (and – be honest – who wasn't genuinely surprised when he revealed he'd discovered 'a way to comb his hair to cover the bald patch' and discarded the rug?), there was nothing we wanted to save up our pocket money for more than to buy another one of Paul Daniels TV magic tricks. It was, of course, marketing genius.[1]

Each trick would be numbered (there were over 30 to collect), rated by difficulty (blue – easy, red – fairly easy, purple – slightly harder, black – master magician... that sort of thing) and packaged in oddly shaped plastic and card fold-out tubes containing props and instructions. Of course, as the tricks became more and more sophisticated up the dark (and expensive) end of the scale, the props became more and more straightforward (whereas the instructions became inversely more complicated). One of these contained only a length of rope and a massive booklet depicting the entire cut-and-restore routine.

The more simple tricks included a drinks coaster from which magically appeared a coin, some gold rings on a red velveteen square under which playing cards would vanish, and the crazy cube that we don't know what it was supposed to do.[2]

Paul urged us in the accompanying leaflets to develop our own 'patter' and learn the art of misdirection, although with an audience comprising only the family pets, this wasn't strictly necessary. Forget dodgy compendium packages, bloody 'mind control' or hanging around in Perspex boxes – these were real magic and highly addictive. We liked 'em. Not a lot, but we liked 'em.

1 From genius Cream-era marketeers, Dubreq, need you be reminded. For some reason, they continued to use the same photo of Daniels on all their magic products, despite the fact that the range spanned four years. As icing on the cake, at one point Paul and Rolf starred in a telly ad double header to promote both the tricks and the latter's 'magic' squeezy paint-filled brushes. We had them as well, by the way. They were rubbish.
2 Not a Paul Daniels effort, but many people remember the contemporaneous it's-a-sort-of-magic-wand-isn't-it?-style *Trick Stick*. Nowt but a cheap majorette's twirling baton fashioned in yellow plastic (with red weights on the end), this was supposed to float and dance around the owner's body as if enchanted by the fairies themselves. Obviously, it was attached to a length of fishing wire and always ended up spinning out of control, but the TV ads (starring *Grange Hill*'s Fay Lucas) etched themselves on to the memory of a generation. Now *that's* magic.

Perfection
Plastic-shapes-spitting mania

Tick... tick... tick... Match shapes – and yourself – against the clock. Variously marketed by Denys Fisher in collaboration, as they so often were, with MB Games and Action GT (which sported TV Cream's favourite ever ball-busting logo, that 'GT' seemingly hurtling off all of their products at high-speed), this was a nasty piece of work, guaranteed to up stress levels in the back seats on that long and boring journey to Swaffham – that's if you had the *Travelpax*[1] edition, of course.

The concept was simplicity itself: slot different shapes into their corresponding holes in the playing board. Easy, eh? But where *Perfection* really scored was with the inclusion of a distractingly loud clockwork timer. If you hadn't got all the shapes safely home before this thing wound down, the board would ping up, spewing plastic stars, circles, squares and pieces of cheese all over the shop. And that's when the screaming would start. More than once we would take to playing the game without the timer on (which rather defeated the point) because it could wind us up into such a state of nervous terror.

Variation on a theme came from *Mr Pop*, a similar set-up but this time the game required assembly of a face (to match an illustration on the chosen card) from an assortment of random features, again against the clock. Run out of time and *Mr Pop's* face would spring disconcertingly forwards and shower you with more noses, ears, lips and eyelids than the bloke who fills the mincing machine at the Val-U-Beef burger factory.

Then there was *Superfection*, which added to the mix an extra dash of mental agility by requiring the player to assemble two congruent pieces before they could be fitted into identical square slots. Or *Computer Perfection*, a fantastically futuristic transparent plastic dome that slid back to reveal '4 electronic games in one' (all of which, sadly, were no more than riffs on the follow-me schtick of *Simon* – but at least *Computer Perfection* invited us to 'probe' his memory, impudent little globe that he was).

Thanks to such self-destructive programming, we reckon it's probably rather difficult to obtain a complete working example of any of these games from their '70s/'80s heyday.[2] But wouldn't it be great to present someone with an edition of *Perfection* missing that one final piece? Oh, the hilarity that would ensue... shortly before the violence.

Born	1973
Batteries	None
Players	👨👩
Breakage	🍷🍷🍷
Ads	▪️▪️
Envy	🏆🏆🏆
eBayability	🖱️
Overall satisfaction	👍👍

See also *Pocketeers, Operation, Buckaroo!*

1 Nifty trademarkable name that, eh? It wasn't MB's first effort, though. They also tried the less-successful *Travelil-lets*, *Ko-travelex* and *Travelways Ultra*.

2 *Perfection* was thoughtfully manufactured in practically indestructible yellow plastic – a decision that, we fondly imagine, emerged from studying a focus group's tendency to chuck the bloody thing across the room in sheer incontrollable fury.

Peter Powell Stunter Kite
Is it a bird, is it a plane?

It was Britain's own Peter Powell – not the DJ, another one – who popularised the dual-line stunt kite. Powell was a Cheltenham-based entrepreneur with a knack for knowing a good bit of PR when it fluttered by. Initially gaining fame winning awards at a Geneva exhibition of inventions (and then the British Toy of the Year in 1976), Powell never turned down the chance to appear on TV flying one of his own durable plastic kites with its distinctive tubular tail.[1] Always dressed in a suit, he could often be seen running along blustery hilltops with an airborne triple stacker or hoisting his granny off the ground with pure kite power before steering her back down to a soft landing (we assume). Such showboating attracted the attention of a Japanese investor and, sure enough, within months, Powell's cottage industry was churning out millions of pounds' worth of kite.

The craze literally flew around the world, for some reason appealing to adults as much as kids. John Noakes crashed a Barnstormer kite on to Shep's nose on *Blue Peter* (although in truth each looked as nonplussed with the whole stunting obsession as the other). Powell received endorsements from the likes of Jimmy Stewart and Mohammed Ali, even appearing on the front page of the *New York Times* at the height of his fame. Then, as quickly as it had taken off, the kite fad came back down to earth with a bump.[2]

Despite the fact that Benjamin Franklin had plainly documented one of the major drawbacks of kite-flying with his storm-powered discovery of electricity in 1752, the powers-that-be deemed it necessary to issue a special public information film. This terrifying warning of the dangers of running your kite or *Frisbee* into overhead power cables (and then stupidly clambering up a pylon to free it) ran on children's television in 1979 as part of a government-sponsored Play Safe campaign. Whether down to this or the persistent rumours of 'a bloke' who ran off the edge of the cliffs at Beachy Head while trying to keep his kite aloft, the wind was well and truly taken out of the kite industry's sales.

When Powell's business collapsed, he burned all evidence of it ever having existed – scrapbooks, cuttings, stock, the lot went up on a bonfire. Powell himself was the biggest casualty, however, declaring bankruptcy and becoming a virtual recluse, which he has remained ever since.

Born	1972
Batteries	None
Players	👤
Breakage	🍷🍷🍷🍷
Ads	▪️▪️
Envy	🏆🏆🏆🏆
eBayability	🪁🪁🪁🪁🪁
Overall satisfaction	👍👍👍

See also Swingball, Flight Deck, Spacehopper

1 The tail held a big wow factor for us kids, as we were told that, with a bit of skill and practice, we could use it to skywrite our names. This was true, if only for that lad at the end of the road called Oooooo.

2 If you think that's a clumsy kite-flying metaphor, wait 'til you see the corker we've got in store at the bottom of the penultimate paragraph.

Petite Super International Typewriter
Clackety clackety clackety clack – ping!

Born	1976
Batteries	None
Players	👤
Breakage	🍷🍷
Ads	📺
Envy	🏆🏆🏆🏆
eBayability	🖱🖱
Overall satisfaction	👍👍👍👍

See also Commodore 64, Girl's World, Speak & Spell

When the pre-Christmas powers-that-be ran out of ideas for training the housewives of tomorrow (see, among others, the 'A La Cart Kitchen'), someone had a bright idea: let's train the secretaries of tomorrow! But let's do it covertly, so that they don't know what they're doing.

Actually manufactured by Byron International (itself a division of super-conglomerate mining corp., Dobson Park Industries), the Petite brand was a front for a range of portable toys including cash registers, sewing machines and various pretend shop fronts that all came in suspiciously typewriter-shaped cases.

We suspect that Petite's moment of glory may have coincided with the rise of the *Superman* films – suddenly journalism was a glamorous career and, with one of these babies, an adventure-packed life as the next Lois Lane or Clark Kent (or, failing that, Julie Burchill) seemed only a Caps Lock away. The *Super International* was the foremost in a series of fully functional toy typewriters (although time would deliver the *De-Luxe*, *Electronic* and *Talking* versions), which differed from its grown-up Silver Reed, Olivetti and Brother – erm – sisters only in its, well, petiteness (and sometimes its colour – snazzy blue if you were lucky, dull grey if you weren't). At any rate, it was far more businesslike and chic than the crappy pink *Barbie* typewriters that followed. (Although, was it just us, or did the red half of the ribbon always dry out after about two days?) Anyway, had you wanted to use it to write a sequel to *The Bitch*, you probably could have done so.

Really enterprising kids probably supplemented their pocket money by knocking out a spot of porn and sending it in to *Mayfair*. Most of us, however, just sat banging away for hours at the asterisk key, giving our parents a migraine. The novelty really wore off when we realised that all it was good for was typing thank-you letters to our gran, and now we had no excuse not to. Drat!

Play Doh Monster Shop
Inspired clay-based depilation

The origins of this wallpaper cleaner made good are documented in lumpen detail elsewhere (feel free to Google... we'll wait), but our favourite fact is that it was first manufactured by a company called Kutol Chemical Products – a name that wouldn't have sounded out of place in one of those post-apocalyptic '70s BBC dramas like *Survivors* or *Doomwatch*.

Another oft-ignored feature of *Play Doh* was its extremely evocative smell. To be frank, they might as well pump the cavity walls of the nation's primary schools full of this stuff, such is its odour so particularly associated with one time and place. Show us an infant school play area and we'll show you a vibrant marbled snake of branded modelling compound. Not to mention a few *Sticklebricks* matted with brown-grey morsels of the stuff.

The newly rechristened Rainbow Crafts Co. swiftly introduced additional accessories to help control and contain the enjoyment. First there was the *Play Doh Fun Factory* – a sort of press wherein a lump of the brightly-coloured clay was deposited and then extruded out into a variety of cross-sectioned sausages, to the great amusement of countless young children still harbouring a vestigial toilet fixation.[1] The real genius, though, was the decision to ally this abstract device to a model person with holes in the top of their head (and chin, in the male instance), thus creating endless opportunities for 'cut 'n' grow' streaky purple dreadlock shaving fun. Thus was the *Play Doh Barber's Shop* born.[2]

Despite there being something slightly skin-crawl-inducing in the way the clay tendrils wormed their way out of each Playperson's scalp, it would be years before such an image would be capitalised upon by the British horror industry (and we're only thinking about the *Hellraiser* films here). *Play Doh* was not so slow, however, and released the *Monster Shop* playset. Here, a mad-professor type resurrected Frankenstein from deep within his plastic coffin, twisted a handle and... cut his hair. Hmmm... already, the limitations of the format were becoming evident.

The *Play Doh* playset went away for a bit but has now resurfaced as the *Barber and Beauty Shop*, so we presume the obligatory TV tie-in version endorsed by Toni & Guy can be only just around the corner.

Born	1956
Batteries	None
Players	👤
Breakage	🍷🍷🍷🍷
Ads	▪️▪️▪️
Envy	🏆🏆🏆
eBayability	🖱️🖱️
Overall satisfaction	👍👍

See also Silly Putty, Shaker Maker, Slime

1 Did we say children? We meant infantile Americans too: log on, if you'll pardon the phrase, to www.turdtwister.com for a veritable catalogue of joke poo-squeezer shaped products.

2 We've covered this before, by the way, in the first TV Cream book. But if something's worth writing about, it's worth writing about enough times that people start to worry we've developed a sexual *Play Doh* fetish.

Pocketeers
Clockwork arcade games

Born	1975
Batteries	None
Players	👤
Breakage	🍷🍷
Ads	▪️▪️◪️
Envy	🏆🏆🏆🏆
eBayability	🖱️🖱️
Overall satisfaction	👍👍👍👍

See also *Remus Play-Kits, Screwball Scramble, Game and Watch*

Possessing a playground collectability factor to rival that of Panini sticker albums and *Top Trumps*,[1] *Pocketeers* were initially teensy-ball-bearing variations of bagatelle, magnet-based racing games or against-the-clock mazes. A Japanese invention (thanks Tomy – now take your *Pokemon* and fuck off!) – in fact, nothing more than a bonsai version of that old parlour game Pachinko – they were marketed by Palitoy in the UK and were, naturally, just big enough to fit into a school-blazer-sized pocket (which was handily now empty of money).

The imagination behind every game was astounding (nearly every field sport was adapted to handheld size at least once), and each new title was just different enough from previous editions to make purchase a necessity. But, basically, a game would consist of a coloured, illustrated plastic box with a clear lid, some additional buttons or triggers, and sometimes a small wind-up timer that would click down to zero with a disproportionately loud whirr. No potential genre was ignored: *Pocketeers* embraced the fruit machine, the casino (cards and dice), duck-shoots, golf, *Pac-Man* and *Smurfs*, before finally meeting their nemesis in the form of *Space Invaders*.[2]

The advent of the video game limited how impressive even the most sophisticated of moving parts in a *Pocketeer* could be made to look. Miniaturisation and the silicon chip rendered them archaic at best (and, for some reason, kids nowadays just don't get that same nostalgia buzz from old toys). Tomy re-entered the market in the mid '80s with the rebranded *Pocket Games* and later *Pocketmates* (although neither has the implicit excitement of the clearly *Rocketeer*-influenced original name), with less success. But, in the wake of your *Nintendo DS* and *Game Boy Advance*, surely these hardy originals are long overdue a twenty-first-century eco-makeover by the likes of clockwork radio guru Trevor Baylis?

1 Full-page ads in late '70s kids' weekly *Look-In* offered free collectors' badges to early adopters for the price of a tenpenny stamp, further fuelling the schoolyard stampede for *Pocketeers*.
2 The writing was already on the wall for *Pocketeers* when Tomy introduced the electromechanical combo game *Blip* on to the market in 1977, followed swiftly by *Demon Driver*. Well, it would be once the price of these part-clockwork, part-LED arcade-style games started to come down. Architects of their own downfall, Tomy, we reckon. That, or just always one step ahead of the game('s market). They were right there at the spearhead of electronic handheld games too.

Racing Bike
Two-wheeled transport of delight

Born	pre-C20
Batteries	None
Players	🚹
Breakage	🍷🍷
Ads	⬛⬛
Envy	🏆🏆🏆🏆🏆
eBayability	🖱
Overall satisfaction	👍👍👍

Judging by the number of Cream era dads who spent Christmas Eve wrestling a flat pack box from the garage to the living room (and the rest of the night attempting to piece together cogs, wheels, mudguards, derailleur and brake cables into something resembling a Raleigh six-speed), getting your first 'proper' bike was hardly the sumptuous fantasy of a generation of shoeless urchins but more an achievable, almost inevitable, Chrimbo Day rite of passage. But why would any child ask for one of these built-for-speed, not-for-comfort bikes, rather than a *Chopper* or *Grifter*? Like the man in the Yellow Pages ad said, just look at that saddle. It'd be like sitting on a razor blade.

Well, there are two reasons. First, consider the sheer desirability and range of two-wheeled vehicles on offer (ferchrissakes, let's make it clear, no-one ever bought a trike). Saturday afternoons were made for covetous browsing of Halfords' window and comparative studies of tube-grips, spoke types, Sturmey Archer gears, cantilever brakes, pearlised paints, stickers, accessories, and (literally) bells and whistles. We're into the realm of the 'spec' here, you may note.

Second, and most sacrilegiously, it's because we just grew out of those iconic sit-up-and-beg bikes because they were, well, childish. The big seats, handlebars and tiger tail ribbons weren't meant for serious bike-riders. Lean, mean teens needed lean, mean wheel trims and lean, mean drop-handlebars (to lean on). Puch, Merckx, Claud Butler – the racer was an elegant bicycle for a more civilised age. That louche, leather-jacketed lad from the estate could ride such a bike at a menacingly slow speed, circling the bus stops like a shark, fag in mouth. You can't do that on a Sunbeam, kid.[1]

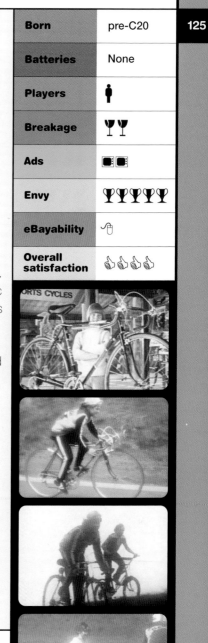

These days, we'd rather walk. Raleigh are back and doing well with a Mark 3 *Chopper,* MTBs, tourers and full sus/hard tails (surely they're making this up?). But for everyone who ever forgot the combination on their chain lock, or scraped a shin on metal-toothed pedals, or wrapped luminous masking tape around chrome handlebars,[2] we're slotting the front wheel of a Cream-era bike into the concrete block of immortality.

We were right about that saddle, though.

See also *Chopper, Peter Powell Stunter Kite, Top Trumps*

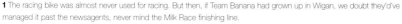

1 The racing bike was almost never used for racing. But then, if Team Banana had grown up in Wigan, we doubt they'd've managed it past the newsagents, never mind the Milk Race finishing line.
2 Drop handlebars served many purposes. There were, of course, the two standard riding positions (hands casually across the top bars or, forward, gripping the front) but they could also be repositioned to face upwards in a rebellious 'ram's horns' posture. This look was particularly effective in communicating the owner's pride at having perfected the art of riding none-handed.

Rainbow Brite
Lurid squidgy rag-doll and all her friends

Born	1983
Batteries	None
Players	👤
Breakage	🍷🍷
Ads	▪️▪️▪️▪️
Envy	🏆🏆🏆🏆
eBayability	🖱️🖱️
Overall satisfaction	👍👍

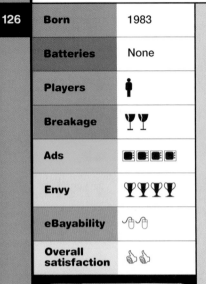

Like *Care Bears*, *My Little Pony* and many, many more, this overpriced doll and her garish companions were more like a worrying cult-in-the-making than a toy, born of an obsession with pretty colours and rainbows and cutesy names and everyone being bloody happy all the bloody time. Chances are, if you remember *Rainbow Brite* with fondness, you're not into David Cronenberg, Bret Easton Ellis or Cradle Of Filth. Vinyl-faced, with knitted dreadlocks and a clown's wardrobe, she arrived backed by at least four multinational corporations and, in the States at least, her own breakfast cereal.

According to the mimsy-flimsy back-story,[1] *Rainbow Brite* lived in Rainbowland in a rainbow-shaped house (available separately) and had seven individually coloured friends, including Red Butler (can you see what they did there?) and Patty O'Green (we can hear the cod Oirish accent still, begorrah).[2] Each doll also came with a cushion and a 'Sprite', which was sadly not a free can of fizzy pop but in fact a sort of over-engineered pet gonk (*Ms Brite's* Sprite was called Twink – now there's a name to keep defensive parents on their toes). There was also an egomaniac horse named Starlite and a human friend called, erm, Brian.

In the obligatory cheapo 'toon tie-in, she would fight the dismal forces of Murky and Lurky and bring happy colours to the world. In the real world, however, her nasty squishy consistency and scratchy woollen texture made for a doll that even the soppiest of softies would find hard to love. She lacked the homespun patchwork cosiness of similarly greetings-card-inspired *Holly Hobbie*, the novelty air-freshener stinkiness of *Strawberry Shortcake* and even the leftfield Angela Rippon involvement of *Victoria Plum*. She was, basically, just too darn dull. And it didn't take the most imaginative of brothers to start dreaming up alternative variations on her surname either.

However, that didn't stop *Rainbow Brite* from shifting over one billion dollars' worth of 'product'. The appeal of Americana to little ones is strong – and the one thing *Rainbow Brite* wasn't was British – especially when it comes peddled with much philosophical moralising of the 'if you believe you can do it, then you will' school (well, it was either this or *Star Wars*). Speaking of Americana, thanks to their 'unique' way of spelling, this doll was probably directly responsible for the annoying flood of neon 'Nite Club' signs that appeared in Essex back in the day. You must remember – it was around the time Reagan was in the Witehouse.

See also Strawberry Shortcake, Barbie, Tiny Tears

1 What? You expected something in-depth? The *Rainbow Brite* character was invented by Hallmark cards, so Tolstoy it ain't.
2 You'd think they'd've run out of inspiration after the seven colours of the rainbow but, in a move that proved irrefutably that American toy giants are more powerful than the very laws of physics themselves, the range continued to expand.

Raving Bonkers Fighting Robots
Genius heavyweight metallic mash-up

Born	1967
Batteries	None
Players	👫
Breakage	🍷 🍷 🍷
Ads	▣ ▣
Envy	🏆 🏆 🏆 🏆
eBayability	🖱 🖱
Overall satisfaction	👍 👍 👍

See also *Stop Boris, Tank Command, ROM the Space Knight*

The Americans sure knew how to name toys. We, to be honest, didn't. So, while this boxing automaton chestnut went under one of the best names for any game, or indeed anything, ever, in the States,[1] the rather rarer British version was renamed... *Raving Bonkers Fighting Robots*. Quite.

This un-American activity came courtesy of Marx Toys Ltd., who, aside from seemingly employing the cast of *Whack-o!* in their marketing division, did actually do a neat enough job of making the toy over here. Within a sturdy boxing ring, two square-jawed robots (named, in the English version, Biffer Bonker and Basher Bonker, but let's not dwell on it) rounded on each other by means of an initially hard-to-master combination of two under-ring levers and laid into their opponents with button-fired 'rocking, dodging, punching action'.

Embarrassing ads further encouraged the use of 'deadly Jupiter jabs' and 'astro punches' in progressive pugilistic bouts, although we should point out these are not recognised under the Queensbury Rules.[2] Bobbing and weaving were virtually non-existent. A successful knockout – not always following a connected punch thanks to Marx's overly delicate engineering – was signalled by the losing robot's head flying up on a ratchet. The resultant 'zing' remains one of our most cherished childhood sounds.

The late '70s *Star Wars*-demanded makeover (because clearly just being robots wasn't sci-fi enough) resulted in *Clash of the Cosmic Robots*, to all intents and purposes the same game but with streamlined-looking combatants and – allegedly, in some editions – a bit of crude 'sampled' surrender dialogue. Given the sheer bloody British politeness of it all, we presume our version went 'By jingo, sir! You've bally well got me in the seven-and-nines and no mistake! Care for a bun?'

Rock 'Em Sock 'Em Robots is still available today courtesy of Mattel and, in an astounding lazy-comedy-endorsing move, is actually smaller than the original. Nevertheless, in the absence of actual prize-fighting robots taking to the ring for our entertainment (why do you always let us down so, boffins!?), these red and blue *Raging Bull*s will have to make do.

1 *Rock 'Em Sock 'Em Robots*, as if you didn't know already. Starring the 'rollicking' Red Rocker and 'beautiful' Blue Bomber – altogether more Rumble-in-the-Jungle sort of names if you ask us.
2 Neither were they much use in real-life scraps. If you found yourself cornered by Slugger Benson's gang near the tuck shop, it was always best to surrender your pocket money or try to make him laugh. Admittedly, threatening a deadly Jupiter jab did have exactly that effect.

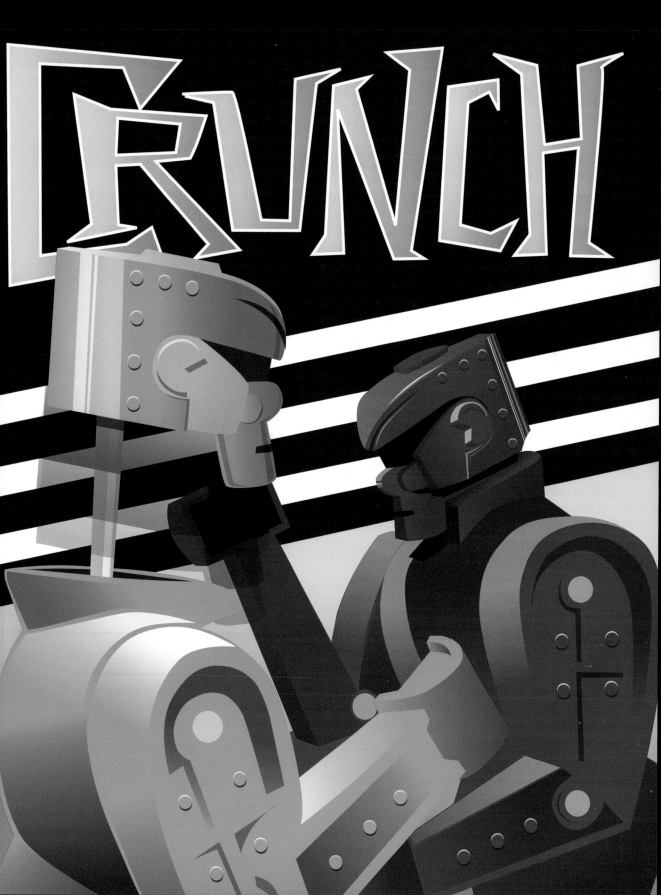

Remus Play-Kits
Bargain-bin gifts from aged benefactor

Born	1975
Batteries	None
Players	👤
Breakage	🍷🍷🍷🍷
Ads	▣
Envy	🏆🏆
eBayability	🖱🖱🖱
Overall satisfaction	👍👍

See also Pocketeers, *Shrinky Dinks, Paul Daniels TV Magic Tricks*

Concealed inside a thin card wallet bearing the illustrative image of the professorial titular 'uncle', these budget-priced kits generally strove to adhere to the notorious adage about 'making learning fun', more often than not involving 3D plasticine pictures from *Aesop's Fables*[1] or a selection of to-be-coloured-in fact sheets about dinosaurs.

However, there were some stray examples that leaned decidedly more in the direction of 'fun', including adaptations of such tried-and-tested favourites as the iron-filings/pen combination for drawing ridiculous combinations of facial hair and hats on the visage of a cheery gentleman[2] (and the cunning variant on same, featuring a man in profile but with his features missing from nose to chin, replaced instead with a chain that could be shaken into comical shapes). There was also a flimsy primitive precursor to *Magna Doodle* in which indentations were made on silvered plastic with a very hard drawing tool and then 'wiped' by running a badly aligned plastic bar across it.

In actual fact, the sheer breadth of activities *Remus* provided was astonishing: jigsaws, paint-by-numbers, model aeroplanes, finger puppets, doodle-pads, trump cards – he had the lot. Surely this Disney-esque patriarch must've been a reclusive genius, dishing out toys and games with vim and vigour from his tiny cottage at the edge of the magic forest? (Think about it: you never see 'Uncle' Remus and Dr Snuggles together, do you?) No way could he have been a cartoon cipher for Halifax-based Mars Ltd. (and that's not even the multinational snack-food one, although they do own the Uncle Ben's brand, which is where it gets confusing). Uh-uh.

Remus Play-Kits score highly, though, because they became desirable by their scarcity. For some reason, the damn things only ever seemed to be on sale at motorway service stations and chemists, meaning that requests for one could only ever be made at times when parents were in 'absolutely no bloody mood' to buy toys or games.

1 Push the clay into the plastic tray and – voila! – it's The (orange) Tortoise and The (blue and pink) Hare.
2 In the States, this fella's got a name – Dapper Dan, the Magnetic Man – and a back-story. He's a secret agent, chosen, you understand, for his skills as a magnetic master of disguise. Not much use on spy missions involving computer disks, tape recordings or credit cards, mind, but brilliant if you want your telly degaussing.

Ricochet Racers
Weapon-propelled miniature cars

Only one word for this Palitoy production – inspired. The original *Ricochet Racer* set took the two things closest to the heart of every ten-year-old boy – cars and guns – and combined them with an effortless genius that West Coast gangsta rappers can only dream of. The high-tech white-and-red rifle, resembling a failed auditionee for the part of Starbuck's fighter in *Battlestar Galactica*, was breech-loaded with 'cartridges' containing a miniature car, which could be fired at great (theoretical) speed along the floor.

But, as ever, what sounded like a dream product was scuppered by the twin toy demons of safety (to avoid potential lawsuits, the gun would fire the cars only when resting on the ground, thus putting paid to mischievous dreams of airborne car assaults from top-floor windows)[1] and the mundane reality of your average '70s house – instead of the acres of just-polished parquet flooring possessed by the parents of the children in the ads, a few square yards of traffic-calming nylon carpet was the deal more often than not, severely restricting the duration of any prospective race. Still, you could always gain limited fun by firing them from the top of the stairs when your mum was on the phone in the hall.

The many variations included a 'speed duel' double set, a 'sharpshooter' gun with a stack of little barrels to knock over, *Spiderman* and *Captain America* branded comic tie-ins and a glow-in-the-dark model. The Wild West saloon version, on the other hand, was just confusing and anachronistic.

Similar firing mechanisms were later developed for the wind-up ERTL *Wrist Racers* ('Snap 'em on! Rev 'em up! Blast 'em out!'), which strapped to your arm watch-style and boasted a permanently wheelie-ing General Lee from *The Dukes Of Hazzard* among their car range. Knickerbocker's *Finger Racers* were the tiniest option (well, they couldn't go any smaller, could they?) and were designed to break apart on impact, presumably to further remove that troublesome firearm association.

Born	1974
Batteries	None
Players	🧍
Breakage	🍷🍷🍷
Ads	▪️▪️
Envy	🏆🏆🏆
eBayability	🖱️🖱️🖱️
Overall satisfaction	👍👍👍

See also *Evel Knievel, Scalextric, Corgi 007 Lotus Esprit, Johnny Seven*

Wrist Racers
A one-off?

[1] We'll come clean here, 'cos the safety-pad mechanism was easily overridden by taping it up on the barrel. Bingo! Instant bazooka. And suddenly we could find out what the racers sounded like ricocheting off walls, shed windows and the neighbour's cat.

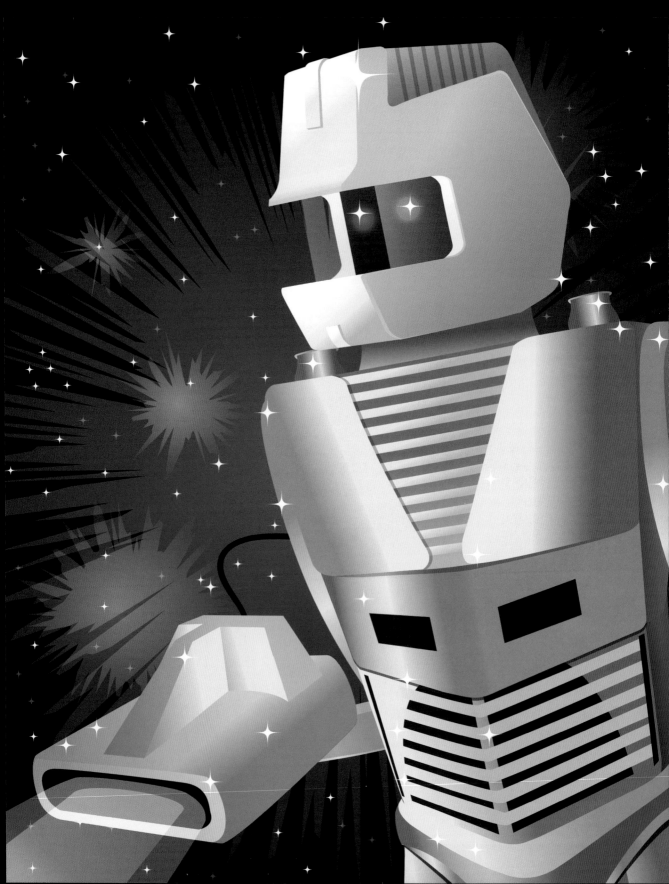

ROM the Space Knight
Futuristically armoured action android

Our first exposure to Parker Brothers' easy-to-spell *Space Knight* came courtesy of the Bullpen Bulletin page in Marvel comics, bigging up the antics of this new cosmic character. We have to confess that at the time we thought him to be yet another also-ran from the pantheon of rubbish second-string comic characters such as *Ghost Rider, Ka-Zar, Deadlock* or any of the other losers who'd appear for an issue in *Spider-Man Team-Up*,[1] and we were totally unaware of his exciting action-figure origins. For some reason, we also had him mixed up with REM, the robot bloke off TV's *Logan's Run* series.

Jam-packed with LEDs (two for his eyes, two in his chest, two in his rocket packs plus an extra one in his utility cable – whatever that was), *ROM* could also boast the essential space knight additions of an Energy Analyzer, a Translator and a Neutralizer. All in all it made for high-octane action around the sandpit at lunchtimes. Better yet, *ROM* could also make electronic noises thanks to two buttons on his back, one of these being the sound of heavy breathing. We're wondering whether latter additions to the *ROM* kit included a space-age inhaler.[2]

The best thing about *ROM the Space Knight*, however, was that in the UK he was marketed as an ally of the *Action Man Space Ranger*.[3] Quite what a space knight's contributions to the war effort could be is open to debate (rescuing space princesses and slaughtering space dragons, perhaps?), but popular suspicion had it that *ROM* was just another alias for *Action Man* himself. Cue hundreds of kids trying to pull his space head off to cop a look at the familiar fuzzhead-with-a-duelling-scar visage beneath.

ROM's real-life creator, Lawrence 'Bing' McCoy, was not one for resting on his laurels. He also invented *Computer Battleship* and *Star Bird* – that's three of our wish-list toys in just two years! All hail the patron saint of the Cream-era electronic bleep.

Born	1979
Batteries	
Players	👤
Breakage	🍷🍷🍷🍷🍷
Ads	▪️▪️
Envy	🏆🏆🏆🏆🏆
eBayability	🖱🖱🖱🖱
Overall satisfaction	👍👍

See also *Action Man, Cyborgs, Six Million Dollar Man, Star Bird*

---

1 And, no, we didn't just make those up. We've done extensive research! Read the rather wonderful *Ultimate Book of British Comics* by Graham Kibble-White for more on the Marvel invasion of Britain.
2 *ROM the Space Knight* is US patent number 4267551, granted in May 1978, and described with glorious pedantry as 'An electronic toy doll including electronic circuitry for selectively generating a number of simulation sounds typically associated with a

mystic or science fantasy character.' Cor! Talk about taking all the romance out. *ROM* was originally intended to be an Egyptian mystic, and then a cyborg called *COBOL*, before Parker Bros. streamlined his look and renamed him.
3 This may well have been to militate against anticipated poor sales. *ROM* was a palpable flop in his US homeland.

Rubik's Cube
54 multicoloured facets of misery

Born	1980
Batteries	None
Players	🧍
Breakage	🍷🍷
Ads	⬛⬛⬛⬛⬛
Envy	🏆🏆🏆
eBayability	🖱
Overall satisfaction	👍👍👍👍

See also *Black Box, Remus Play-Kits, Mercury Maze, Pocketeers*

We figure that if we're listing executive toys and abstract logic puzzles in our catalogue, then this iconic brainteaser has to count double. For a start, it was one of those so-easy-to-manufacture products that shops down the precinct would have countless knockoffs for sale at pocket-money prices. Hence, we don't think we ever knew anyone who owned a branded version and, naturally, that's what we really wanted.[1]

We're still unsure whether Professor Rubik actually endorsed the barrel, ball, hexagon or key-ring incarnations of his original cube-shaped arthritis-provider, but we are confident that both *Rubik's Magic* and *Snake* are canon. Second, the sheer amount of peripheral merchandise that the cube craze generated qualifies it for inclusion, principally the section of John Menzies devoted to 'solution' books that offered anything but. Inevitably written by either precocious 12-year-olds who shared a tailor with antiques freak-boy James Harries or spatial engineers from Brunel, they all amounted to a single set of incomprehensible instructions: get two sides sorted then somehow magically conjure up the remaining four.[2] Cue many lost childhoods as the cube's victims disappeared into near-focus hell for months on end. Ah, sorry, you must excuse us – we've missed our stop...

The hilarious dad-joke method of cracking the puzzle ('peel all the stickers off and put them back on in the right order') was rubbish and, in any case, impossible. And although there was always one kid in the class who could finish the thing fast enough to qualify him a spot on the local evening news, the only option for mere mortals was to take a screwdriver to it. Rubik did, however, spark a short-lived interest in the wider potential of the geometric riddle, so we probably have him to thank for origami kits, 3D chess and those bloody tangled-steel-wire puzzles that turn up in crackers to this day.

1 Brand recognition didn't kick off when Levi's, Apple and Nike rolled into town, you know. Beyond a certain age (let's say seven years old), nothing screamed out 'povvy kid with rickets' round our way more than cheap replica toys. Worst offenders were those unnamed featureless dolls (featureless, you understand, in the sense that they didn't do anything – cry, wet, blink – rather than that they had no face: this isn't some nightmare Hammer Horror toy catalogue), *Action Man* rip-offs (especially the ones with fewer-than-standard limb joints or plastic hair) and remote-controlled cars that still had a wire connecting the car to the controller. But it was also blisteringly important not to show up at school with something called a *Puzzle Cube* or *Magic Cube*. Christ, it all seems so weird

now, eh? It's not like there were gangs of kids who actually thought Erno Rubik was, like, the raddest professor behind the Iron Curtain. Great name for a Bond villain, though.
2 The most celebrated book was called *You Can Do the Cube*, by Patrick Bossert (although we prefer the sneery French title *Le Cube: c'est facile*), which shifted one and a half billion copies. Where is he now? Teaching molecular biology at Oxbridge? Chairing MENSA? Undergoing extensive therapy? Nope. According to his website, he's a business consultant 'experienced in managing multi-disciplinary bid teams for high-value client projects and providing governance in deal development and transition phases'. So still writing impenetrable stuff then, Patrick?

Scalextric
Slot machine

Here are our three favourite spurious claims made about this, the self-proclaimed 'most complete model motor racing system in the world'.[1]

One: at least five Australians were admitted to casualty last year with *Scalextric*-related injuries. Oh really? What happened? Did they get their tongues caught in the slots? Confused by the 1/32 scale and tried to drive through 'the bush' on one? Suffered carpel tunnel syndrome from gripping the speed controllers too hard? We're guessing that, in common with all hospital-related horror story stats, the nationality of the unfortunate slot-car victims changes depending on where this oft-repeated tale is relayed. All it really tells us is that people love to hear anecdotal evidence that others are more stupid than them.[2]

Two: there are now more *Scalextric* sets sold each year to baby-boomer adults trying to recapture their youth than to children. This little nugget comes courtesy of the BBC, which, we can quite confidently claim, is unlikely to have carried out the research itself. Leaving aside the significant probability that this statistic was seeded by *Scalextric*'s marketing department to attract an untapped demographic, we ask: since when did kids go out and buy their own bloody presents anyway?[3]

Three: if your holiday flight to Playa de las Americas is delayed, it's probably because a team of overpaid lad-mag journalists have built a Guinness World Record-breaking *Scalextric* track on the runway and are busy spraying champagne around and snorting coke off Z-list celebrities' arse-cracks. That, or some *Top Gear* presenter has chartered an Airbus to push a full-sized Formula One car out of the back to see whether it will reach *Scalextric*'s measured 'scale speed' of over 600mph, the idiotic, mid-life-crisis-gripped bigot. Maybe it was always your boorish future petrol-heads that were attracted to *Scalextric* at the expense of more recreational pursuits. Show us the boy at seven, and we shall show you the boy-racer.

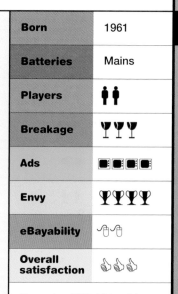

Born	1961
Batteries	Mains
Players	👤👤
Breakage	🏆🏆🏆
Ads	▪▪▪▪
Envy	🏆🏆🏆🏆
eBayability	🖱🖱
Overall satisfaction	👍👍👍

See also TCR, Matsushiro Knight Rider Radio-Controlled Car, Top Trumps

---

1 Our top three songs that reference *Scalextric*: The Housemartins' *The Light Is Always Green*, Godley and Creme's *Freeze Frame* and Half Man Half Biscuit's *All I Want For Christmas Is a Dukla Prague Away Kit*.

2 And – come on – five isn't a very high number is it? Out of a population of 20,579,913, it's a pretty poor effort.

3 'Parents in purchasing-children's-toys shame'? It must surely have been a slow news day.

Scrabble
Never a cross word

Born	1948
Batteries	None
Players	👤👤👤👤
Breakage	🍷🍷
Ads	▪️▪️
Envy	🏆🏆
eBayability	🖱️
Overall satisfaction	👍👍👍

See also *Trivial Pursuit, Monopoly, Speak & Spell*

'In the beginning there was the word,' wrote St John. 'And the word was God. And the word was worth five points, just one more than "nod" and actually one less than "mod".'[1] But then, that just goes to show how long *Scrabble* has been around.

For some reason, this lexiconic leviathan has been criminally ignored when it comes to compiling lists of the greatest games.[2] Put it down to years of family fights over the *OED* (they might as well have called it Squabble) or a reputation for attracting po-faced, serious and worthy players – that's 'word slingers' to you, sunshine – at international tournaments. Or that covert, crafty, it's-good-for-you quality (as you improved your game, you expanded your vocabulary – up to a point. No one ever dropped a 'qat' or 'zek' into a conversation at the grocer. Not unless they wanted bruised spuds and a stunted cucumber). There are no hilarious, fondly recalled *Scrabble* anecdotes, no childhood bonds forged through arguments over a triple-word score, no debauched tales of Y–F swapping at the Thornton Cleveleys Catholic Club. *Scrabble* was a drab, middle-class game played in drab, middle-class households by the drab middle-classes.

And yet... it's a game that has starred in some of the biggest sitcoms ever made (from *Seinfeld* to *The Simpsons*, they've all warmed over the 'pass off a made-up word as real' *Scrabble* schtick for cheap laughs). It numbers Keanu Reeves and Mel Gibson among its devotees and has been issued in 28 different languages. Including Welsh.

Our greatest literary figures have invoked *Scrabble* (look up Shakespeare's *Merry Wives of Windsor*, Act II, Scene I, where the mistresses check out Falstaff's gigantic set: 'I warrant he hath a thousand of these letters, writ with blank space for different names'[3]). Lewis Carroll reckoned he invented it. Douglas Adams had it determining the Ultimate Question of Life, the Universe and Everything (which was 'What do you get if you multiply six by nine?' apparently). So we salute *Scrabble*, game of champions and the only place you'll ever score with benzoxycamphor, diazohydroxide or oxyphenbutazone. Unless you're outside Camden Market on a Tuesday afternoon, that is.

---

1 Ignoring double-letter and triple-word scores and so on. Part of this Bible quote is not authentic, in case you were wondering.
2 Don't bother playing the word 'lexiconic' in *Scrabble*, either. We just made it up. That said, the modern-day version of *Scrabble* was christened *Lexico* by its originator, Alfred Mosher

Butts (that was his real name, by the way, not just what they called him down at Rockworld on metal night).
3 Actually, no one ever did play *Scrabble* with Shakespeare, 'cos they could never dispute any of the words he put down. In his lifetime, he invented over 1700 of the buggers.

Screwball Scramble
Ball-bearing-in-a-maze madness

Another one of those games that we would only ever glimpse across the classroom, on someone else's desk. With a concept latterly reinvented as *Marble Madness* for your new-fangled microcomputers, *Screwball Scramble* was a genuinely addictive race-against-time affair from Tomy. Your job was to guide a ball-bearing through a crazy maze via the use of a button, a lever and a knob.[1] Could you get it from start to finish before the tick-ticking timer wound down one minute? Cue much tongue-out, steely-eyed determination as kids would queue up to outdo their own and each others' fastest times.

But the fun didn't stop there. Never a company to leave a game horizontal when it could (with judicious addition of some magnets) be rendered vertical, Tomy went on to release the Nintendo-apeing *Kongman*. Yet another assault course for the plucky ball-bearing – this time the aim was to 'conquer mighty Kongman's kingdom' by means of a perpendicular onslaught across bridges and ramps (and, at some point, via hot air balloon), again against the clock. The game has since acquired scientific endorsement as a cognitive tool in psychiatric research.[2]

Screwball Scramble (and derivatives thereof) previously went by the names *Run Yourself Ragged* (which is perfectly acceptable) and *Snafu* (which, given it's an acronym of 'Situation Normal: All Fucked Up' is possibly less so for a kiddies' toy). Whatever they called it, this clockwork nail-biter was always destined to ratchet up the rage and tweak the odd nerve-ending. *Screwball Scramble*'s life expectancy shortened rapidly as the game became regularly sighted sailing across the room following yet another maze-traversing failure. It's still in production today, but we do have to wonder how many of those gobstopperish ball-bearings actually ended up taking the rather more 'screwy' route through some child's rectal canal. Particularly on the last day of the school term. In Moss Side.

Born	1979
Batteries	None
Players	👤👤
Breakage	🏆🏆
Ads	▣▣
Envy	🏆🏆🏆
eBayability	🖱
Overall satisfaction	👍👍

See also *Pocketeers, Mousetrap, Domino Rally*

---

1 Pre-wireless networks, all kids had a dream that they could rig up their home with an intricate Heath Robinson series of levers, pivots, gulleys and pulleys, thus operating everything in the house without ever having to leave their bed. Although *Screwball Scramble* gave some form to this dream (and an opportunity to practise at the controls), it wasn't until the opening moments of Aardman Animations' *The Wrong Trousers* that we got a glimpse of how it might work in reality. Ah, the epiphany.

2 *Kongman* was used in a clinical trial investigating 'habitual prospective memory in schizophrenia'. They're pretty dextrous, those schizos. For a full copy of the paper, contact BioMed Central Ltd, Cleveland House, London. We won't remind you again. (Ha-ha! Just a little joke for the cognitive scientists among you.)

Sea-Monkeys
Protozoan pets

Born	1962
Batteries	None
Players	👤
Breakage	🍸🍸🍸🍸🍸
Ads	▪️▪️▪️▪️
Envy	🏆🏆🏆🏆
eBayability	🖱️🖱️
Overall satisfaction	👍

See also *Magic Rocks, Shrinky Dinks, Squirmles*

Winner of the TV Cream award for Largest Disparity Between Portrayal in Advertising Materials and Reality. It is with some pleasure we see these fishy fraudsters continue to be sold to this very day. Yet, who has ever owned a family? Far from the apparent hierarchical society of tiny grinning mermen and mermaids presented in illustrated form on the packaging, *Sea-Monkeys* were in fact tiny – and we mean microscopic – crustaceans of the *Artemia salina* family. Yet we were, as youngsters, encouraged to believe that they inhabited a mysterious world of sunken treasures, kings and queens, castles and adventures, in a brazen example of spin that surely should have invited the full punitive powers of the Advertising Standards Authority.[1]

1 Actually, a '70s episode of *That's Life* was devoted to exposing the whole *Sea-Monkey* racket. They were originally marketed in 1957 by one Harold Von Braunhut, who can list *X-Ray Specs* and *Invisible Goldfish* among his other 'discoveries'. The British manufacturing licence for *Sea-Monkeys* currently lies with Benjamin Toys Ltd., whose other ranges include, we're delighted to note, spin-off merchandise and kids' costumes from *The Bill*! Surely it's only a matter of time before

Devoid of any anthropomorphic qualities, less still any simian behavioural patterns, 'Sea'-'Monkeys' lived in a freshwater tank of tap-water rendered habitable by the addition of packeted solutes, 'instant life' eggs (or brine shrimp to you and me) and powdered aphids (for food). The extent of the fun that could be derived thenceforth can be listed firmly under the category of 'observation' (hence the accompanying plastic magnifying viewer), although this tended to appeal more to the family cat than impatient kids.

But, for a time in childhood when keeping a tropical aquarium wasn't considered retro-kitsch in an Austin Powers kindofaway, Sea-Monkeys qualified as a genuine first pet of one's own and thus were desirable. Rumours that they grew to massive size in New York sewers after being flushed away by errant owners only added to the fascination. Most interesting, however, was the prospect of overpopulation. As some of them died, the surviving monkeys would cannibalise the bodies of their fallen comrades! Now, if only they'd put a cartoon picture of *that* in the adverts, we'd have definitely bought some.[2] For now, we must file them away alongside ant colonies, worm farms and stick insects under 'things that died of neglect'.

someone at ITV hits on the idea of a series that combines the two.
2 For more *Sea-Monkey* mania, dig out *The Ultimate Guide to Sea-Monkeys* by Susan Barclay (so called, we believe, to distinguish it from the lesser-regarded tomes The

Definitive Guide to Sea-Monkeys, A Complete Sea-Monkey Manual and *Sea-Monkeys For Dumb-Asses*). The book debunks some great *Sea-Monkey* myths, including a couple of the ones we've repeated here.

Shaker Maker
Oasis-inspiring make-and-paint gnome set

Born	1971
Batteries	None
Players	👤
Breakage	🍷🍷🍷
Ads	▪️▪️▪️
Envy	🏆🏆🏆🏆🏆
eBayability	🖱🖱🖱
Overall satisfaction	👍👍👍

Cast very much from the mould of the parentally approved toy, even your basic *Shaker Maker* knocked plaster-of-Paris modelling into a cocked hat due to (a) its novelty shaking method of construction and (b) its chemically imbalanced colour scheme.

Common to every *Shaker Maker* kit was the bag of 'magic mix' (all too easily confused with mum's spare Bird's Trifle sachets, with often unpleasant results). This served one function – to be stirred up in water, poured into a bright-orange plastic mould, dropped into a lemon 'n' lime Tic-Tac-coloured cocktail shaker and shaken vigorously until your arms ached so much you burst into tears.[1]

And the fun didn't even begin there – the whole apparatus had to be left overnight to set, and only then were you starting to get somewhere! Opening the mould revealed a blancmange-like model with all the wet slickness of cold sick and a not dissimilar smell. Vintage *Shaker Makers* covered the usual suspects, from farmyard animals through to horror characters and those perennial favourites, telly cartoon tie-ins. However, the excitement generated when you first removed a big, fat, wet Womble from the mould was matched only by the disappointment when you returned later[2] to find that the statuette had shrunk to a third of its original size and turned from a dazzling pink to an anaemic white.

If you weren't completely jaded by the whole experience, you could attempt to paint the by-now foam-shrimp-style models so that they matched the stunning but impossible-to-achieve photographs on the box. Tears of frustration were inevitable as Tobermory refused to look like his TV counterpart no matter how many of the thumbnail-sized plastic pots were mixed, preferring to sit there in unremarkable imitation of a shrunken, crumbly knoll.[3] Posh kids could acquire the highly prized *Roto-Cast* kits that came with a marvellous tombola-like device for shaking the maker without getting tendonitis but, despite the surplus of plastic, the end results were just as pitifully stunted.

Forget the Gallagher brothers: *Shaker Maker* was first immortalised in song by Mud in their minor 1976 hit *Shake It Down*, or possibly AC/DC's 1983 power-chord corker *Landslide* (sample lyric: 'He's a shaker, he's a breaker, he's a maker'). Perhaps the definitive *Shaker Maker* anthem is yet to be written.

See also *Shrinky Dinks, Play Doh Monster Shop, Mr Frosty*

---

[1] How come that never happened to Tom Cruise, eh?

[2] Note how we drop in casual terms like 'overnight' and 'later', words that would have cast a huge shadow of despair over a child's heart in the Cream era. *Shaker Makers* often took a whole week to set properly. That is one hell of a chunk out of your summer hols.

[3] Wombles no longer cut the mustard, it seems, making way instead for a set called *Disney Princess*. That's not even a proper Disney character – it's just a sort of... archetype. 'What did you make today, darling?' 'A Disney Princess, Mummy!' 'Really? Snow White? Cinderella? Sleeping Beauty?' 'No, Mummy, just a generic one.'

Shrinky Dinks
Make-and-bake marvel

Born	1973
Batteries	None
Players	👤
Breakage	🍷🍷🍷
Ads	📺📺
Envy	🏆🏆🏆🏆
eBayability	🖱️🖱️
Overall satisfaction	👍👍👍

See also *Shaker Maker, Play Doh Monster Shop, Remus Play-Kits*

Shrinky Dinks sat at the end of the hobby scale marked 'high concept'. We can only imagine the phone call that took place when these puppies were pitched over the phone. In fact, we're going to. (Well, in all honesty, we're just going to bastardise the famous Bob Newhart 'Walter Raleigh' monologue to make our point for us. Anyway, here goes...)

'Yeah, Bob, so you get the kids to colour in a line drawing that's been preprinted on what looks like an overhead projector transparency, right? Okay, then what? You get them to cut it out? Fine. So it's like a window sticker, right, Bob? No? Okay, so what do the kids do then? No, wait, lemme guess... they stick it in their ear? Oh, they put it in the oven! Right, of course they do. And the whole thing shrinks! Bob, why haven't we thought of this before?'

Like most high-concept ideas, though, *Shrinky Dinks* scored well with kids. Turning floppy plastic shapes into solid, hardened, frosted keyrings was industrial alchemy of the finest kind (and although the adverts might have led you to believe that you could use them for badges, fridge magnets and all manner of ingenious purposes, at the end of the day we all knew they were good for bloody keyrings and nothing more). The choice of designs was much the same as that for every other kids' art range, with superheroes for the boys and animals for the girls, plus a movie tie-in at every available opportunity. In the UK, in fact, many a Cream-era kid's first exposure to *Shrinky Dinks* was those given away in special packs of Shreddies to market Disney's syrupy space saga *The Black Hole*. Sci-fi, cereal, *Shrinky Dinks*... what's not to love?

However, it wasn't too long before the younger generation figured out that the plastic used to make crisp packets was pretty much the same as that employed for ver *Dinks*[1] and so took to baking them too. Thus, bicycle-lock, suitcase and school-locker keys the land over soon had mini-bags of Outer Spacers, Smiths Tubes and Football Crazy dangling off them. We're not sure, but we think it was also around this time that schoolkids took to sticking their conkers in the oven in the hope that they would go hard and be more useful for playground combat. (Please insert your own double entendre here.) And we still don't understand what a 'dink' is, in any case. (Please insert another one here.)

---

1 Not any more, thanks to the 'foil fresh' revolution. For God's sake, don't get us started on crisps and snacks. That's a whole other book. The top-secret *Shrinky Dink* plastic traded under the name Frosted Ruff 'N' Ready, which in itself sounds like a rogueish sugary snack.

Silly Putty
Gooey toy and cheap Xerox machine stand-in

Dateline 1943 (or thereabouts) and with war raging across the globe what the world needed was a right good laugh. The US government's War Production Board, aware that the Japanese were apparently staging a systematic invasion of any and all rubber-producing countries, charged its boffins with finding a new synthetic substitute. One, boss-eyed Scots engineer James Wright, reckoned he might have just the thing, combining boric acid with silicone oil in a test tube to create... something gooey.[1]

Blowed as to what this new sticky gunk could actually be used for, samples of it were sent out around the globe to see whether anyone could give it a sensible use. In 1949, a toy-shop owner did just that and started flogging it as a fun new toy. By 1950, the moniker 'Silly Putty' was coined and soon the useless stretchy stuff was being shipped out in Kinder Egg-like containers to millions (of, initially, adults).[2] And so another overnight success entered the American pantheon.

The reality, on the other hand, is that *Silly Putty* was just another one of those toys that you coveted for ages but tired of almost immediately. Get a lump of putty from Santa and the chances are you'd fully expect to find some car primer in your stocking the following year. Okay, it bounced and that was grand enough. But what was less good was the habit it had of lifting the ink off your *Beano*, thereby emblazoning a reverse-image of Little Plum across your palm. Pointless, surely? Well, you could then stretch his face into all kinds of weird shapes, but do it too often and it made the putty all dirty!

Despite any number of US patents preventing copies, pots and pots of the stuff appeared under different names: *Gupp*, *Tricky Putty*, *Nutty Putty*, *Potty Putty*, and (acknowledging the one classroom-pleasing use it could be put to) *Fart Putty*. More recently, *Thinking Putty* has cornered the market with metal tubs of the stuff – sold, once again, to (nostalgic) grown-ups.

So, credit where it's due: *Silly Putty* has endured decades of sweaty palms. In the '90s, a new version was created that changed colour with the heat from your hands and, 50 years after its creation, a commemorative metallic gold-coloured putty was introduced into the range. Apollo 8 astronauts even took *Silly Putty* into space in 1968 to use as a stress reliever. And to make copies of Little Plum, naturally.

Born	1949
Batteries	None
Players	🧍
Breakage	🍷🍷🍷
Ads	▪️▪️
Envy	🏆🏆🏆
eBayability	🖱️🖱️
Overall satisfaction	👍👍

See also *Slime, Play Doh Monster Shop, Magic Rocks*

1 Actually polydimethylsiloxane. If you want to get really scientific about it, you can pin all the unusual characteristics of *Silly Putty* on its nature as a viscoelastic liquid. Study the fluid mechanics and you will surely agree. Now, that's not to say it's a dilatant – not at all; that's your basic *Slime* toy, that is. No, viscoelasticity is where it's at, baby. (See, kids? Science is cool!)

2 Why an egg? 'Cos when it first hit the shops it was Easter. No, really, it's that simple. That toy-shop owner, Peter Hodgson, died in 1976 worth around $150 million.

Simon
Studio 54 on your living room floor

Born	1978
Batteries	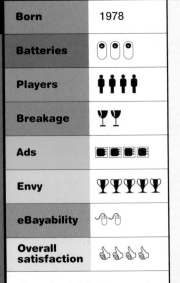
Players	
Breakage	
Ads	
Envy	
eBayability	
Overall satisfaction	

See also Merlin, Game and Watch, Mastermind

In the mid '70s, arcade giant Atari came up with a novel idea for a cabinet-based game – four flashing lights illuminated in a set order, which the player had to copy by pressing the appropriate buttons. Unsurprisingly, it sank without trace, perhaps not helped by Atari's chosen title for this meisterwerk – *Touch Me*. A couple of years later, Milton Bradley happened upon the idea and churned out a round, tabletop version of the concept, gave it the (relatively) more macho name *Simon*[1] and cleaned up in the Christmas of '78.

Its resemblance to the final scene of *Close Encounters* has been often remarked upon and, just like that effects tour-de-force, *Simon* was visually hypnotic and staggeringly pointless. In fact, the ideal conditions in which to play the thing – in a quiet, darkened room, with your face right up against it, dead to the world, finger poised ready to jab – could well have provided the catalyst for the whole 'computer games are rotting our kids' minds' movement. The TV ads[2] actually pitched the game at a relaxed, suburban, after-dinner crowd and families, although no-one ever played competitive *Simon*, did they? For a start, there never seemed to be the right kind of batteries in the house.

Towards the end of the decade, imitators aplenty came out, often hedging their bets by offering more games, with more and various coloured lights – anyone recall Mego's *Fabulous Fred*? Of course not! They all forgot the simplicity that was the key to the original game. Just four lights, a tune and a disapproving low farty beep when you cocked it up. The handheld *Simon* made it to the market eventually,[3] but the simple design of the original was – oh, go on then, if we must – iconic.

---

1 Simon Says... right? Just checking. This toy was considered educational by some on account of the fact that it, notionally, improved memory, taught eye–hand coordination and enabled parents to demonstrate increased self-control... by not smashing the bloody thing to pieces with a mallet.
2 That accompanying memorable jingle in full: 'Simon's a computer, Simon has a brain. You either do what Simon says, or else go down the drain.' Okay, so it's not Baudelaire, but it did the trick. In the States they had an excellent pastiche Police track, with a

vested Sting-alike singing 'Just do de-do what I do da-do!'
3 Additionally, *Super Simon* was the two-player rectangular effort with bars instead of quadrants. *Simon²* was a more recent attempt to cash in on the nostalgia boom but suffered at the hands of the not-dissimilar *Bop-It Extreme*. It seems the public appetite for 'computer-controlled' games has dimmed – although this was considered such a plus-point at the time that a photo of *Simon's* circuit board innards featured on the rear of the box.

Sindy
Foot-high fashionista

Pedigree's answer to that brash American vixen *Barbie* came in 1963, between the end of the *Chatterley* ban and The Beatles' first LP.[1] With rosebud lips, wide blue eyes and prominent brow, *Sindy* epitomised girl-next-door cutesiness for a generation of British 'gels' in need of an 11-and-a-half-inch role model.

In the 40-odd years since, *Sindy*'s weathered many storms. There were those nasty rumours about being inserted into a popstar's bottom, unfounded accusations of racism, criticism of her body shape and a whole series of facelifts that have redefined the phrase 'plastic surgery'. Oh, the price of staying young. Yet despite the endless assaults on her territory (there were some inroads made by rivals such as Palitoy's *Tressy* and *Pippa* dolls), *Sindy* has always held her own.

'Active', Cream-era versions came with the ability to pose, ride a bike and dance. Top-of-the-range accessories included her very own MGB sports car (which *Action Man* often had to 'borrow') and crazy playsets like the *Super Sindy Electronic Spaceship* and the *Wall of Sound*. The latter effort, nothing to do with Phil Spector's Gold Star Studios, was a sonically accurate miniature of a madman's living room. Like an old-time shooting gallery, every feature hid a hitherto unexpected racket, from the none-more-'70s stoneclad chimney-breast (*crackle!*) to the unnamed kitten on the hearth (*purr!*).

But such gadgetry was for boys. What little girls wanted were clothes, clothes and more clothes. Skirts, dresses, suits, coats, capes and shoes – there were thousands of outfits to choose from. *Sindy* was probably paying off one credit card with another.

Recently, the doll has become decidedly more almond-eyed and *Bratz*-influenced, whilst the older ones largely star in 'adult' photo-story action strips on websites run by porn-obsessed nerds. Mind you, there is something very Jilly-Cooper-sultry about *Sindy* in her horse-riding outfit.[2] It's always the ones you least suspect, isn't it?

See also *Barbie, Tiny Tears, Chic-a-boo*

Born	1963
Batteries	None
Players	👫
Breakage	🍷🍷🍷🍷
Ads	▪️▪️▪️▪️▪️
Envy	🏆🏆🏆🏆🏆
eBayability	🖱️🖱️🖱️
Overall satisfaction	👍👍👍👍

1 *Sindy* actually hit the shops just before *With The Beatles*, the band's second studio album, but we couldn't resist quoting Philip Larkin.
2 We'd speculate further on the nature and depth of *Sindy*'s sexual proclivities only we live in constant fear of reprisal from her legal team. All we're saying is – take a look at the first three letters of her name. Surely no coincidence, eh?

Six Million Dollar Man
Lee Majors' pension fund

'Gentlemen, we can rebuild him – we have the technology.' Yes, and every last cent of it was funded by sales of the spin-off merchandising. In red-tracksuited action figure form, Steve Austin came complete with an impressive array of pseudo-bionic features that included a magnifying-lens eye (sadly with none of those cool bar-chart things that appeared when we 'saw' through his eyes in the series),[1] an arm with easily torn fake skin that rolled back to reveal various plastic fittings and a 'bionic grip' operated by pressing a substantial red button that protruded awkwardly from his back. Rich kids could also invest in a set of interchangeable limbs, namely a Laser Arm (which shone a red light), a Sonic Neutraliser (some sort of karate-chop/ray-gun combination) and the self-explanatory Oxygen Supply Arm.

Six's main corresponding playset was the *Bionic Transport and Repair Station*, a thermos-flask-like contraption that stood a full foot and a half tall and opened to reveal all manner of mock computer equipment (then, when closed, doubled as a rudimentary spaceship with barely enough room for the rebuilt one to swing a cat).[2]

In a bid to ensure that girls didn't miss out on the action, a *Bionic Woman* Jaime Sommers doll was also produced, although her main accessory was – gasp! – a purse, along with disturbingly tanglesome blow-wave hair. Jaime's range of extras – sports car, dream home, and the downright baffling *Bionic Beauty Salon* – suggests that the manufacturers weren't exactly busting to break down the barriers of gender stereotyping.

Also available were several villains – *Maskatron*, who apparently had only one million dollars spent on him and was so haunted by the fact that he sought to wreak revenge by wearing interchangeable masks of Steve Austin and Oscar Goldman; the *Fembot*, who did much the same for Jaime; and the unforgettable *Bionic Bigfoot*, a strange ape/robot hybrid with more than a passing resemblance to Dave Lee Travis. Even boss Oscar got a look-in, complete with a booby-trapped briefcase and cardboard office. Frankly, did Steve really need any of these hangers-on and freeloaders? Yeah, like he needed a hole in the head.

Born	1975
Batteries	None
Players	👤
Breakage	🍷🍷🍷🍷
Ads	▪️▪️▪️
Envy	🏆🏆🏆🏆
eBayability	🖱️🖱️🖱️
Overall satisfaction	👍👍👍

See also *Cyborgs, Action Man, Dr Who TARDIS*

---

1 In fact, everything looked further away. We reckon this was the toy equivalent of the TV series demonstrating the speed of 'bionic action' by running everything in slow motion.

2 Bionic grease-monkey Austin was never seen without his internal combustion engine. And he could never lift it unless he was looking right at it.

Slime
Synthetic goo

Born	1977
Batteries	None
Players	👤
Breakage	🍷🍷🍷🍷🍷
Ads	▪️
Envy	🏆🏆🏆
eBayability	🖱️🖱️🖱️🖱️🖱️
Overall satisfaction	👍👍👍

See also Silly Putty, Shaker Maker, Magic Rocks

Most toys were no use to an only child. There's not much mileage in playing *Monopoly* alone. Even games with no format, no rules and no board – the kind that challenged the imagination – 'playing *Action Man*', say, were more fun with two or more people. Precious few of our most-wanted Cream-era toys were not only aimed squarely at the solitary child but also made absolutely no sense in company. Mattel's *Slime* was one of 'em.

Dreamed up by some toy-making genius (and we'd put our last dollar on that being one of those American dreams we keep hearing about), presumably after watching too many '50s B-movies, this viscous mixture of latex, wallpaper paste and food colouring (the actual ingredients may have differed slightly, but that's what we're guessing)[1] hit the shops at roughly the same time the *TISWAS* gang were chucking buckets of water and foam flans at each other and basically making a right old mess on telly every week. Although no parent would normally leave his or her offspring unsupervised with just any old gunge, the restrained anarchy of *Slime* (water-based, non-staining on wipe-clean surfaces such as the kitchen lino) was perfectly suited to out-of-the-way play.

Disappointingly, once the contents were emptied from the Oscar the Grouch-type 'trash can' container (*Slime* came in different colours, some with plastic eyeballs, some with rubber worms), there was precious little play to be had. Sure, it could slowly ooze and bubble (a satisfying trick was to trap some air in a glop of the stuff and slowly force it out with a pop),[2] but an hour with your hands in the stuff was pretty much the limit.

Thus, it has been constantly revived and reinvented for each new generation: in the '80s, as *Masters of the Universe Slime* and again as *Nickelodeon Slime*. The *Ghostbusters* fire-station set came with a tub of *Ecto-Plazm Slime* to gloop down the walls. In the '90s it re-emerged as *Teenage Mutant Ninja Turtles Retromutagen Ooze* (which surely gains extra points just for the name) and, most recently, as the amniotic fluid inside *Goosebumps Monster Bags*.

Although all of these are to be commended for continuing the lineage of a once-great toy, nothing could match the joy of opening that plastic garbage can for the first time. Similarly, nothing could match the misfortune of finding an accidentally left-open pot of the stuff, dried to a husk and rendered useless to both man and beast. But, oh! That evocative smell! Oh! That clammy touch! *Slime* was but a fleeting pleasure, and all the better for it.

---

1 Do you really want the full SP? Okay, technically it's a reversible, cross-linking gel made from guar gum and sodium borate. Yeah, you think our guesswork was more fun, now, don't you? *Slime* behaves exactly the same as quicksand – under stress it will expand – so if you had enough of it and a deep paddling pool, you could drown someone.

2 This, unsurprisingly, has been embraced as a positive marketing point for the new range of *Slime* (made by British toy company FEVA), which comprises *Original*, *Magic* and *Ooops!* (pardon me) *Pffft Slimy* varieties, plus the obligatory *Spiderman* and *Spongebob Squarepants* tie-ins. Doesn't it make you proud?

Slinky
Spring roll

Born	1945
Batteries	None
Players	👤
Breakage	🍷🍷🍷
Ads	📺
Envy	🏆🏆
eBayability	🖱🖱
Overall satisfaction	👍👍

See also *Newton's Cradle, Magnetic Wheel, Mercury Maze*

The Queen owns one of these, you know. Having bought it at the British Industries Fair in 1954, she was reported to have dubbed it 'amusing'. Presumably she couldn't wait to set it off walking down the Grand Staircase at Buckingham Palace.[1] Rumour has it too that when, in 1982, Michael Fagan broke into the monarch's bedroom, she kept him occupied by delivering a physics lecture on compression-wave principles illustrated with a *Slinky*.[2]

Not the strangest non-toy use of a *Slinky*, mind. Not by a long chalk. The US military used them as impromptu short-range antennae in Vietnam. The pecan-pickers of Texas and Alabama used them in farm machinery. Lazy mid-westerners stuck them in their rain gutters to keep out leaves (although, actually, that's not such a bad idea). It's also the Official State Toy of Pennsylvania (where they still make 'em). Fancy having to dress up as a *Slinky* for the Independence Day parade, eh?

Invented in the '40s by maritime engineer Richard James, who later disappeared to become a preacher with a Bolivian religious cult, the *Slinky* was 80 feet of flat steel wire machine-wound into a short column of 98 coils. In its heyday in the States (during the '60s, when a catchy ad sent sales spiralling), there were *Slinky* dogs, *Slinky* trains and those funny specs with *Slinky* eyeball goggles.

Back in boring old Britain, we were similarly attracted to this big loose spring, although the brand-name original never seemed to arrive in our Christmas stockings. Say hello instead to the *Merit Springer*, *Magic Spiral*, *Rainbow Coil* and 1000 other patent-infringing copies just waiting to be tangled to buggery by Cream-era kids. Worse still, there was a plastic version that didn't even behave like a *Slinky*. One of the hidden secrets of the metal original was that, when dangled full-length and held to the ear, wobbling it about would recreate the laser-blast sound effects from your favourite sci-fi films.[3]

Ultimately, though, all *Slinkies* suffered a fatal calamity, whether through accidental treading-on, overoptimistic stretching or rust. A bent *Slinky*, like Prince Naseem Hamed, is never going to get back into shape. Thus, the career of this mortal coil would come to an end at the back of the wardrobe. Isn't that where they always wound up? Or down.

---

1 This is just an absurd flight of fancy, of course. We know for a fact that the steps of the Grand Staircase are simply too wide to walk a *Slinky* down. Here's a tip: never set off a *Slinky* down an 'up' escalator unless you've got a few hours to spare.
2 Want more? Look up Hooke's law, which states that the force applied to a spring is related directly to its stretch. Or, to put it another way, how to knacker your *Slinky*.
3 It wasn't just us who noticed, either. Some enterprising company glued a *Slinky* inside a bit of drainpipe, called it the *Zube Tube (the Ultimate Cosmic Sound Machine)* and sold it back to us all over again.

Smoking Monkey
Mail-order pocket-money sapper

In addition to the adverts for unfamiliar and strange-sounding confectionary such as Twinkies and Reese's Pieces, imported American comics held an additional attraction for British readers in that they provided exposure to all manner of gimmicky novelty items, normally promoted by sizeable adverts that occupied two-thirds of a page and yet included only microscopic illustrations of literally dozens of different products. The most fascinating of all these curios was the *Smoking Monkey*.

A plastic chimp that exhaled smoke of some description when one of the special mock cigarettes was inserted into its mouth, the *Smoking Monkey* was seriously politically incorrect on many, many levels at once.[1] It was also the source of much confusion for British youngsters, who could neither understand nor appreciate why anyone would actually want a toy chimpanzee dragging on a pretend Woodbine, or indeed what possible use or purpose it might serve.[2] Was it some sort of tribute to a legendary primate? Perhaps in the days of the British Raj, a top-hatted monkey-wallah did indeed climb down from the trees and trade bananas for Bensons. Or is it a comment on man himself? Are we literally the smoking monkey? Whatever, mass non-ownership of this toking tamarin burned it into our collective memory.

Other classics of the novelty genre included: *X-Ray Specs* (promoted by an illustration that suggested that they gifted the wearer the ability to see animal skeletons and women's legs, but in fact they merely produced a hazy outline around objects through suspiciously rose-tinted lenses); *Whoopee Cushions* ('emit a real Bronx cheer!'); itching powder; unrealistic plastic ice-cubes with unrealistic plastic flies embedded in them; equally unconvincing squirting buttonhole flowers; more unconvincing still plastic chocolate digestives (which were not only the wrong texture and hue but also nowhere near the standard size of a biscuit); fake dog poo; fake chewing-gum packets that snapped the finger of anyone who tried to remove their contents with a spring-loaded metal paddle; black face soap; and, most unforgettably of all, the ridiculous arrow-thru-head.

Most of this stuff – the ciggie-sucking simian included – was in fact available in the UK, visible alongside the usual quota of glow-in-the-dark stars in the legendary 'stocking fillas' catalogue and even occasionally advertised in the likes of *Whizzer and Chips* (using the same microscopic illustrations), but for some reason it suited everyone better to believe that they were known only to our Stateside counterparts. There is some comfort to be had in thinking 'only in America', eh?

Born	1950ish
Batteries	None
Players	👤
Breakage	🍷🍷🍷
Ads	📺
Envy	🏆
eBayability	🖱
Overall satisfaction	👍

See also *Finger Frights, Squirmles, Lone Star Spudmatic Gun*

1 There were actually negro-monkey drawings on the packet!

2 Tell you what, though – it works. 'Blows smoke rings' says the packet, and that's what the little fella does (at least until his fag goes out). Sorcery! Witchcraft! Burn him! (Oh, we have.)

Sonic Ear[1]
Digital spy

Born	1979
Batteries	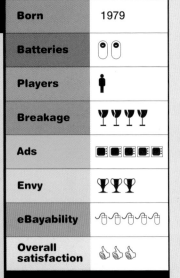
Players	
Breakage	
Ads	
Envy	
eBayability	
Overall satisfaction	

If ever there was an MI5-standard surveillance gadget mistakenly marketed as a children's plaything, then *Sonic Ear* was it. In fact, it was such a covert piece of military hardware that there are now only 14 people in the UK who know this existed. They remember the telly ads featuring a lad spying on his family and neighbours from 50 feet across the garden. They remember the shape and size of the thing, something like a cross between a rifle and a trombone, fashioned in silver and red plastic (and not to be confused with the US 'super' version, which parabolically anticipated Murdoch's micro-satellite dishes). What isn't known is whether anyone ever owned one.

Seemingly on sale for about a fortnight in the summer of 1978, although never spotted on toyshop shelves, the *Sonic Ear* was hastily erased from history – clearly as part of some government cover-up or national security conspiracy. Sure, it might have been possible that the ability to eavesdrop on the confidential conversations of people up to 200 yards away contravened some kind of privacy law, but – hey – that's what they wanted us to think, right? There was obviously a more sinister agent at work, possibly connected to the nanny state's wider scheme to prevent us kids from 'breaking out' and becoming telepathic, paranormal *Tomorrow People* (while at the same time denying us the high-tech equipment we, as homo superiors, would require for our intergalactic adventures).

The *Sonic Ear* (and the more we think about it, the more we can convince ourselves that the 'E' on the logo was shaped like a human ear) was just the tip of the iceberg in that respect but, of course, you won't hear any of us saying this out loud. You never know who might be within earshot.

Those who rashly claim to have owned the *Sonic Ear* talk of the toy's stethoscope-like set of earphones and disappointing inability to pick up even the noisiest conversation without standing in plain sight of the very people you were supposed to be snooping on. But then, they would say that, wouldn't they? We're living in the age of hidden webcams, remote-controlled spy trackers and GPRS-enabled phones. There are 14-year-old boys being trained in abseiling, rifle-shooting and martial arts, just so they can be put to work as secret agents.[2] What's some sneaky old plastic bugging equipment anyway? Well, to the kids of the Cream era, it was everything we could have ever wanted. So Santa, why weren't *you* listening?

See also *Tasco Telescope, Armatron, Johnny Seven*

---

1 Something of the tautological about that name, no? Maybe there were plans for other toys? The *Optical Eye*, perhaps, or the *Smelly Nose*.
2 Since this entry was written, it has been pointed out to us that this may actually be the plot to the film *Stormbreaker* and not some government conspiracy after all.

Sorry!
Ludo for bastards

Much as we hoped otherwise, sadly this board game owed little to the Ronnie Corbett sitcom of the same name. Even the politeness of the title was only a front, as this otherwise unremarkable plastic pawns 'n' ludo-style makeweight appealed largely to the nastier side of childhood nature.[1] It was gloriously mean-spirited, in fact. Lotto meets Russian roulette.

In the time-honoured tradition of the ancient game Parcheesi, from which it descends,[2] the idea with *Sorry!* was straightforward: simply move your pawns round the board to 'home'. So far, so humdrum. Fortunately, a series of randomly drawn instruction cards added variety to the gameplay, as did the magic ingredient – the ability of players to directly, deliberately and with malice aforethought bugger up the game for their opponents. In the words and typography of the instruction leaflet, this primarily involved BUMPING pawns all the way down SLIDES back to the START – a hugely satisfying aspect that, short of kicking over the table and sodding off home, is sorely lacking from most modern board games.

The game's most iconic features were design-led. A mid-Imperial phase ('70s Waddingtons) version had split-screen action photographs on the box (very *24*) and circular cards that were supposed to make shuffling much easier. Early editions featured a cartoon Japanese couple on the box for no readily explainable reason. A distant cousin of the *Mastermind* lady, perhaps?

Meanwhile, in the blue corner was Peter Pan Playthings' *Frustration*, cut from much the same cloth game-wise but with its own unique selling point – the simple addition of a 'popomatic' dice roller, turning what could be a fairly dull children's game into a noisy festival of explosive fun.

Strangely, this brilliant innovation (stick the dice in a plastic bubble) was deemed more important than the game itself. A TV campaign had Richard Briers fervently relating the 'pretty rotten' tale of a North Pole Inuk family that 'keeps cheerful by playing popomatic *Frustration*' and dispensing igloo-specific safety tips. Even the box lid sacrificed the game title in favour of a huge pink arrow pointing to a hole in the middle, with the word 'popomatic' written in bold, bright letters instead.

Yet the clicky little dice device didn't exactly set the world on fire. Admittedly, it prevented arguments of the 'I definitely threw a six' variety, but practically no other games before or since *Frustration* have been 'popomaticised', if indeed that's even a word. Like so many other '80s novelties – Athena prints, Ketchips, EPCOT – it seemed like a futuristic idea at the time but now just looks like an embarrassing relic. But then, don't we all?

Born	1934
Batteries	None
Players	👤👤👤👤
Breakage	🍷🍷
Ads	▪️▪️
Envy	🏆🏆
eBayability	🖱
Overall satisfaction	👍👍

See also *War of the Daleks, Escape from Colditz, Mousetrap*

Frustration Drove us popping mad

---

1 To us Brits, of course, the word 'sorry' barely carries weight. We say it about a hundred times a day – if we nearly bump into someone, cough a bit too loudly, or slightly talk over a stranger at a bar. It's such a flimsy expression of regret that it's practically sarcastic.

2 One in a long line of family-friendly versions (see also *Coppit, Headache, Trouble, Trap the Cap* and so on and so on to infinity).

Spacehopper
Boing 24/7

Born	1968
Batteries	None
Players	👤
Breakage	🍷🍷
Ads	▪️▪️
Envy	🏆🏆🏆🏆
eBayability	🖱️🖱️🖱️
Overall satisfaction	👍👍👍

See also *Swingball, Chopper, Peter Powell Stunter Kite*

Surely not? How can this iconic cliché of the decade that taste forgot (whenever that was, exactly) be in a catalogue of toys that we wanted as kids? Didn't we all just own one? Weren't they handed out by the government on 1 January 1970 along with regulation loon pants, glitter and the pill? Well, no... we're exaggerating, obviously. But we've still got some questions we want answering about this bouncing bloody behemoth.

Although everyone remembers the distinctive carrot-coloured rubber model with horns and a bemused-looking kangarooish expression[1] cartooned on the front, the first *Spacehoppers* in the UK were actually blue. The artwork on these rather larger bouncers simply distorted the phrase 'The Great *Spacehopper*' into a Beatle-esque Blue Meanie face. So what happened? Why the change? The generally accepted theory is that the blue hoppers were meant for adults but failed to catch on, but we suspect something slightly more 'the Walrus was Paul' sinister.

But what is it that has lodged the *Spacehopper* so firmly in the nation's consciousness? We're going to hazard a guess that it's nothing to do with 'everyone had one' and everything to do with 'everyone who did have one lost one'. For what sums up the ephemeral life of childhood toys more than this hippest of hoppers? Well before we'd experienced the cold fingers of mortality, whether personally due to clumsy stewardship of a family pet or vicariously via the procession of animal deaths that was *Blue Peter*, the cold, hard streets were already witness to a litter of ruptured, gored or just plain burst *Spacehopper* carcasses. High-visibility targets for mean kids with penknives, defenceless against Gran's electric fire or weakened by inevitable overinflation (insert Labour government joke here): death à l'orange. No wonder adults still yearn for them.[2]

And, although no longer produced by Mettoy or Wembley, the classic-look *Spacehopper* is back. Surely this is the final redemption. In spite of everything – they're awful shorthand for retro kitsch, they're unwieldy, they're inefficient as a means of transport (even just a short go on one makes you want to have a poo) – they are indomitable, quite literally bouncing back. Maybe one day we will all have one after all.

---

1 Check out that gap-toothed grin. A sign, according to Chaucer's *Canterbury Tales*, that our balloonsome friend here (like the Wife Of Bath herself) had a strongly sexual nature. Inappropriate for a child's toy? Don't blame us, blame English literature.
2 In the '70s we'd buy any old tat as long as it had the word 'space' on it. Cheap plastic *Frisbees* were rechristened *Space Spinners*, fizzy sherbet became Space Dust and vac-

formed corn snackmongers KP begat us Outer Spacers. We sent *Space Oddity* to number one, we watched *Space 1999* (in 1975) and we all holidayed at Walt Disney World (but only for Space Mountain). We also watched the Space Shuttle take off and land, but we'll allow that one, for obvious reasons.

Speak & Spell
Remedial alphabet tutor

Calculators became something of a school obsession in the early teens of '80s kids, although even the most maths-obsessed pubescent would've found it hard to justify a requirement for logarithmic polynomial functions to parents already sceptical that the damn things were actually allowed in the classroom in the first place. This was probably the first generation for whom electronic aids were encouraged and, in some cases, compulsory, as long as the battery compartments weren't being used to conceal various useful formulae in maths exams.[1] (If you attended Grange Hill, of course, you were required by the laws of drama to raise the bar on even this illicit behaviour by attempting to sneak class A drugs into your mock O levels.)

Anyway, it's doubtful that even the most liberal of junior school teachers would've been happy to allow Texas Instruments' *Speak & Spell* into English lessons. Replete with an array of bleeps, parps, toots and tics, this most vocal of educational toys came fully equipped to instruct and comment – in a gentlemanly American way – on the user's ability to spell.

Fashioned in Fisher-Price-friendly orange plastic, with no sharp edges (you get an idea of the target age range) and a built-in carry handle, the *Speak & Spell* displayed design cues that would inform some of today's 'ergonomic' laptops. Certain versions sported a *ZX81*-style touchpad keyboard, others the clicky button type, but all shared the same primitive speech cell (similarly duff voice synthesis was later also popularised by the Currah Microspeech for the *ZX Spectrum* and the thing that Professor Stephen Hawking talks through). The most fun could be had by making him 'laugh' by repeatedly pressing the 'e' key (or the 'o' key if it was Christmas), and even though the educational value of spelling what sounded like 'beurellaux' or 'sinflaps' was suspect to say the least, some of the words did seem a bit rude.

Joining the range later were *Speak & Read* and *Speak & Music*. Collect the set! *Speak & Maths* tried the same trick by making numbers seem sexy or fun but, as noted, by this time the kids had tired of LED-based arithmetic and moved on to the charms of the slimline calculator (ooh – all vinyl wallet and solar-powered liquid crystal display).

Born	1978
Batteries	🔋🔋🔋🔋
Players	🧍
Breakage	🍷
Ads	▪️▪️▪️
Envy	🏆🏆🏆🏆
eBayability	🖱️🖱️
Overall satisfaction	👍👍👍👍

See also *Little Professor, Commodore 64, Stylophone*

---

1 In the days before GPS wi-fi hotspot-enabled PDAs made it possible for kids to hold the processing power of a Cold War-era battle computer in the palm of their tiny hands, they were already experts in miniaturisation – specifically, writing extensive cheat notes on wafer-thin tissue paper. Folded tightly, these sheets could then be smuggled into even the most conscientiously invigilated test and secreted under the desk as required. Other favourite hiding places included: inside chewing gum or Polo wrappers; on slide-rules or other geometry equipment; as microdots beneath fingernails; and as part of forged *Urlaubscheine* documents to pass through the German/Swiss border.

Spirograph
When fun and geometry collide

Born	1966
Batteries	None
Players	👫
Breakage	🍷🍷
Ads	▪️▪️▪️
Envy	🏆🏆
eBayability	🖱
Overall satisfaction	👍👍👍

See also *Etch-A-Sketch, Shrinky Dinks, Meccano*

Spirograph was a junior engineer's wet dream, comprising many plastic gear shapes, each with tiny teeth round the edge and tiny holes round the centre, and a whole load of rings, teeth again protruding from the outside and inside edges. The idea was to lay the gears on to a piece of paper pinned to a board (or, indeed, Mum's fine oak dining-room table) and then roll your chosen ring around it, pushing a pen through one of the holes. Thus, with no artistic talent beyond the bare minimum of coordination, anyone could 'draw'.

Once the artist-powered cog system was mastered, the resulting unimpressive spiral on the paper could be reproduced to create more unimpressive spirals on top. This carried on and on with different-sized plastic pieces – eventually producing something not unlike a knackered *Slinky*. Every. Single. Bloody. Time. In point of fact, the name *Spirograph* is a portmanteau of the Greek words *graph*, meaning 'drawing', and *speira*, meaning 'knackered *Slinky*'.

You may also be surprised to learn that such spiral graphs have a basis in maths, being used to solve polynomial equations of a higher degree. Their application as a toy, however, has to be called into question. For instance, no-one ever explained what you should do about the little holes left in the paper by the drawing pins. Of course, you could try to hold the various rings in position manually, but only the slightest movement meant that the spiral effect was ruined completely.[1]

The original *Spirograph* hit the shelves in the mid '60s but was relentlessly improved, modified and reissued in a new guise every couple of years. Before the '70s were out, a bewildering array of spin-offs included *Spirotot, Super Spirograph, New Spirograph* and *Spiro 2000*. When they released the *All New All Star Super Spirograph*, we began to suspect the involvement of Hanna Barbera in the product development department.

That didn't stop the copycat toys, mind you. *Dial-A-Design* attempted to solve the slipping paper problem by including a loading cartridge, although the paper used had to be of a fixed size and entirely circular. So, handy for making those oh-so-desirable geometric paper coasters then. Even more obscure was *Rotadraw*, plastic discs with stencil-like holes in a dot-to-dot style. When you'd rotated the wheel and filled each one of them in – lo! – there was an almost-joined-up picture of a Disney character. So-called, of course, because it disnae look anything like it was supposed to.

---

1 TV's Tony Hart never had this problem. He'd achieve a similar pattern on a grand scale, filling up a huge funnel with paint and suspending it over a floor-sized sheet of black card. Neither of these was ever available at Toymaster, mind, which put such art beyond the means of the average eight-year-old.

Squirmles
Pipe cleaner with personality

Born	1975
Batteries	None
Players	👤
Breakage	🍷🍷
Ads	■■■■
Envy	🏆🏆🏆
eBayability	🖱
Overall satisfaction	👍

See also Smoking Monkey, Finger Frights, Paul Daniels TV Magic Tricks

The archetypal 'spontaneous dad present', we're saying, insofar as it's the sort of thing he'd spot in Toy & Hobby one night after work – usually because of an endlessly looped demo commercial playing on a telly in the window – and decide to bring home to thrill the brood. Although having barely learned the rudiments of its 'secret instructions', the breadwinner of the house[1] would still be able to make Squirmles do just enough to have your baby sister squeal with excitement and run off into Mummy's arms.

Then, with a paternal wink, you'd be taken to one side and shown exactly how it worked – on a bit of bloody fishing line nicked off your junior angler rod! The secret instructions themselves didn't break any Magic Circle code either: basically, you were supposed to tie the 'invisible thread' around your shirt button and move your hands across it to and fro. Not easy for a t-shirt-dwelling mite of the '70s.

Any actual fun evaporated after a few hours of practising and failing to make Squirmles do anything it said on the packet. Maybe master prestidigitators could get him to go in and out of jacket pockets and that, but for kids with all-fingers-and-thumbs first-grade piano hands, even the sliding-back-and-forth-across-the-tabletop manoeuvre was a big ask. Plus, you would inevitably attempt to pull off the in-and-out-of-the-glass trick before remembering to drink your Vimto, leading to what we believe they call in the toy trade the 'wet fuzz scenario'.

The high concept idea behind all this nematode nonsense was to fool other kids into believing Squirmles was a genuine pet ('Everyone's got them in America'); this despite the fact that the toy, rather like the 'invisible thread', was clearly on view and on sale in the high street. Luckily there was always one gullible short-sighted girl in the class who'd be suckered in as it twirled around your finger. Sadly, the critical come-on line 'Would you like to see my furry worm?' barely extended into adolescence without headmaster's-office-visit repercussions.

[1] Apologies to children from broken homes, single-parent families and orphanages, but look on the bright side: you got all that government benefit money.

Star Bird
Sonic boon

Truly a masterpiece of timely '70s toy design, proudly marrying X-Wing-influenced rear spoilers to a swan-like stem and detachable cockpit fighter. The first remarkable thing about *Star Bird* was its sheer size. Forget buzzing around the garden with Matchbox or Dinky toys clutched in your tiny paw: this monster was a serious piece of space hardware.[1]

Once assembled (a process in itself reminiscent of some gung-ho, muscle-rippling AK-47 lock 'n' load film montage) and fully liveried with the enclosed stickers, the *Star Bird Space Avenger* (as it was later to be rechristened) weighed in at a couple of kilos and stood over a foot long. It was, however, perfectly balanced – meaning it could be cradled with one hand gripping the neck and thereafter making it simplicity itself to swoop and zoom into interstellar battle on the patio. Which is where the real unique selling point came in, because the second remarkable thing about *Star Bird* was that buried somewhere in its plastic hull was a motion-sensitive gizmo (something gyroscopic or mercury-based, perhaps, but possibly just a marble in a tube) that could tell whether the ship was in a 'dive' or a 'climb' (or, at least, whether you were pointing it up or down or not) and emit the appropriate rising or falling drone.[2] The currency offered by such a feature in the playground pecking order was almost immeasurable, marking a clear line in the sand between those who had the incessant hum of galactic ion engines literally in their grasp and those who had to resort to oral simulation of same.

MB later introduced the *Star Bird Space Intruder* to the range (a smaller, blacker and, therefore, evil iteration of the toy), which added insult to injury for kids who weren't even lucky enough to own the *Avenger* and moved the pleasure even further from reach (insofar as it was idiocy to consider owning the latter without the former). The combative relationship of the two ships extended to in-flight scenarios, with each being able to 'react' to the LED laser cannon attacks of the other and a couple of flat-pack targets. Totally minted kids could also get the cardboard *Command Base* but, seriously, by this point it was just rampant consumerism.[3]

Born	1978
Batteries	(1)
Players	(1)
Breakage	YYYY
Ads	▣▣▣▣
Envy	YYYY
eBayability	🖱🖱
Overall satisfaction	👍👍👍

See also Big Trak, Computer Battleship, LEGO

---

1 We're quoting Billy Bragg. *That's* how serious we are about *Star Bird*.
2 Either considerably better or just not the same, depending on whether you were a fan of sci-fi or real-life fighter dogfights, was a surprisingly faithful *F14 Tomcat* model with a joystick attached to the back to fly it around the house. If you were prepared to avoid growing up until the '90s (what, that soon!?), then the Kenner *Talking X-Wing* did a better job on every level.
3 Did we really expect our parents to shell out for a simple box full of slotted cardboard shapes so that we could assemble them into a tower and landing pad for *Star Bird*? Too right, we did.

Star Wars
May the toys be with you

Born	1978
Batteries	None
Players	👤👤
Breakage	🍷🍷🍷🍷🍷
Ads	▪️▪️▪️▪️▪️
Envy	🏆🏆🏆🏆🏆
eBayability	🖱️🖱️🖱️🖱️🖱️
Overall satisfaction	👍👍👍👍👍

So we'll take it as read that everyone had at least one *Star Wars* figure, because otherwise this is just going to be an uphill struggle – the card-mounted Kenner character was the standard unit by which all collections were measured and/or founded, whether you owned just Luke Skywalker or a whole squadron of Stormtroopers. The fact of the matter is that entire 3000-page catalogues have been published detailing the merchandising history of the Lucas franchise,[1] but at least that leaves us free to skip to the top end (at least in our neighbourhood) of the desirability stakes and miss out the soap-on-a-rope C3POs, Leia earmuffs, Darth duvet covers, etc.

In reverse order, then, those toys that we all would've happily been born a spoiled only-child for (or that are still stored in airtight containers by over-zealous fan boys), wish-fulfilment light-sabre Photoshopping aside.[2] We loved the 'pipework' detail on those massive chunks of moulded beige or grey plastic that formed AT-ATs, the Millennium Falcon and TIE Fighters (especially the

---

1 *Star Wars: From Concept to Screen to Collectible* by Stephen J. Sansweet and Steve Essig is a good place to start. And, really, it's a good place to end too. Seriously, do you know how many items there are for sale on eBay alone? There's no way of catching up now.

2 For the avoidance of doubt, we here at TV Cream Towers (along with any right-thinking adult) define *Star Wars* as being the three films that were released between 1977 and 1983. And, to be honest, *Return of the Jedi* wasn't that much cop. In fact, the best thing about the entire franchise was the exploding TIE Fighter clip in the opening titles of *TISWAS*.

ones with 'hidden' compartments or 'secret' buttons that would make parts spring off), although the varying scales they were constructed to meant for confusingly incorrect-perspective battles.

Conjuring up a similarly surreal David-and-Goliath fight potential were the 12-inch figurines of popular baddies Vader, Boba Fett and so on. These guys had an advantage over their more miniature fellows (not just in terms of size), insofar as their clothes/capes weren't fashioned from vinyl, they were more accurately detailed and their light-sabres, etc. need not be awkwardly retracted into their arms. However, we do understand that for anything other than display-and-admire purposes, they were pretty impractical.

By far the most coveted toy, however, was the cardboard-and-plastic hybrid that was the *Death Star Playset*. Oh *Death Star*, how we desired thee. Shall we count the ways? The most thrilling parts of the first film could be re-enacted with ease (from 'TK-47' to 'Run, Luke, run!'). The seemingly bottomless tractor beam control duct, rendered by simple means of a mirror at the base, was confirmed (as we suspected all along) to be slap-bang in the middle. And the working trash compactor even had the eye-on-a-stalk alien thingy drawn on it. In fact, the only thing really wrong about this *Death Star* is that it was way too cool and expensive for us to even consider returning to later, shooting a couple of plasma bolts at and destroying. If it had been down to us, the Rebellion would've been crushed just so we could carry on dropping Han Solo down the cell-block chute.

Another teensy problem was the lack of a corresponding Kenner Grand Moff Tarkin to stand on deck and say 'You may fire when ready.' Walrus Face and Death Star Droid, yes, but no Tarkin. In fact, let's quickly remember some of the other cack ideas trolled out in the name of merchandise. The 'droid factory'. The inflatable light-sabre. The Jawa figure (surely it should've been half price?). The completely unnecessary cardboard-flavoured gum packed in with the *Topps* trading cards. And the quaint notion of providing adhesive 'battle damaged' stickers to apply to the space ships.

You see, ironically, it was the damage so easily sustained to that cardboard *Death Star* that has made it such a collectable today. If there's one thing kids do really well, it's 'battle damage' – and even those who did own one thought nothing of burning, battering or breaking it. Mind you, all that carelessness did not go in vain – it has at least given us the opportunity to watch completist Americans taking out second mortgages to acquire one now, eh?

Death Star Playset
Battle stations

See also Dr Who
*TARDIS, Zoids,
Star Bird*

124318

Stay Alive!
Chinese chequers with trapdoors

Born	1971
Batteries	None
Players	👤👤👤👤
Breakage	🍷🍷
Ads	📺📺
Envy	🏆🏆🏆
eBayability	🖱
Overall satisfaction	👍👍

See also *Sorry!*, *Hungry Hippos*, *Hangman*

A possibly too-panicky title for a pretty good last-one-left-on-the board strategy game. Essentially what we had here was a variation of Chinese chequers with bloody great holes in the board to make things a bit trickier. Up to four players took it in turns to move plastic slides under coloured marbles in an attempt to line up openings that would cause their rivals' balls to drop[1] out of the game.

It didn't take long for the serious *Stay Alive!* player to work out that, if the tabs were whipped about with great speed, inertia would prevent one's own balls from dropping[2] while still securing a gap into which an opponent's balls might drop.[3] Furthermore, the home advantage to the owner of this game was that, despite giving the appearance to the young mind of having an almost infinite number of combinations, the board could in fact be learned. Dropping your mates' balls at will appeared to give you almost Kasparov-level powers of mental acuity.

A good game for the last day of term (as it was one of those games that was not only useless to play alone but also improved with extra players), the marbles could also be adapted (i.e. stolen) to replenish those that'd gone missing from *KerPlunk* and *Hungry Hippos*. Much was made of the 'ultimate survival' element both on the box blurb and in the accompanying TV ads, which made the game an unpopular choice of gift in hospital intensive-care units. On the bright side, it clearly inspired elements of TV favourite Rob Curling's daytime quiz show, *Turnabout* (as did, we suspect, both *Connect Four* and *Othello*). However, rumours that a version endorsed by the Bee Gees, called *Stayin' Alive*, to be used as a really awful pun on which to finish this entry, are, we understand, much exaggerated.[4]

---

1 The first one to make 'Ooh err missus!' remarks will be sent to the back of the book until break time. Now just simmer down. I can wait all day. It's your own time you're wasting.
2 I've warned you once. If there's any more of this sniggering, you'll all be staying behind after the book has finished.

3 That's it! Detention, everyone. Write a 200-word essay entitled 'Why *Stay Alive!* ironically lost its appeal to kids around about the time they hit adolescence'.
4 This was a much funnier joke before the 2006 schlock horror film *Stay Alive* came out. Why does Hollywood have to ruin everything so?

Stickebricks
Lo-fi *LEGO*

Benjamin Franklin wrote that nothing in life is certain except death and taxes. Closely challenging those two in bronze medal position, however, is the likelihood that you would always find a couple of stray *Sticklebricks* at the bottom of your primary-school toy box. Ubiquitous in the Cream era, the part-filled bucket of *Sticklebrick* squares, triangles and oblongs was a stalwart of the wet-break-time classroom scramble. Ironically for a set of plastic toy blocks whose whole *raison d'être* was to stick together, pieces would inexplicably find themselves strewn all over the place (as any parent or teacher carelessly wandering around in stockinged feet would confirm).

Designed to appeal to toddlers (the UK version was well-named for infant pronunciation: they literally are sticky lickle bricks),[1] these coloured building bricks proved both a visual and a tactile delight. Fringed on all sides with flexible plastic brushes, they held together purely by friction grip. Fine when stacking them end-to-end and making a sort of Tootie-Frootie Wicker Man,[2] but not so fine if sandwiching them flat on top of one another – thereafter, pulling them apart became a near impossibility for a grown-up, never mind someone still coming to terms with their own opposable thumbs.

Sadly, beyond a certain age, a kid's awareness of the statute of *Sticklebrick* limitation became all too apparent. Whether used as a makeshift bed of nails for a teenager's *Action Man* or fashioned into a *Blade Runner*-style skyline on a university hall of residence window ledge, there came a time when everyone put a *Sticklebrick* to its final use.[3] To be fair, though, they were never much use for playing with anything other than themselves. Unlike *LEGO* or *Meccano*, you couldn't really construct yourself additional prop cars or houses – well, not of any discernible shape anyway. More recent sets have attempted to remedy this by including useful pieces such as wheels, lights and, erm, teddy bears. However, we are delighted to confirm that *Sticklebrick* sets of the present are much like *Sticklebrick* sets of our past (and, for that matter, Ron Jeremy, Seymore Butts and Ben Dover): they still come in buckets.

Born	1969
Batteries	None
Players	👤
Breakage	🍷🍷
Ads	▣
Envy	🏆🏆
eBayability	🖱
Overall satisfaction	👍👍

See also *Fuzzy Felt, LEGO, Fisher-Price Activity Centre*

---

1 The USA had 'em called *Bristle Blocks* (sensible), *Nopper*, *Clipo* and *Krinkles* (not so sensible). UK manufacturer Denys Fisher stuck with the name *Sticklebricks* – 'an easy new way to build big toys'.

2 The colour palette of *Sticklebricks* has expanded over the years, but they still have that chewy sweet E-number influence. Perhaps they should be called Skittlebricks?

3 Not to be confused, we should note, with those little fish you used to net in the local reservoir and keep in jam jars. Those were sticklebacks, and we spent a good 15 minutes composing an entry based on them before realising our error.

Stop Boris
Eight-legged, battery-gobbling freak

Born	1979
Batteries	● ● ● ● ○ ○
Players	👤👤
Breakage	🍷 🍷 🍷
Ads	▣ ▣ ▣
Envy	🏆 🏆 🏆 🏆
eBayability	🖱 🖱
Overall satisfaction	👍 👍 👍

See also Tin Can Alley, Crossfire, Raving Bonkers Fighting Robots

Like some crazy one-off *2000AD* strip come to life, this game's star was a huge battery-operated plastic spider on wheels, with vicious-looking teeth and a pulsing green brain and stomach that glowed eerily in the manner of a backlit monster from a cheap BBC teatime sci-fi show. Boris, for 'tis he, had one job and one job only: to progress stealthily down a cardboard ramp... and get you! He could, however, be repelled by the beam of a rather slick-looking infrared 'Photon Phaser' gun. Hit him squarely in a small target located directly between the eyes and he'd scuttle back up to his PVC web. And that was it. Corgi weren't messing about when they came up with the name for this. Those were all the words of explanation you'd need. Just get the job done, sunshine, so we can all go home.[1]

According to the instructions, you could shoot Boris only when he was moving towards you, so that meant the quicker you shot at him the further back he'd retreat. Miss and he'd keep creeping down until you were firing anxiously at anything and everything. Talk about tension: *Stop Boris* could turn a Zen Buddhist into a babbling, trigger-happy psychopath in minutes.

Now, we say he moved stealthily. What we actually mean is shakily (and, in some cases, not at all). If truth be told, Boris was a bit portly looking, and slightly erratic. But, by jingo, he didn't half shift when you landed one on him. Of course, these days, we know him better for slating Liverpudlians and hosting some classic episodes of *Have I Got News For You?* (Ha-ha! You thought we were still talking about Boris the Spider,[2] but we were talking about Boris Johnson. Geddit? Satire! *Private Eye*, eat your heart out.) Later, more sophisticated variants on the formula – mid '80s effort *B.A.R.T.*[3] for one – came across like the punch line to a pointless joke when compared with the mighty, menacing spider. Thus, for one glorious, endless summer in 1979, *Stop Boris* was the toy that everyone had to have. In reality, it was also the toy that hardly anyone got, the high incidence of rampant arachnophobia among more sensitive siblings being enough to persuade parents to allow pleas for ownership to fall on unheeding ears.[4]

1 Weren't the '70s didactic? Lots of bossy people telling you what to do. *Stop Boris*. *Get Carter*. Enjoy Coca-Cola. Do the Shake and Vac (and put the freshness back). Why didn't they just leave us alone?

2 Also the name of a 1966 track by The Who, from which we're not going to quote the lyrics in this book. John Entwistle's already dead and we'd rather keep the money, thanks. Plus, it's not that great a song.

3 Bio Automated Roaming Target apparently. *B.A.R.T. Laser Challenge* featured 'High speed drive system with 50 escape patterns', which means he was actually trying to run away. Such a coward when compared with the belligerent bastard Boris.

4 The bloodcurdling screech Boris was prone to emitting may have not gone unheeded by those same ears, however, which could be another reason parents were reluctant to shell out.

Strawberry Shortcake
Creepy, aromatic, fruit-inspired dolls

So, let's sling 'em in with your *Cabbage Patch Dolls*, *Rainbow Brites* and those two rather disturbing naked *Love Is...* kids as another example of an apparently acromegaly-afflicted cutey that made little girls go mad in the '80s.

Yet another craze that doubtlessly inspired a weary and bitter 'and finally' on the teatime news around Christmas – cue pictures of mental parents battering the crap out of each other in toy shops up and down the land. Everything about the *Strawberry Shortcake* empire smelled of big bucks. And we make that point deliberately, because the high concept behind '*Shortcake* and pals (that line-up including Blueberry Muffin, Plush Custard the Cat and – phwoar, this one sounds like a goer! – Raspberry Tart[1]) was that they whiffed of fruit. Which was quite clever, we have to admit.[2]

The *Strawberry Shortcake* franchise was mega, spanning your expected crap Saturday morning cartoon through to lunchboxes, porcelain trinket-sets, books and – well – bins. And it still goes on. We were predictably despondent to discover that this pre-pube girly favourite is still cutting a huge marketing swathe across the globe, with hundreds of websites flinging out new '*Shortcake* merchandise on a daily basis. Worse than that, the range seems to be somehow linked to other insidiously marketed toys of the '80s, joining hands across the World Wide Web with your *Care Bears*, *My Little Ponies* and any other ugly little goblins that provoked 'I-want-one-of-those' temper tantrums of Violet Elizabeth proportions back in their heyday.

Although singing from the same 'let's celebrate the joy of life' hymn sheet as *Rainbow Brite*, *Strawberry Shortcake* wasn't limited by the need to fight against a darker power. However, a delightful coda to this cloying brand franchise is the tale of Web comic, *Penny Arcade*, receiving cease-and-desist letters from *Strawberry Shortcake*'s intellectual property-rights lawyers, for producing a parody subtitled 'She's a sweet girl with a taste for pain'.

So not so friendly after all? Sounds like a case of Sour Grapes to us.

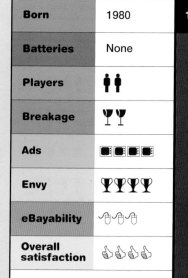

Born	1980
Batteries	None
Players	👫
Breakage	🍷🍷
Ads	🎞🎞🎞
Envy	🏆🏆🏆🏆
eBayability	🖱🖱🖱
Overall satisfaction	👍👍👍

See also *Rainbow Brite, My Little Pony, Chic-a-boo*

---

1 The potential for double-entendres is rife in Strawberryland. Even the official website describes La Cake as 'a sweet and spunky redhead'.
2 Whoever it was who worked out how to infuse polyvinyl toys with a plethora of tempting aromas was a genius. That no-one stopped to ask why – why make little girls want to eat their dollies? – casts that brilliance into even sharper relief.

Stretch Armstrong
Elastic lump in blue underpants

Born	1976
Batteries	None
Players	👥
Breakage	🍷🍷🍷🍷🍷
Ads	🎞🎞🎞🎞
Envy	🏆🏆🏆🏆
eBayability	🖱🖱🖱🖱🖱
Overall satisfaction	👍👍

On the one hand, it's hard to understand the appeal of this giant of the Cream era, but that's only if that hand belongs to a kid who never owned one. The other hand we've got here – the one that lusted after *Stretch Armstrong* with an unremitting passion – says that, yeah, he might have looked like *He-Man*'s soppy cousin but he had the amazing power of s-t-r-e-t-c-h to make up for it. (So amazing, in fact, it necessitates the use of dashes between the letters of the word 'stretch'.) This is the hand that knows what it's talking about.

The play opportunities were boundless. You could pin his legs to the floor with your feet, then try and pull his arms above your head. Get a friend round and the two of you could try and make *Stretch* stretch from the front to the back of your house. If you did this outside, and tried stretching him round the corner of a brick wall, you would probably also find out the other awesome secret of *Stretch* – that he was filled with some weird carcinogenic ooze. Split *Stretch* in this way and your fun would be short-lived as the ooze was the source of his power. Once that ooze oozed away, your bendy-limbed friend would go limp and leave you holding what might as well have been a large, human-faced rubber johnny.[1]

He may have had a thing or two in common with that bloke out of the *Fantastic Four*, but while he was still s-t-r-e-t-c-h-y and getting pulled more often than Britt Ekland in a Carnaby Street cocktail lounge, *Stretch Armstrong* had no equal. Unless, that is, you count *Stretch Monster*, the lurid green but crap 'enemy of *Stretch Armstrong*' (crap due to his snot-like appearance at full pull), *Stretch Octopus* and *Stretch X-Ray*, the incredible orange-coloured, slightly-see-through version who already resembled a rubber johnny even before he split.[2]

Stretch always seemed destined to provide an instant, unoriginal nickname for any kid in the class with the surname Armstrong,[3] so it was quite something to see the original Denys Fisher '70s model undergo a WWF wresting-style makeover in the early '90s, gaining himself a manic cheesy grin, blond mullet and natty black vest outfit in the process.[4] His modus operandi remained the same, however, and – even better – this time his mate was a dog called *Fetch Armstrong*. Surely the revival was worth it for that gag alone?

See also *He-Man and the Masters of the Universe, Six Million Dollar Man, Silly Putty*

---

1 Rubber Johnny, we're thinking, was probably among the rejected names for this toy.
2 The serious collector can amass quite a *Stretch* army. We hope their wives never file for divorce. Can you imagine the heartbreaking tug-of-love such a separation might instigate? It'd go on for ever. And it'd be about six feet across at least.
3 Who was he named after, though, really? Neil Armstrong? Louis Armstrong? Or is it, as we rather suspect, just a fairly lame play on the words arm/strong?
4 Hulk Hogan, we're blaming you. Again.

Stylophone
Rolf-endorsed, pocket-sized electronic organ

Born	1967
Batteries	
Players	
Breakage	
Ads	
Envy	
eBayability	
Overall satisfaction	

See also *Merlin, Electronic Project, Magna Doodle*

What to say about this harmonic, monophonic, iconic artefact? If you didn't own one, then you wanted to – fact. And it's proved a must-have prop for pre- and post-ironic tunesmiths like Jarvis off of Pulp, Phil 'Orbital' Hartnoll and Tin Machine's David Bowie. Apparently profiting from the onset of the microelectronic revolution, the *Stylophone* was to all intents and purposes the iPod of musical keyboards.

This 'electronic organ in your pocket'[1] was invented by Brian Jarvis around 1967, after a bionic repair job on his niece's toy piano. Essentially a slim keyboard packed with oscillators, resistors, diodes and the like, you'd operate it with a small stylus and thereby emit a rather reedy, nasal BBC Radiophonic Workshop-type sound. The overall effect was not unlike that of a drunk wasp merrily burrowing its way into your ear canal on a kazoo. All that was needed was a big name to sell it.

With Rolf Harris at that time king of light entertainment in the UK (and – let's face it – isn't he still?), Brian and co. approached him to promote their product.[2] The Antipodean animal-lover was only too keen to get involved and, despite an

1 Ooh er, missus. No, stop it. Hands up who thinks they should've had Frankie Howerd's face on the box instead?

aborted attempt to launch the *Stylophone* on David Frost's ITV show, Rolf was soon noodling away with it alongside *The Young Generation* on his own titular BBC teatime extravaganza.

With such enthusiastic Aussie endorsement (his bearded phizog bedecked the packaging and he even recorded an instructional flexidisk to go with the product), things naturally went mental. The *Stylophone* became the must-have accoutrement for – well – anyone really, even though it cost an absolute bomb. Over the years four million units were sold in the UK alone as differently clad variations were introduced – one sporting a fake wood veneer. Now there's posh.[3]

In truth, one *Stylophone* did not a career in pop music make, and for most kids the lonely drones quickly grew unsavoury. Nine times out of ten the 'electronic organ in your pocket' became more commonly regarded as the 'six months' pocket-money-sized hole in your pocket' as the instrument was consigned to bottom-of-toy-box oblivion. Rolf, how could you lie to us? Your face was on it and everything!

In 2003, Brian Jarvis' son Ben resurrected the family business, apparently with the sole purpose of constructing a giant *Stylophone* in the shape of a Gibson Flying V guitar. Rolf played it with a celebrity *Stylophone* orchestra at the Royal Albert Hall. Yikes! Who would've thought it? Nearly forty years on and the bloody thing still won't buzz off. (That's the *Stylophone* we're talking about, not Rolf Harris. Mind you...)

2 According to legend, Rolf was literally approached in a Television Centre rehearsal studio and the prototype *Stylophone* thrust into his hands. As historic meetings go, it's right up there with Lennon and McCartney, no?

3 There was also a dual-stylus model called the 350s. As well as being two-note polyphonic (duophonic?) it had an infrared light beam that you could wave your hand across to control vibrato. Heady stuff for the '70s.

Subbuteo
The champion game of all!

Born	1947
Batteries	None
Players	👤👤
Breakage	🍷🍷🍷
Ads	🎞🎞🎞
Envy	🏆🏆🏆
eBayability	🖱🖱🖱🖱
Overall satisfaction	👍👍👍

See also *Test Match, Top Trumps, Screwball Scramble*

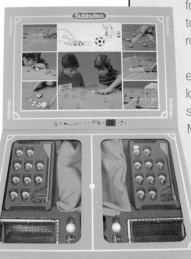

This famous tabletop baize-cloth 'flick-to-kick' football interpretation needs no introduction. From the £2.49 scale replica of the FA Cup to the full-on World Cup sets bursting with teams, referees, balls, a fence surround, an 'electronic' scoreboard and little manager and coach figurines (you could tell them apart because one was wearing a sheepskin jacket), most young football fans[1] encountered this at some point. Whether they stuck with it was a different matter.

Although the range offered all sorts of goodies for you to collect, and the eventual introduction of pre-packaged real-life teams brought an air of partisanship, the twin problems of a) finding someone else to play with (mums being curiously reluctant) and b) fathoming out the over-complex rules ('you can't do that, see Rule 7F!') meant that it only ever found lasting appeal with adolescent football fanatics of the let's-collect-it, update-your-*Shoot*-league-ladders ilk.[2] Along with all the equipment necessary for the actual game came extraneous items of tat such as scoreboards, linesmen standing attentively with their flags in the air and the famous floodlights (always the centrepiece of TV ads featuring highly excited young boys slotting one home with a flick of the finger). On the plus side, it allowed the young fanatic to revel in his own football fantasies, creating (and meticulously recording) super-leagues, tournaments and reprising classic fixtures of the past, all with a full rota of staff, press and TV chaps watching on.

Talk in the '90s of TV coverage and a bid to become an Olympic event (the twin goals of all joke sports) depicted *Subbuteo* as more loved than it actually was. The brand was a strong one, however, and several different sports were similarly miniaturised over the years.[3] Most famously there was *Subbuteo Rugby*, which, among the usual paraphernalia, sported an odd device used to simulate scrums – the Scrummage Machine. A big old bit of rugby ball-shaped beige plastic, this had six holes in the sides and one in the top. Place players next to holes, put the ball in top and see who wins possession. They also tried *Subbuteo Hockey* and *Subbuteo Cricket*, the latter eventually being eclipsed by *Test Match*. There was even a *Subbuteo Angling* set once, although on inspection this turned out to be a rather drab board game instead of little plastic men sitting on the sides of a fish tank dangling tiny rods into the water.

1 And even non-fans may well have stumbled across the odd piece. If this were the TV Cream Book of Toys You Stood On, *Subbuteo* would be top of the league.
2 In the mid '80s *Subbuteo* produced a poster displaying all the available accessories along with all the different teams. In the pre-Champions League days, this was the first opportunity to get acquainted with some foreign teams.
3 Nomenclature nugget: the name *Subbuteo* comes not from some mythical Brazilian full-back but from the Latin name of the hobby falcon because the inventor of this new 'hobby' was a birdwatcher.

Swingball
Perpetual tennis machine

Always the preserve of the Cream-era family with a luxuriant and well-groomed lawn, *Swingball* was truly king of the outdoor games. It was also one of those great games of our youth that could honestly pass the test of time, thus explaining why our prowess as a nation of tennis players isn't what it should be, 'cos on the grass courts of SW19 you never get that 'I'll catch it on the next rotation' second-chance element.

Nothing more complicated than a pole, a helical screw and an old tennis ball fastened on with string, *Swingball* came to dominate well-to-do British back-garden summertimes like no other. Okay, we'll give you a paddling pool, the odd climbing frame and putting the tent up ('we're not even going anywhere!'), but in the sparsely sown field of home-for-the-holidays sport,[1] *Swingball* towered above all-comers. They should have covered it on *Grandstand*.

Inevitably, of course, there were inadequacies. For a start, the string would always get horribly tangled, requiring the more grown-up of the participants to step in and sort things out (at which point, the other player could, with a quick flick of their bright-orange racquet, whip the ball and string around to imprison their opponent, Red Indian style). Playing one taller versus one shorter would invariably lead to what professional athletes call 'diagonal play'. Uncorrected, this style would result in 'vertical play' and, ultimately, the dead-ball scenario.[2]

The game's pop-up 'you've won' top eventually broke, due to either snappage from an overzealous forehand or sheer clumsiness when dismantling the pole from its sand-filled ballast base. (The more portable, take-it-to-the-beach version just had a spike to jam into the ground, which usually meant a secondment to windbreak duty later.) Continued application of the broken set for either yoyo-style footie practice or as 'the hammer' in Geoff Capes-aping mini-Highland games was never encouraged.

Further ball-on-string fun could be had with *Whizz-Ball* (or *Rocket Ball* or *Zoom*, depending on where you bought it), a plastic rugby ball commanded by two competitors with opposing pairs of stunt-kite-style handgrips. Cue much frantic Bullworker-type aerobic activity as each player strove to prevent the ball from hurtling down the line to their 'end'.

Like most outdoor games, *Swingball* and *Zoom* were really just exercise regimes in disguise. Once we'd cottoned on to this hidden agenda, it wasn't long before the arsenal of water-pistols was broken out for that vital 'cooling-off' period.

See also *Binatone TV Master, Subbuteo, Spacehopper*

Born	pre-C20
Batteries	None
Players	👤👤
Breakage	🏆
Ads	▣ ▣
Envy	🏆🏆
eBayability	🖱🖱
Overall satisfaction	👍👍

---

1 What are we talking about here? Competitive Wendy-house hurdling, Formula One ride-on tractor racing, the slide and kicking the bright-orange Wembley Trophy football over the fence to next door's. Gold medallists all, weren't we?

2 *Swingball* scores over other bat 'n' ball games because it did allow for a certain amount of one-player fun. However, it's probably not too uncharitable to suggest that the *mal-de-mer*-inducing back-and-forth solo play is best thought of as 'whacking off'. You'll go blind!

Tank Command
Desert Storm in a box

Born	1975
Batteries	None
Players	👫
Breakage	🍷🍷🍷
Ads	▪️▪️▪️▪️
Envy	🏆🏆🏆🏆
eBayability	🖱️🖱️
Overall satisfaction	👍

See also Flight Deck, Chutes Away, Crossfire

A noble entry into the looked-cool-but-was-in-fact-shite pantheon, this strategy game's object eludes us even now. The limited gameplay itself was strangely reminiscent of that most-scratched of nostalgic itches, TV programme The Adventure Game's vortex, with which it shared a basic set of rules.

Young Rommels would face off across the mile-long board, taking it in turns to advance a battalion of (four) tanks move by move into 'enemy lines'. Counter-attack plans were hidden behind covers and took the form of positioned pegs intended to trigger so-called mines under the opposition's contingent. After all moves were completed, a complicated series of levers and pulleys coordinated the ground strikes, requiring each player to sharply yank a toggle on a bit of string. The force of the assault could often send rival tanks flying into the air, which always looked terribly exciting on the television adverts – but, once again, we must confess we're left scratching our heads as to the purpose of all this. There was a bunch of red and blue flags in the box but, frankly, we'd have been better off with a white one.

Tank Command took its cue, we imagine, from WWII films – those protracted scenes of stiff-upper-lipped minions deep in darkened underground bunkers, shifting tanks and planes across huge scale models of El Alamein like so many croupiers of war. As Tank Command was a bloodthirsty game generally played only by boys, we can only assume it led to a taste in women with bright-red lip-gloss who wore buttoned-down collars, hairnets and gravy-browning lines down their legs in lieu of stocking seams.

Those who did get their hands on one were invariably disappointed as all the marketing spiel had led us to believe there was real ammunition involved somewhere along the line. Those spectacular slo-mo 'explosions' and suitably dramatic sound effects turned out to be naught but telly trickery. Bitterly ironic, 'cos if there was one game screaming out to be ramped up with electronics, flashing lights and, well, just some damn noise, it was this one.

That said, Tank Command almost made up for its quite considerable shortcomings by providing the lucky owner with a whole squadron of reasonably well-detailed plastic tanks with which to menace his not-too-out-of-scale Airfix H0:00 soldiers. Originally blitzing shops in 1975, the game lost ground almost immediately in a real-life board-game war with MB's Tank Battle, a Stratego-like thinker's game (yet still featuring more ballistic action than its Ideal cousin). Neither of these games is likely to make a return post-Diana and her attendant anti-landmine campaigns, we feel.

Tasco Telescope
Watch the skies

It must've been tough for a grown-up with a genuine interest in astronomy but an income that could only support it on the never-never. Fancy having to flick through the kids' pages of Kays to indulge your hobby. Skipping past the Spiderman suits, Wendy houses, climbing frames and paddling pools in among the 'outdoor activity' toys before finding the fishing rods, binoculars (and, sorry, Patrick Moore – a sturdy pair of binoculars simply isn't good enough) until, ultimately, the page with the telescopes on it. Although, thinking about it, perhaps the catalogue folk placed them there deliberately to effect a slight embarrassment – a fair indication of their associated nerdiness, perhaps? This was, after all, a hobby that numbered among its ambassadors *Newsround* stalwarts Reg Turnbull and Heather Couper, and Curly from *Coronation Street* (none of whom had ever received a particularly thorough scrubbing with the glamour flannel).

Although a low-burn enthusiasm for stargazing had been around for donkey's years, the craze reached the zenith of its popularity in the UFO-obsessed '70s. *Close Encounters* was a hit in the cinemas, Erich Von Daniken books propped up the shelves in WHSmith and, well, *UFO* was still on the telly. Millions tuned in to the Beeb and watched Carl Sagan float on a dandelion seed to the strains of Vangelis. How we boggled at him pointing out our insignificant place in the universe while we tucked into potato waffles and poached egg.

If you put one of the 100x magnification – minimum – telescopes on your Christmas wish list, you were reaching for the stars in more ways than one. Often fashioned in Space Shuttle-informed white plastic and black trim, telescopes were invariably astronomically expensive (if you were after the half-decent reflector-type to impress someone with, that is). A further, ironic problem with the really top-of-the-range brand-name jobs made by Tasco and suchlike was the sheer amount of – ahem – space needed to own one. Unless you were lucky enough to live in an observatory, the chances are you wouldn't be allowed to leave it mounted on its tripod in a spare easterly-facing room just on the off-chance Halley's Comet rolled by. Of course, a mate's dad had one. Which us kids weren't allowed to touch.

To this day, there is a generation that still wonders what 'azimuth' means, why one would employ a 'moon filter' and, indeed, what a lunar eclipse actually looks like when projected on to a black piece of card.

Born	1965
Batteries	None
Players	👤
Breakage	🏆
Ads	▣
Envy	🏆🏆🏆
eBayability	🖱
Overall satisfaction	👍

See also *Viewmaster, Sonic Ear, Electronic Project*

TCR
The car's the star

Born	1977
Batteries	Mains
Players	👤👤
Breakage	🍷🍷🍷🍷
Ads	🎞️🎞️🎞️🎞️
Envy	🏆🏆🏆🏆🏆
eBayability	🖱️🖱️
Overall satisfaction	👍👍

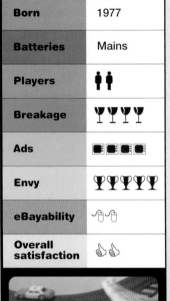

Once *Scalextric* roared off the grid, the slot-car market was left waiting, coughing and spluttering for a new challenger to vie for pole position. Typically it was the American love of motorsport that fuelled interest in scale-model racing (a birthday treat in the States could likely mean a longed-for day of burning rubber at one of the country's many model raceways). Also typically, it attracted the kind of punter who took the whole thing just that bit too seriously and, for a while in the late '60s at least, this kids' hobby was top-heavy with grown adults.

Chief beneficiary was Aurora (they of *AFX* fame), who managed to ride out a worldwide slump of interest by keeping the faith with little 'uns and knocking out home racing sets with plenty of flashy gimmicks. *Stop! Police* grabbed the attention by means of a back-story and a nifty piece of 'squeeze' track that enabled the vehicles to run each other off the road. Their *Daredevil Rally* set included exciting loop-the-loop and wall-climbing sections of track. Yet the cars were still stuck, literally, in a rut.

Cue Ideal and their innovative slotless slot-car system *TCR* (Total Control Racing). Instead of the time-honoured method of keeping the cars fixed to the road, *TCR* used three metal tracks and brushes, thus allowing the cars to switch lanes at the push of a button. The immediate and inherent drawback of this was that the cars would always fling themselves into the outside lane around bends, no matter how much you fiddled with the lane-changing control.[1]

TCR was also the first racing-car system to really push the envelope in terms of track development. Forget boring figure-of-eights – there were mammoth double-tracks with four-lane crossover interchanges, 30-feet long L-shaped loops and gravity-defying banked curb corners. Cor! Stick a bikini-clad babe on this page and you could be forgiven for thinking you were reading *Max Power*.

TV and movie tie-ins weren't far away. Matchbox's *Race and Chase* attempted to cash in on *Cannonball Run* back-axle action with a Corvette and cop-car U-turning double act plus a tilting swing-bridge ramp in the middle of the track.[2] Tyco, meanwhile, threw in their lot with the darling of the Indy scene, and all-round international playboy jetsetter, erm... Nigel Mansell.

See also *Scalextric, Vertibird, Ricochet Racers*

---

1 *TCR* sets came with a lot of plastic 'banking posts' and billboards to help prevent the cars skidding off the track altogether. Matchbox's *TCR* clone *Lanechanger*, on the other hand, allowed you to fight that centrifugal force and hug the corners, meaning you could sometimes even overtake your opponent on the inside track. Magnets may have been involved. We don't know.
2 It was, of course, Ideal who landed the official licence to issue a repro *Dukes Of Hazzard* Dodge Charger. Further tricks up Ideal's sleeve included cars with working headlamps, the Electronic Super Booster (which allowed one driver to slingshot past another) and the Jam Car – a congestion-instigating additional vehicle that idled around the track of its own accord.

Terrahawks Action Zeroid
Spherical metallic Windsor Davies

Born	1983
Batteries	None
Players	👤
Breakage	🍷
Ads	📺 📺
Envy	🏆🏆🏆
eBayability	🖱🖱
Overall satisfaction	👍

Surely any right-thinking merchandiser scanning through the enviable Windsor Davies CV would realise that the prime plum to squeeze here was tied up in *Never the Twain* and churn out those Oliver Smallbridge Toby jug figurines double-quick? Alas not, and doubtlessly beguiled by the brand awareness that comes with anything Gerry Anderson, Bandai threw their lot in with that *World of Sport* warm-up, *Terrahawks*.

Never a real TV viewers' favourite in the *Thunderbirds* league (bar that cool Zeroid versus Deadly Cubes noughts-and-crosses tournament across the end credits), this puppet series did at least usefully contribute the word 'Zelda' as a pejorative term to describe any particularly wizened old ladies. The toy line, however, was another matter altogether. With Bandai putting together what was basically a low-rent version of the hugely successful Kenner *Star Wars* action figure collection, there was some top stuff on offer here. Aside from fairly representative models of Tiger Ninestein, Kate Kestrel et al., there were also bags of great hardware knocking about – none more so than the *Action Zeroid*.

This was a Bandai 'deluxe' toy, featuring a 5.25-inch-high model of the '*Hot Mum*-star-voiced Sergeant Major Zero sat atop his pedestal and poised for action. Winding the thing around cranked up a spring below, which would then launch the spherical Zero off the pedestal, on to the floor, where it would wobble around for a bit. 'The Zeroids are fighting and reconnaissance robots' read the underside of the box.[1] Alternatively, they were also relatively expensive playthings for cats once they'd been pinged into action.

For many, however, the *Action Zeroid* represented a bridge too far in *Terrahawk* toy-collecting, as Mum and Dad refused to shell out for that 'bauble' that would complete the set. Those wishing to salvage some level of kudos among their peers might have also considered investing in the real-life Kate Kestrel single *SOS*[2] or any one of the smaller die-cast spaceships. (*Battlehawk*, *Treehawk*, *Hawkwing*, etc. – you can see what they were doing there, right?)

Ultimately, what killed both the TV show and the toy range was the curse of relatively low production values (although it's probably worth mentioning the excruciating comedy of the scripts and lack of ready catchphrases – 'Stroll on' and 'Expect the unexpected' aren't exactly up there with other Anderson favourites 'Stand by for action' or 'Thunderbirds are go'). By 1986, it was a goner. Time to chalk up yet another one to George Lucas and his gang.

See also *Star Wars, Dr Who TARDIS, Six Million Dollar Man*

---

1 Other nuggets included: 'A Zeroid weighs 100 tonnes' and 'Battlehawk can carry up to 100 Zeroids'. We hope you're making a note of all this.
2 Actually pop moppet and session singer Moya Griffiths shoved rather unconvincingly into a pink fright-wig and 'space-age' jumpsuit. Sadly, according to the chronology of the TV show, the record isn't actually due to chart until the year 2020.

Test Match
Tiny Oval fun

From Peter Pan Playthings (of Peterborough – feel the cricketing heritage). Authentic! Action-packed! Officially endorsed by the England cricket team with a picture of a fully padded Freddie Trueman on the box! (Are you a bit younger? Then the photo was probably a mid-game Botham or Gower, no?) A fair stab at board-game cricket, this – the box was stuffed with a plastic pitch and boundary fence as standard (no ball-off-table antics here), plus nine fielders, a batsman, a bowler, a wicket, some (steel!) balls and a little scoreboard.

The mechanics of play were fairly simplistic. The bowler had a long piece of drainpipe attached to his hand, and the batsman was connected to *Subbuteo*-keeper-style handle for bat movement (there was only one type of shot available in this game – the straight drive). Roll a ball down the pipe (a grass-cutter every time) and, with a flick of the trigger, the batsman would, in theory, hit it. The pitch was divided into sectors, worth more runs the further out they were. Wherever the ball landed dictated the number of runs scored. The fielders had little 'cups' between their feet, simulating a catch – your batsman was out if the ball landed between a fielder's legs.[1]

Fairly exciting at first, but too many innings and the game was bound to get tedious – and some games were very long.[2] It wasn't long before *Test Match* would find itself at the bottom of the pile of board games and, in time, it became a very popular mainstay of regional jumble sales. The pitch was also prone to riding up, causing ripples here and there – an annoyance when your ball was hit 'for six', only to roll back into a 'two' sector.

Like any miniature sport, though, whatever it was that attracted you to the game in the first place was unlikely to be replicated in a tabletop version.[3] No thwack of leather on willow here. No parading the Ashes around on a red double-decker bus. No getting fitted for your first box at the sports shop. Possibly the most interesting part (for yer stat-obsessed young cricket fans) was updating the scoreboard, a full-on proper pavilion-end effort with many little wheels denoting overs, teams, batsmen's scores, etc. But, really, who gets their kicks out of obsessively cataloguing stuff, eh? Not us! Oh no.

See also *Subbuteo, Escalado, Palitoy Cue Ball*

Born	1960
Batteries	None
Players	👤👤
Breakage	🍷🍷🍷
Ads	📺📺
Envy	🏆🏆🏆
eBayability	🖱🖱
Overall satisfaction	👍👍

---

1 That and hitting the wicket were the only two ways to get out. The players were so small no umpire could ever call LBW convincingly. Canny players could consistently kick the ball away for four leg-byes, which was rather against the spirit of the game, we think.

2 In fairness, every game should've been five days long. And against Aussie kids.

3 As any fule kno, the bestest cricket game is the one where you draw the runs and fouls on the six different sides of HB pencils and roll them along the table. Play that anywhere, you can. Mind you, the toy manufacturers didn't miss a trick and even marketed that back to us kids as 'luxury dice game' *Owzthat*. Other attempts to jump on the bat 'n' ball bandwagon were *Wicketz*, Ideal's *Super Cricket*, *Capri Knockout Cricket* (a sort of card game really) and, somewhat inevitably, *Subbuteo Cricket*.

Tin Can Alley
Electronic hillbilly outfit

Ideal's *Tin Can Alley* reeked of the transatlantically exotic.[1] Everything about it was 100 percent American and alien to these shores. Rifles were still largely the preserve of farmers and the SAS, and rugged, homesteading types like the game's '80s TV patron Chuck 'Rifleman' Connors were similarly absent from your average Kettering cul-de-sac.

As, indeed, were the 'targets' in the game – empty cans of that nefarious industrial sealant that got lucky, Dr Pepper, a brew so intrinsically bound to the States that even one of the mightiest multinationals in the world still hasn't persuaded anyone else to drink the stuff.[2] The game itself is a simple affair. A sawn-off plastic gun containing about 90 batteries fired a beam of red light at light-sensitive pads in holes on a plastic representation of the top of a rickety fence, which then flipped up little platforms upon which were balanced said tin cans. Of course, the advertising wisely omitted the mundane mechanical explanation, so impressionable kids did, for a brief while, really believe that a toy company was selling a high-tech James-bond-style laser weapon as a children's toy – a misconception that Ideal would not be the last company to exploit.

Inevitable copies abounded, such as *Marksman* – which projected targets on to a wall and made a noise when you hit 'em – and Chad Valley *Shoot Out In Space* – where silver foam rocket ships replaced the cans of pop. An official *Tin Can Alley* Colt 45-style handgun edition was also launched, although purists prefer the original 'cocks like a real target rifle'[3] version. However, the awkward side-effect of training a generation of would-be soldiers to always aim three inches below the target might explain why Western coalitions take so long to finish wars these days.

See also *Lone Star Spudmatic Gun, Johnny Seven, Stop Boris*

Born	1976
Batteries	◖◖◖◖
Players	🧍
Breakage	🍷🍷
Ads	▪▪▪▪▫
Envy	🏆🏆🏆🏆🏆
eBayability	◖◖◖◖
Overall satisfaction	👍👍👍👍

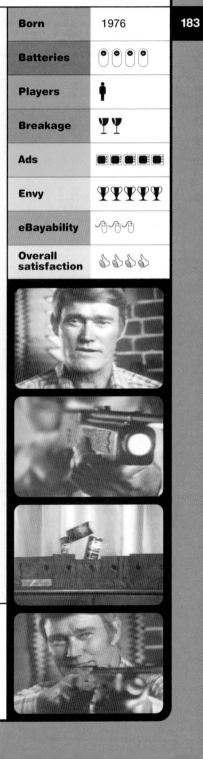

---

1 The name, if you need reminding, was a play on words. Tin Pan Alley was the district of Manhattan where many Broadway songwriters set up shop in the late 1800s. The best-known inhabitant was Irving Berlin, composer of such classic show tunes as *White Christmas*, *Heat Wave* and *Let's Face the Music and Shoot Cans*.

2 Later versions replaced the cans with lip-smackin', thirst-quenchin', ace-tastin', motivatin', good-buzzin', cool-talkin', high-walkin', fast-livin', ever-givin', cool-fizzin' Pepsi.

3 Always one for boasting, that Chuck Connors... Ironically, *Tin Can Alley* was yet another example of a toy that looked much bigger on telly than it actually was. Anyone over the age of seven probably couldn't get their chubby fingers around the trigger.

Tiny Tears
Blubbing, enuresis-afflicted doll

Born	1965
Batteries	None
Players	👤
Breakage	🍷
Ads	■ ■ ■ ■ ■
Envy	🏆 🏆 🏆 🏆 🏆
eBayability	🖱 🖱 🖱
Overall satisfaction	👍 👍 👍 👍

Are there any vintage girls' toys out there that aren't just plain creepy? The vacant-eyed, H_2O-seeping *Tiny Tears* is yet another case in point. A cross between *Play School*'s Hamble and a hospice in-patient, Palitoy's innovative doll was nevertheless an acknowledged Rolls Royce in the field of plastic surrogate children.

A blaze of pee-pee-powered publicity accompanied the doll's launch (and won Palitoy a coveted Toy of the Year award the following Christmas). Initially sporting a hard plastic head, which made for a weighty cosh if younger brothers became annoying, the doll's novelty came in its ability to both cry and piss its pants.[1]

Promoted via an insidious advertising campaign as an actual new member of the family to be placed in the care of all little girls, it seemed as though Palitoy was advocating keeping tots miserable and permanently soiled. And because of that, *Tiny Tears* was an absolute must-have, a real stayer that hadn't floated in on the back of a Saturday morning cartoon and wasn't about to lend its name to a flotilla of spin-off merchandising (although a *Tiny Tears*-endorsed travel rubber bedsheet would have made childhood sleepovers at friends' houses a little less fraught).

As all dolls pretty much conformed to the standard human baby size range, *Tiny Tears* opened the – ho-ho! – floodgates for 1000 accessories: clothing (mainly frilly rock-a-bye nightgowns but also the occasional themed outfit), stuff you could put her in (prams, cots, rockers and high chairs) and stuff you could shove in her mouth (notably those miraculous 'disappearing milk' bottle feeders).

Potential crossovers into the world of boys' toys never happened, alas. Instead, some small concession to gender was made with the introduction of Chucky lookylikey *Timmy Tears*. Blessed with anatomically correct genitalia (albeit ones that confirmed the 'Tiny' brand, the poor sod), he was manufactured by then brand-holder, Tonka, which made him altogether more rugged than his sister.

If *Tiny Tears'* perpetual incontinence didn't stifle the maternal instinct, the following decade saw ever-more realistic dolls crawling on to the market with their own interesting USPs: Fisher-Price *Bonnie* (with follow-me eyes), Rainbow *Baby Talk* (gurgled unintelligibly), Hornby *Baby Hush-A-Bye* (slept for a bit, woke up and cried) and Hasbro's *Oopsie Daisy* (crawled, fell into a convulsive heap, crawled again). Without fail, all were guaranteed to make little girls squeal with delight and give boys of any age a real case of the heebie-jeebies.[2]

See also Barbie, Sindy, Girl's World

---

1 Of all the characteristics of a baby, why decide that a soiled nappy was the clincher to sell to kids? Was it a conspiracy to introduce the toy as a premeditative contraceptive device?

2 Never feed *Tiny Tears* with Ribena, unless you want to see some real pant-wetting action come bedtime. There was also supposed to be a version that could be fed with semisolid food, with predictably sloppy results...

tiny tears

Tip-It
Balance-of-power tower

Born	1965
Batteries	None
Players	👫
Breakage	🍷🍷🍷
Ads	📺
Envy	🏆🏆
eBayability	🖱
Overall satisfaction	👍

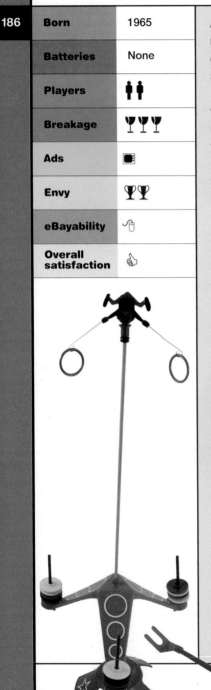

As if in futile tribute to the sheer towering greatness of this Ideal game – but mainly to keep ourselves amused – we're going to attempt to complete this entry without using the word 'balance' or any derivative thereof. Oh, and the subtitle doesn't count. Do you think we'll manage it? Place your bets now.

Tip-It seemingly gained inspiration from ye olde plate spinners of '70s variety entertainment telly, centring as it did around the eternal battle between man and gravity.[1] That little plastic fella perched on top – perhaps himself some vestige of the circus speciality act – wouldn't have looked much out of place on *The Paul Daniels Show*. Supported only by his nose and the equal weight of two rings clutched in his hands, we'd stare up at him slowly rotating and just hope he didn't fall, at least not on our go.

The object of the game was to remove a collection of tokens from the lowest tier of this strange spinning plastic construct (or possibly just move them around – it's difficult to know; there was a special fork in any case) without upsetting the acrobat above. A *Twister*-like spinner indicated which counters had to be gotten rid off on each turn, thus pushing the lean-to of the whole thing to its extremity.

Like an extraordinarily complex version of *Jenga*, and with a similar reliance on Newton's laws, *Tip-It* was all about cause and effect. Cause the tower to topple and the effect was nerve-shattering (see also *KerPlunk*). But, like *Jenga*, plate-spinning and even our toy gyroscope, much of the pleasure was divined in anticipation of that final collapse. The cathartic submission was addictive – or are we giving too much away regarding our adult pastimes? After a while, even the gameplay felt like it was getting in the way and, in the end, you'd find yourself building the thing up just to knock it down.

Hmmm... that's got us thinking. Although we said it was a great game back at the start, we're beginning to realise that it wasn't all that hot at all. In fact, all things considered, we've come to the conclusion that it was probably a bit rubbish all along. But then, that's the problem with being too positive about nostalgia: sometimes it can seem a bit one-sided. So, to avoid accusations of bias, we're saying boo to *Tip-It*, the toppling toy of tedium. Not necessarily because we believe it, but in the interests of impartiality and balance.

Doh!

See also *KerPlunk, Mousetrap, Operation*

1 Let's just say there is at least one good reason they didn't take *Tip-It* with them to the MIR Space Station – it doesn't half ruin the money shot.

Tomytronic 3D
Solar-dependent shoot-'em-ups

The coin-op arcade explosion of '79/'80 (which you knew had gone mainstream when Arthur Daley played *Space Invaders* on *Minder*) led to a boom in the tabletop electronic game, as we've noted elsewhere in this book. The *Tomytronic 3D* range gets its own entry, however, due to the unique binocular portability and playability of the games.

For the record, they were: *Planet Zeon* (pilot your X-shaped starfighter down a narrow trench),[1] *Thundering Turbo* (drive around an endless rally circuit) and the *TRON*-indebted *Sky Attack* (tank-based overhead target-practice). The two later additions to range were the restyled *3D Stereo Skyfighters* (incomprehensible aerobatics involving balloons and a biplane), with twin speakers and a colour backdrop screen, and *Shark Attack* (which was basically *Sky Attack* again, but upside down, the cheeky bastards).

Unlike the cabinet constructs around the likes of *Astro Wars*, a *Tomytronic 3D*'s in-built colour LCD meant no more shielding the screen from the sun – in fact you actually needed the sun (or some strong, steady light source shining through the top at least) to play these babies. The practical upshot of this was that those 3xAA batteries tended to last double the time they would in a 'normal' handheld.[2] Even if they did run out, the unique design of a *Tomytronic* meant you could pretend it was a spaceship instead.

Top-mounted left/right, accelerate and fire control buttons meant that these were among the few electronic games that truly demanded to be handheld – with both hands. It was no easy feat to wrestle *Thundering Turbo* from the iron grip of a classmate when it was your go. The neck-strap attachment didn't help matters much either, inviting incidents of near-strangulation. That said, there was something about the essentially private, immersive nature of *Tomytronic 3D* that precluded them from end-of-term games days. They were more likely to be seen accompanying their owners on holidays and daytrips out in the car (with the sound off).

Some misleading television adverts implied that each *Tomytronic 3D* employed smooth-scrolling vector-like graphics and spectacular over-your-head explosions (arcade *Battlezone* stylee), although the games themselves simply followed that image-appears-in-one-of-three-places-only drill (see also *Game and Watch*) that we believe warrants a name all of its own.

Born	1983
Batteries	◖◗ ◖◗ ◖◗
Players	🧍
Breakage	🍷
Ads	▪️▪️▪️
Envy	🏆🏆🏆🏆
eBayability	🖱️🖱️🖱️
Overall satisfaction	👍👍👍

See also *Galaxy Invader 1000, Game and Watch, View-Master*

1 Where do they come up with these kerazy ideas for game scenarios, eh? In the States they also got two more: another 3D stereo game, *Sherman Attack*, and *Jungle Fighter* (another, like *Skyfighters*, which promised more actual fighting in the name than there was in the game).

2 This was back in the day when we thought battery life of a few *days* was short. Days!? We didn't know we were born. Just try taking more than five shots with your new-fangled AA-powered digital camera without getting 'battery low' warnings.

Tonka Trucks
Mini JCBs

Born	1949
Batteries	None
Players	👤
Breakage	🍸
Ads	📺📺
Envy	🏆🏆🏆
eBayability	🖱🖱🖱
Overall satisfaction	👍👍👍

See also Corgi 007 Lotus Esprit, Top Trumps, Evel Knievel

Tonka was *the* name in building-site toys. The hardwearing, hard-hitting (particularly when one was dropped off a wall on to your head) playthings were the delight of young boys (and tomboy girls) everywhere. Best known for their trucks, Tonka made rock-solid, cold-rolled steel[1] vehicles, with real-rubber tyres and tough-as-old-boots paint jobs. And, to paraphrase Henry Ford, they came in any colour you liked, as long as that colour was yellow.

Unlike the toys of today, they were genuinely built to last.[2] If you were to play 'chicken' with a *Tonka Truck* and any other vehicle of the time, there was absolutely no question which was going to come off worst. You could smash them into anything and, though they'd get chipped and dented, they would still outlast your parents' car. You could even leave them out in the rain – actually, that's where most of them ended up. A *Tonka Truck*'s natural habitat: the sandpit. Although they would rust eventually, by such time you'd have grown up, moved home and forgotten about them.

Every boy wanted one – to be in charge of such a destructive construction vehicle is genetically hardwired into the Y chromosome – but such engineering quality came at a price. If you were lucky enough to get the *Mighty Loader* or *Crane* for Christmas, you probably didn't get much else that year. But it was worth it, because they'd still be there the following Christmas, battering hell out of any new trucks on the block.

In some ways, though, *Tonka Trucks* were just too big for their own good – for a start, they couldn't be stored or paired with similar 1:18-scale toys for an integrated play experience. Simply nothing else was *Tonka Truck*-sized. And who owned a complete set? No-one. Somewhere out there is a scrap yard, filled to the brim with six-inch-high hulks of slowly degrading *Tonka Trucks*. Presumably there's also a driver, sitting bored in the cab of the huge bulldozer that's shifting them, who just can't see the irony.

1 That's the same stuff they used to make real cars with. Tonka parent company, Mound Metalcraft, originally made garden spades and that. The toy-truck trade was just a sideline.

2 How times change. Tonka is still in business today, but now they offer 'diversity': plastic versions for the under-twos, talking *Thomas the Tank Engine*-style human-faced tow-trucks, and birthday-cake decorations.

Top Trumps
Fight-initiating card game

Top Trumps was an idea so simple that it bordered on exquisite – an adaptation of that schoolboy collector's perennial, the themed cigarette/bubblegum card, into the world's piss-easiest card game.

Fifty pee bought you a round-cornered red-plastic box containing 32 cards with pictures of warplanes, ships, dragsters, et al. After dealing them out on the table/playground/bit of waste ground, players would take the top card off their stack, study it with baroque expressions of intensity, before one of them confidently declared 'Number of cylinders... eight!' Through such ritual did many a bonding experience occur.

The makers were always keen to hype up the 'educational' aspect – never before or since did so many children know the precise dimensions of the HMS Ark Royal – although the basic impulse of the game was less noble: to use that knowledge to get loads of cards off your mates for free. This (the bridge-pilfered act of 'trumping' – a name itself riotously amusing to prepubescent minds) was the sole point of the game.

Quirks of the more eccentric editions are imprinted on many a memory – one ships edition ('Tonnage... eighteen hundred!') was, for some reason, printed lengthways. The horror edition ('Fear factor... five!') showed a bit of imagination, as among the usual suspects (Dracula, Werewolf, Skeleton) was The Incredible Melting Man[1] and, er, a maggot. The downside was that the pictures were drawn rather hastily in magic marker.[2] The prehistoric monsters set fared slightly better, with photos of unconvincing plastic models instead.

The range expanded for the next ten years or so, eventually mutating into *Supertrumps* (which had snazzier boxes and slightly better pictures); celebrity endorsement reared its head (*Mike Brearley's Batting Aces!*), until variations (the hopelessly fiddly *Minitrumps*) and poor rivals (the *Ace Trump Game*) sprang up.

Unfortunately, an escalation in the cost of licensing decent pics for the cards led the makers to move the '*Trumps* on to the backburner, where they stayed until only recently. As far as we're concerned, however, if the pattern on the back isn't a white-and-blue image of a racing car, a boat and a plane, it ain't *Top Trumps*.

Born	1977
Batteries	None
Players	👤👤
Breakage	🍷🍷
Ads	▪️▪️▪️
Envy	🏆🏆🏆🏆
eBayability	🖱️🖱️
Overall satisfaction	👍👍👍👍

See also *Scalextric, Airfix Kits, Hornby Railway Set*

USA

Boeing E-4
control system aircraft

Max. power output	96000 kg thrust
Max. speed	960 km/h
at height	12800 m
Wing span	59,64 m
Length	70,51 m

---

1 Yes! TV Cream's favourite never-seen horror movie of the 1970s, as glimpsed in a friend's brother's video collection, or in paperback form (with graphic stills from the film on the back!) on a newsagent's revolving book stand.

2 Cribbed from classic horror pics, too. Dracula is lawsuit-temptingly close to Christopher Lee, and The Hangman is clearly traced from that famous Lon Chaney *Phantom of the Opera* still. Confusingly, the phantom cropped up as a different card in the set, but illustrated as a bandaged bloke.

Transformers
TV and comic tie-in robots

Born	1984
Batteries	None
Players	👤👤
Breakage	🍷🍷🍷
Ads	▣▣▣▣
Envy	🏆🏆🏆🏆
eBayability	🖱🖱🖱
Overall satisfaction	👍👍👍

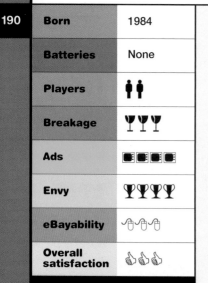

No prizes for guessing *Transformers'* gimmick. They were, the vocoded jingle reminded us, robots 'in disguise' – i.e. figures that could transform into cars, trucks, aeroplanes or (at the less sane end of the spectrum) cassette tapes.[1] Stupidly collectable, these die-cast anthropomorphs had an in-built double-the-value argument for kids eager to pressure a parent into parting with their hard-earned. It's a model VW Beetle! And it's a robot reconnaissance soldier! It's two toys in one! It is *not* a rip-off.

Transformers were testament once again to the fact that the Japanese knew how to knock up a battalion of warrior toys with a noble mythology and great gimmick. Oddly, the first *Transformers* were in fact predated by a good year or two by *RoboMachines* (later renamed *Gobots* to tie in with their similarly *TV-AM*-favoured cartoon series) – a slicker and less plastic range of chameleonic constructions that failed to catch on with the general public – and were followed by a load of long-forgotten five-minute wonders (*Grandstand Convertors*, *Robot Anti-Terror Squad... RrrrrrrrrrrATS!*) that are now remembered only by... well, us really.

There was also the obligatory comic-book back-story: Autobots (the 'good' *Transformers*, initially all road vehicles of some description led by top articulated-lorry bloke Optimus Prime), waged a battle to destroy the evil forces of the Decepticons (the villains, headed by Megatron – boo, hiss). Such fictions – along with the tie-in cartoon – bent to the whim of whatever additional toy Hasbro decided to foist on us. Every character had a name, and so the range soon expanded to include transforming cameras (Reflector), bulldozers (Bonecrusher), dinosaurs (Sludge) and a space shuttle (Omega One Prime). Best of all were the triple-changers, where three or more from the standard range could be combined to make one giant gestalt *Transformer*. Now they really *were* cool.[2]

1 Technically it was a Walkman-style tape player with additional cassette *Transformers*.
2 Not surprisingly, they always looked *mega*-cool in the TV

Such was the magnitude of '80s T-mania that, soon, chunky digital watches appeared with flip-up *Transformer* fascias, Ocean Software produced a fairly rubbish computer game, and the TV show finally begat its own feature film, boasting the disparate vocal talents of Orson Welles and Eric Idle.[3] In 2004, when retro kitsch finally reached the advertising industry, Citroen used whiz-bang CGI and a Les Rhythmes Digitales track to create a dancing, transforming version of their new C4. So if you want to blame the recent Spielberg-financed revival on anyone, blame them.

See also *Zoids, Cyborgs, Ricochet Racers*

dverts, seamlessly and smoothly effecting their own transformation
a super-fast stop motion style.
Guess what happened in the film? All the 'old' *Transformers* were

killed off and a new 'generation' of robots took their place. Canny way of getting the kids to splash out all over again, eh?

Trivial Pursuit
Fact hunt

Born	1982
Batteries	None
Players	👤👤👤👤👤👤
Breakage	🍷🍷
Ads	▣▣
Envy	🏆🏆🏆
eBayability	🖱
Overall satisfaction	👍👍👍

See also Monopoly, Scrabble, Mastermind

For all its dressing up as a grown adults' game (those Victorian line-art pretensions, foil-embossed board and extravagant citrus plastic stylings), *Trivial Pursuit* was never going to replace *Rummikub* or backgammon as the contemplative post-prandial pastime. Its sole purpose was to foster family arguments about obsolete world-record-holders and how many James Bonds there've been, and reduce even the most mature player to childishly smug remarks like 'I'm sorry, that's not what it says on the card'. Ironically, a game that contained often wildly out-of-date information about various national borders has driven a wedge[1] between more relatives than any previous board game in history.

Blessed with a cover quote from *The Rape of the Lock* by Alexander Pope, *Trivial Pursuit* featured your archetypal designed-on-a-beermat game board (particularly fitting, since it was a direct forerunner of the pub quiz machine),[2] intricate 'playing piece is also the scoreboard' counter system and 6000 questions per box. But let's not kid ourselves these were *University Challenge*-strength general-knowledge teasers – more a battle of half-wits. When the expensive, Dad-purchased 'Genius Edition'[3] first hit the coffee table back in the early '80s, it all seemed ridiculously complicated, even though half the time the clue was pretty much given in the question. Gameplay typically progressed in one of two ways: the pedants' revolt insistence that all pronunciation of questions and answers must be to the letter, including foreign accents if necessary; or the 'let's just let the next correct answer win' school of giving up early 'cos *EastEnders* is starting. As time passed, even the makers decided to go all po-mo-fo wacky, leading to such recently annoying questions as 'Was Humpty Dumpty pushed?' Ho-fucking-ho.

In the intervening years, the trivia game craze took hold, requiring the supposed purchase of refill boxes for the *Master Game*[4] or the purchase of duff competitors such as *Genius* – seemingly inspired by that old Guinness advertising campaign – and BBC's *The News from the BBC*. (Oh, how we would've loved to have seen a couple of sequels to that one: *The Weather from the Met Office* or *From the North: the Great Granada Game*, perhaps.) None ever really caught on. Originators Horn Abbot (founded by the two pornalike journalist *Triv* inventors, one of whom was nicknamed 'The Horn', although we'd hope that was 'cos of his voice or

---

1 No pun intended. No really, even we wouldn't sink that low. How cheesy would that be? And how easy? As easy as pie?

2 Alcohol and competitive one-upmanship – quite a potent mix: some people make a living beating 'quizzies' in various boozers. *Give Us A Break*, *Hangman*, *Millionaire* – they can drop the jackpot in all of them. We know a bloke who can do it. He keeps getting

barred so we don't take him out much these days.

3 Oh yes, 'Trivial Pursuits' suffered from the common Cream-era curse of parent-added extra-letter pronunciation. Like Cliff Richards and Peter Davidson. Blame the twiddly writing on the box. Speaking of which... point of order: *Trivial Pursuit*'s international licensor was called Sans Serif, which is a bloody cheek, considering how many swirls

something, not because general knowledge gives him a stiffy) kept up demand for their own brand by issuing ever-more genre-narrowing editions, including *Silver Screen*, *RPM* and *Baby Boomer*, although nowadays there are so many knocking around you can probably go online and order *Trivial Pursuit: Top 40 Hits Of February 1984*.[5]

Forsooth, *Trivial Pursuit* was a triumph of the cerebral over the athletic. Appropriately for an indoor Olympiad that promoted fat backsides and furring arteries, the 1990 BBC TV version was hosted by comedy chubster Rory McGrath (who himself was succeeded by the even more porktastic Tony Slattery). In 2005, Christmas boxes of After Eights chocolates (they're not mints, that's a disguise) even featured mini-*Triv* packets to test sedentary relatives while you stuffed your face before the big film. No wonder sport and leisure are in the same category.

and strokes there are on the logo. (And it was run by a bloke called Richard Gill, which is an even more hilarious joke, if only for all you typographers out there. Do we have any font fans in the house tonight? No?)

4 Inevitably, you would come down one morning to find your dad reading all the cards and flipping over to memorise all the answers.

5 Which Top 40 act was named after the two bumbling detectives in Hergé's comic strip *The Adventures of Tintin*? Give up? It was The Thompson Twins. Right, our go.

Twister
Arthritis-inducing floor game

Born	1966
Batteries	None
Players	👤👤👤👤
Breakage	🏆
Ads	📺 📺
Envy	🏆🏆🏆
eBayability	🖱
Overall satisfaction	👍👍

See also *Domino Rallly, Cascade, Operation*

Invented by Chuck Foley and Neil Rabens in 1966, *Twister* revolved around a small and somewhat slippery plastic mat decorated with equidistant coloured circles, on to which players were supposed to contort their limbs in correspondence with the demands of a handy spinner ('left foot on blue', etc.). Well, that was the plan.

Apparently initially derided as immoral smut on the basis that it involved minor contact between fully clothed human bodies, *Twister* hit the big time after being featured on *The Johnny Carson Show*, when the host was seen to play it with guest Eva Gabor, and from then on it became a favourite at frat parties, on Playboy TV specials and in Michael Stipe lyrics the world over. However, the game was always conspicuously avoided and consigned to an inaccessible shelf once child owners had become awkward adolescents who found the whole idea faintly embarrassing (and not without good reason). When we were growing up, the only people playing *Twister* beyond the age of 12 were Russian gymnasts and perverts.

Twister is many things,[1] but it is not a game for fewer than three people, nor many more than six people. It is also not a game for naked people, despite what a thousand teenage fantasies might lead us to believe. Come on! Who really wants to see a load of tangled up boobs and bums? That's what the Internet was invented for – to keep people like that away from family games.

Various rip-offs and rehashes included *Funny Bones*, an impossibly complicated and almost unplayable card-game effort derived from the traditional spiritual *Dry Bones* ('connect knee bone to ankle bone', etc.). See also *Body Boggle*, a combination of *Twister* and the word-based game, using the same floor-bound vinyl mat to connect letters into four-letter words. (Yes, we can think of a few of *those* to describe that particular brainwave.) There was even a long-forgotten reworking called *Bent Outta Shape*, featuring none other than Derek Griffiths on its packaging. To the notoriously rubber-jointed Griffiths, of course, such games of dexterity presented no problem whatsoever, and the box depicted him contorting his body around the board in much the same way he did around the studio floor on *Play School* (and that bike in the public information film about preventing theft). It's a fair bet, however, that the average player was somewhat less able to 'wibble wibble wobble' to the same dramatic extent and thus quite possibly found it no different to *Twister* itself in any case.

---

1 For a start, it's a fish, a rollercoaster and a rubbish Bill Paxton film about tornado hunters. But the game also shares its name with a rather lovely fruit ice-cream lolly made by Walls (which, incidentally, was invented by adapting rope technology to the frozen food market).

Up Periscope
Das board game

For a Cream-era kid, just getting your hands on a periscope guaranteed hours of fun: looking round corners or over fences into next door's backyard, watching *The Man From U.N.C.L.E.* from behind the settee. Oh yes, without a doubt the periscope was a useful and worthy addition to a seven-year-old spy's kit.

Then some genius at Denys Fisher had a brainwave.[1] Why not bolt two of 'em on to a vertical board game? Mix in a bit of turn-taking *Battleships*-style gameplay and you'd have the perfect recipe for some submarine-hunting fun.

On the face of it, therefore, *Up Periscope* was either 'a ruthless war of nerves' (as it said on the box) or a pretty basic chase-me-do – seek, locate and poke a peg through a hole. Move your flotilla of boats undetected across a perforated seascape to 'safe harbour' at the far side. At the same time, sink your opponent's fleet armed only with plastic depth charges and a bit of trial and error.

What the titular periscope apparatus brought to the party, however, took the game to a whole new (sea) level. Some clever double-mirror action gave each player a cracking approximation of a U-boat's-eye view across to their opponent's cardboard horizon. Estimate the range of any ship in your sights correctly and you could 'torpedo' it by pushing your peg through the board's dividing membrane, stretching the rubber and popping it out the other side.[2]

Although the game itself was hardly likely to – ahem – sail into history, it did inspire a taste for nautical annihilation in all those who played on her.[3] A few years on, and a few inches taller, we'd be down the arcade grappling the rubber periscope handles of Midway's top coin-op subsim *Sea Wolf II*. Now just the periscope wasn't enough. What we'd obviously needed all along was sonar.

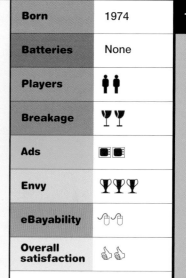

Born	1974
Batteries	None
Players	👤👤
Breakage	🍷🍷
Ads	▪️▪️
Envy	🍷🍷🍷
eBayability	🖱️🖱️
Overall satisfaction	👍👍

See also *Bermuda Triangle, Vertibird, Tasco Telescope*

1 In our fevered imagination, we see them stuck in a cubicle toilet, trying to work out a way of nabbing some loo paper from next door.
2 Cheat's tip: levering a bit of pressure on the periscope when you were looking through it would twist the board and let you count exactly how far away an oppo's merchant schooner was.
3 We think it says something about Britannia and her whole 'rules the waves' thing that maritime-themed games were so damn popular. Talk about naval gazing.

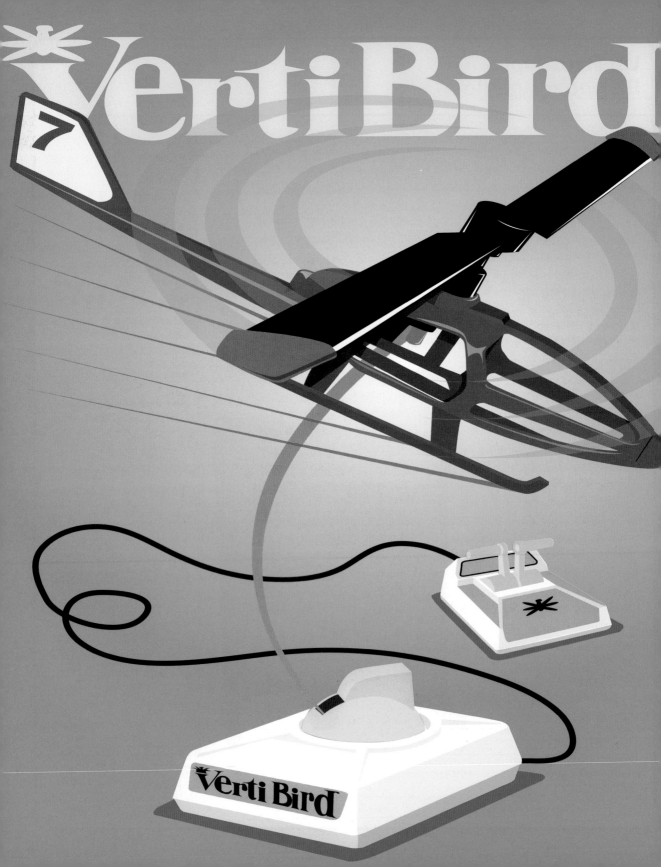

Vertibird
Perpetually spinning indoor helicopter

There had to be a happy medium between your grown-up proper remote-control plane (the likes of which would eclipse many an attempted bonding session between father and son on Britain's windy hilltops as Dad quickly became entranced with the buzzing machine while son whimpered to be allowed a go on the controls) and the worthy, solitary 'merriment' afforded by an assembled Airfix Fokker. And there was, thanks to Mattel.

Vertibird was a small battery-powered helicopter fastened on the end of a wobbly rod, forever circling the same area – a cross between a fairground rockets ride and a battery-powered *Swingball*, really. The small remote-control unit provided joystick-waggling fun and allowed you to 'Throttle fast or slow, buzz high, dive low... rescue the astronaut 'n' whirl away!' (that latter bit referring to a small plastic Christmas-cracker figure who would find himself all too often marooned somewhere within the circumference of the *Vertibird*'s flight-path).[1] Depending on battery strength, this meant either bouncing your chopper along the ground[2] or plotting a practically vertical 'mission' in the manner of a small desk fan.

Vertibird earned its immortality by virtue of hitting the shops early in the '70s and hovering in kids' top-ten-most-wanted-presents list for a solid ten years before mysteriously disappearing off the shelves. In the intervening time, many an inquisitive child's fingers were caught in the prop blades, many a family dog's ears were strafed and many of those vital connecting rods were shattered by a careless parent's size tens. Your first *Vertibird* would thus often retire to the back of the wardrobe until a replacement could be found.

Back in Woolies, various aerial-runway themed playsets were available, from a logging 'copter to a polar icecap base, a Styrofoam rescue ship and glow-in-the-dark adventures. But, for our money, none was finer than the *Space 1999* flying Eagle version.[3] Who's for 'whirling away' with a rescued Barbara Bain? (Actually, shall we just leave her where she is?)

Vertibird is now extraordinarily rare, even in the collectors' market, but check out eBay for stacks of cloned versions: *Chopper Patrol*, Remco's *Star Trek Enterprise* and MB's *Flying Thunder*.

See also *Armatron, Chutes Away, Flight Deck*

Born	1971
Batteries	◖◖◖◖
Players	🧍
Breakage	🍷🍷🍷🍷
Ads	■■■■
Envy	🏆🏆🏆🏆
eBayability	
Overall satisfaction	👍👍👍

---

1 Rescue was fairly easy, however, 'cos the helpful little spaceman was clinging on to a bloody big plastic hoop, a legacy of the fact that he was actually a reused motorcycle rider from another toy. How else can you explain his tiny helmet?

2 We are being exceptionally restrained with the double entendres in this entry. This is only one of two. Can you spot the other? Clue: it's in a footnote.

3 As anyone who's seen the show knows *Space 1999* Eagles weren't renowned for their rotor blades. Neither for that matter was Apollo's Viper in *Battlestar Galactica*. But there they were, all present and correct on the *Vertibird* licensed versions.

View-Master
Low-tech 3D-photo story binoculars

Born	1939
Batteries	None
Players	👤
Breakage	🍷🍷
Ads	📼
Envy	🏆🏆🏆
eBayability	🖱🖱
Overall satisfaction	👍👍👍

See also *Tomytronic 3D, Up Periscope, Top Trumps*

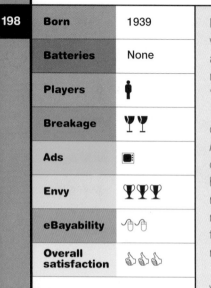

Possibly the toy industry's earliest foray into virtual reality, albeit on a budget and with little chance of any horrific, *Lawnmower Man*-esque side-effects. Originally a Bakelite update of the eighteenth-century stereoscope, *View-Masters* were manufactured by a stack of different companies, but it's the red-plastic GAF 'model J' that became a familiar acme of the Cream era.[1]

Pretty much any story that could be told in no more than seven scenes was depicted on a series of rotating, blister-packed cards (featuring such classics as *Popeye*, *Doctor Who: Castrovalva* and *The Seven Wonders of the World*).[2] The cards slotted into the viewer and, using back-projection to illuminate the slides, held up to the face for scrutiny. Different right and left eye-depth perception resulted in a stereoscopic 3D effect. (The *View-Master*'s unreliable trigger mechanism often resulted in slight misalignment of the two cells used to create the illusion, simulating the kind of imperfect vision normally associated with migraine or astigmatism.)

Stereoscopic images reached their peak popularity in the early '80s, when – for whatever reason – telly companies fell over one another to broadcast a bunch of badly made 3D films. Red-and-blue-lens cardboard glasses were pasted on the front of the *TV Times* (families too poor to pay for that week's issue were told to stick coloured sweet wrappers on their faces instead), and viewers were encouraged to take part in a number of 'experimental transmissions', i.e. would an entire nation sit in front of the TV looking like goons?

Still going strong today, long after the introduction of cine-projectors, home video and Laserdisc, *View-Master* is proof that, as long as there are kids with two eyes, there'll always be work for jobbing actors to recreate scenes from the court of King Arthur. There are also plenty of Web-based shops selling customised viewers and discs, just so that you can send your business clients a copy of those all-important sales figures in 3D. That should stop the annual market report from falling flat!

---

1 GAF? General Aniline & Film, which was – until US entry into the Second World War – a member of the IG Farben group of companies, main suppliers of poison gas to German concentration camps.

2 The photos didn't exist in isolation. Each of the seven frames had an accompanying line of text that would appear in a slot between the lenses. Not much room for editorialising on that *Seven Wonders of the World* set, then, eh?

Walkie-Talkies
Wireless communication

A hundred and one outdoor hobby books showed us kids how to make plastic-cup telephones, stretching a dozen feet of fraying string (or washing line) across the back garden into the den or treehouse. Like pre-infrared remote controls, though, they were deeply unsatisfactory and could cause one or more members of the family to trip up and drop a tray of Sunday tea and Jaffa Cakes.

Some kids were blessed with a slightly more sophisticated intercom system, being able to 'buzz' a close friend or neighbour if the wire could stretch between two open bedroom windows (or maybe that was only the sort of thing that happened in American TV movies). What we all really wanted was a set of walkie-talkies. Sadly, the only type that fell in the range of a child's purchasing power was the kind that had a transmitting range of about six feet and, frankly, we'd have been better off investing in a long cardboard tube to carry out covert conversations. Or just standing closer together.

At the top end of the scale, lucky girls could get pink walkie-talkies, with packaging that depicted their usefulness for gossiping.[1] Boys could get camouflaged varieties or something badged up NYPD style in the time-honoured tradition (plus, every TV cop show from *CHiPs* to *Columbo* produced a tie-in version), although the sound quality usually made any conversation sound like a Dalek playing the bagpipes.

The holy grail, however, was the heavy-duty long-range walkie-talkie that came inside a full 'spy kit' attaché case set, nestling in Styrofoam alongside a mini camera, a Luger complete with twist-on silencer and plastic handcuffs. Especially desirable was the kind that could transmit Morse code and had different channels, frequencies and so on.

The '80s, however, brought the CB radio revolution, with talk of 'smokeys', 'rubber ducks' and '10-4 good buddy', and the bulky, blue Ever Ready-guzzling walkie-talkie fell out of fashion. Kids nowadays are far more likely to have Internet-ready mobile phones and Bluetooth headsets than some crackly old box of plastic crap. Thankfully, the walkie-talkie lives on as the preserve of lowly TV-studio production-floor team members – probably the only people left in the world who still get a thrill from saying 'over'.[2]

See also *Johnny Seven, Action Man, Sonic Ear*

Born	1978-ish
Batteries	
Players	
Breakage	
Ads	
Envy	
eBayability	
Overall satisfaction	

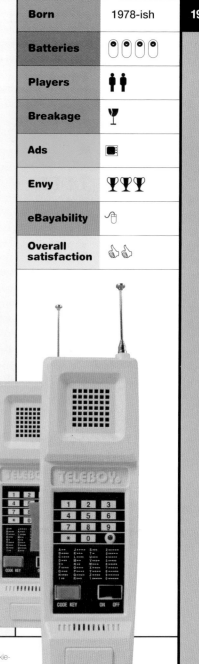

---

1 Lonely, introverted girls could ask Father Christmas for MB's *Electronic Dream Phone* instead. This fun game about dating, chitchat and boys would keep you guessing until you worked out who your secret admirer was. Ring ring! It's for you. Who is it? Nobody. No-one likes you. Start putting out a bit more. Boys like that.

2 Other people you will see using walkie-talkies: staff at bargain-basement clothes shop for grannies, Peacocks; canal-boat holiday-makers stuck either end of a bloody big barge; oh, and the police, naturally.

War of the Daleks
Space ludo with Skaro-centric baddies

Born	1975
Batteries	None
Players	🧍🧍🧍🧍
Breakage	🍷🍷🍷
Ads	▣
Envy	🏆🏆🏆🏆
eBayability	🖱🖱
Overall satisfaction	👍👍👍

See also *Haunted House, Dr Who TARDIS, Stay Alive!*

Arguably the Cream era's most cumbersome feat of paper-and-plastic toy engineering, Strawberry Fayre's *War of the Daleks* was played on a hollow card box-cum-board of roughly the same thickness as the average upholstered sofa cushion. All the better for hiding behind, we feel contractually obliged to add. Featuring Doctor Who's most famous enemies and yet no sign of the venerable Time Lord himself, it relied wholly on the enduring appeal of Davros's tin-plated creations to shift units. Which, in 1975, would've pleased Terry Nation's agent no end.

The game itself involved moving card figures of a nondescript early '70s comic-strip man around a circular playing area and trying to get to the centre while avoiding the Daleks.[1] With nary a staircase in sight to impede their progress, the metal meanies themselves were surprisingly faithful plastic renditions[2] (in non-canonical silver/red and gold/blue colour schemes) that stood a good three-quarters of an inch tall and were inserted into grooved tracks cut into the board. When the even taller pale-blue 'control centre' in the middle of the game was rotated, the card disc underpinning the concentric slots also spun round, causing the Daleks to 'patrol' randomly around the board and subsequently *EX-TER-MIN-ATE!* hapless players (by touching them).

If your man successfully navigated this waltz of death and made it to the centre, he could destroy the control centre simply by lifting it up, although doing so displaced four panels. Three of these bore illustrations of bloody big explosions, but the fourth deployed a hitherto unknown King Dalek, who could invalidate the entire game.

Despite (or perhaps because of) its ludicrous bulkiness, *War of the Daleks* was massively popular, but most of the sets that now find their way into second-hand shops are invariably missing the odd Dalek or two, not to mention the all-important King Dalek panel, which has often thoughtfully been replaced by a child's felt-tip drawing on a flimsy piece of lined paper.

A couple of years later came a straightforward *Doctor Who* game from the same company, which, despite boasting a handful of cut-out Tom Bakers and a plastic TARDIS, was an extremely boring and slow-moving affair. Insert your own joke about similarities with the Sylvester McCoy TV era here.

1 We're sad to report that there was no option to play on the side of the Daleks themselves. The fact that every Cream-era kid tried to work out a way to do so speaks volumes about the popularity of these monstrous mutants (or the bloodthirstiness of youth).

2 Which is more than can be said for the artist's impression on the box. Here, the malevolent pepperpots have been painted with air-horn eyestalks and – blasphemy, blasphemy! – laser bolts coming out of their sucker arms.

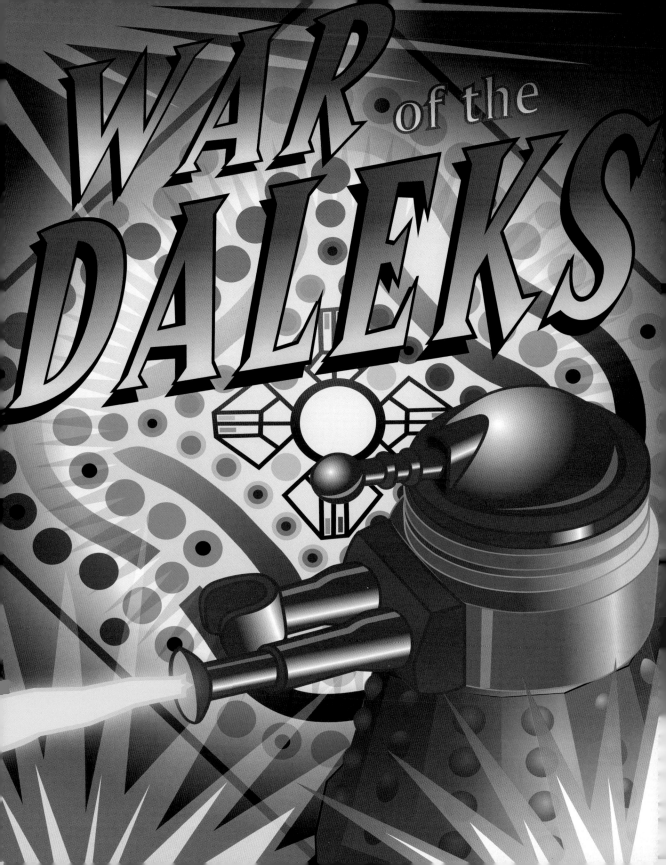

Weebles
Does my bum look big in this?

Born	1970
Batteries	None
Players	👤
Breakage	🍷
Ads	▪️▪️▪️
Envy	🏆🏆
eBayability	🛷🛷
Overall satisfaction	👍👍

See also *Whimsies, Big Yellow Teapot, Spacehopper*

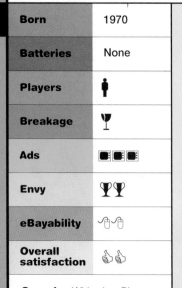

Sporting that 'Billy Bunter as played by Brian Glover in a wig' look to a man (and woman, and child), Airfix *Weebles* were the egg-sized shellac-like cousins of the inflatable 'bop-bag'. Chortling ovoid characters with bulky rump regions, they came to dominate the pre-school toy market in days before fat was a feminist issue. The classic Cream-era *Weeble* was a pug-ugly, smug-grinned, pink-faced buffoon and yet was also blessed with one of the all-time most memorable catchphrases ever.[1]

The initial batches of *Weebles*, however, were simply uniform smooth plastic castings, distinguishable only by a see-through sticker of bodily features attached to the outside. When it became obvious that the stickers were easily shed and wont to unpeel of their own accord, the more familiar moulded plastic, pissholes-for-eyes *Weeble* was introduced.

Initially available only in regular 'family' varieties, the humble *Weeble* race soon proliferated to incorporate various animals, characters from fiction and even the cast of *Sesame Street*. Similarly, their multitudinous playsets started out as simple houses and parks (which included a series of *Weeble* slides, seesaws and roundabouts) and progressed to such unlikely settings as a haunted house featuring a witch, a glow-in-the-dark ghost and, rather disturbingly, two terrified children.

Top dog, though, was *Superweeble*, a figure that could be transformed into a mild-mannered ice-cream man at the flick of a switch, and the *Tumblin' Weebles*, which were weighted at both ends to great Mexican jumping-bean-like acrobatic effect.

The legions of less successful imitators included *Shufflies*, which made their way around tracks with the aid of heavy ball-bearings embedded in their undersides, and the *Good Eggs*, essentially *Weebles* with limbs (and without the wobbling-but-not-falling-down quality).

Best of all, as if anyone was in doubt of their supremacy, *Weebles* made for excellent gigantic replacements for *Subbuteo* players, particularly if you wanted to re-enact your favourite moment from *It's a Knockout*.

---

1 So '*Weebles* wobble but they don't fall down' do they? If ever there was an irresistible challenge to the ingenuity of the pre-teen only child, this was it. The only solution we recall – beyond the unsporting use of *Plasticine* or outright weeblicide – was to place the victims on the *Weeble* roundabout and spin it too fast. They might not fall *down*, but the little buggers certainly fell *off*...

Whimsies
Miniature porcelain menagerie

Not strictly the sort of present any right-thinking kid would write off to Santa for, *Whimsies* were cheap (only a few decimal pence in the halcyon days of childhood), twee (glazed pottery hedgehogs and corgis – puh-lease!) and ubiquitous (hands up who didn't own one – not so fast at the back there, Collins!). However, they maintained a stable and moderate popularity because they were, above all else, collectable. And there are two unassailable truths about anything kids start to collect (Panini stickers, comics, *Star Wars* figures): one, it's almost impossible to complete a collection; two, kids will spend all their pocket money trying to prove otherwise.

Facts not taken too lightly by George Wade Pottery, which, following a huge drop in the demand for industrial ceramics, decided to reintroduce its retail line of pre-War animal figurines in 1953 (and again in 1971). The newly boxed fauna proved to be a far larger success than even Wade could have imagined. *Whimsies*, as they were called, were a damned good way for parents to bribe their offspring to stop fighting/be quiet on a long car journey/visit to the dentist. They could also be presented in their own display case (the germ, there, of a thousand commemorative-plate collections). However, we find it especially ironic that, while encouraging a generation to invest their entire prepubescent income in such (literally) hollow property, it was Wade that attracted kids to the delights of banking as they approached adolescence. For when Griffin was offering dictionaries and sports bags over at the Midland,[1] Nat West responded with a set of collectable porcelain pigs, which themselves were simply overgrown *Whimsies* with a splash more personality.[2]

With these giant freebies on offer in the open market, the *Whimsie* (*Whimsey*?) currency stalled. Wade did deals with PG Tips and Christmas-cracker companies to give their unwanted animals a home. Further 'series' were introduced to reignite the collector's ardour (resulting in ridiculous inequalities of scale – in Whimsieland, a hedgehog is as big as an elephant).

The company survives to this day, producing porcelain figures to commemorate events of national importance. Which is why we're delighted to note the (relatively) recent addition of the England World Cup 2006 Wayne Rooney bulldog. It doesn't look anything like him.

Born	1953
Batteries	None
Players	👤
Breakage	🍷
Ads	▪️▪️
Envy	🏆🏆🏆
eBayability	🖱️🖱️🖱️
Overall satisfaction	👍👍👍

See also Chic-a-boo, My Little Pony, Boglins

1 The relative ease with which these goodies could be obtained (by opening a Midland bank account with £10) led to the great Griffin Savers bag plague of 1982, where school cloakrooms and corridors would be literally carpeted with the things. Such was the ubiquity of identical sports bags at the time, it was commonplace to return home, open yours and find someone else's rough books and PE kit inside.
2 Fact! In the early '80s, Nat West's family of 'beautiful porcelain pigs' were manufactured exclusively by Wade. The idea was that kids would fall in love with the pigs, which in turn would encourage them to save money. The more they saved, the more members of the pig family they could earn. Choose from: Baby Woody, Maxwell, Annabel, Lady Hillary, Sir Nathaniel Westminster and Cousin Wesley. Note that Lady Hillary cannot be Sir Nathaniel's wife (as, according to the honorific order of knighthood, Hillary must be her surname). Saucy bitch!

Yahtzee
No great shakes

Born	1956
Batteries	None
Players	👤👤
Breakage	🍷🍷
Ads	▪️▪️
Envy	🏆🏆
eBayability	🖱️
Overall satisfaction	👍👍

See also Sorry!, Backgammon, Othello

The history of games is a winding Victorian back street scattered with dice. Take a stroll through Limehouse this fine, fog-blighted night and cast your eyes over the human remains that foment in the gutter. There's the drunken, snaggle-toothed harridan crowing over a round of *Hazard* (that's craps in the modern parlance). They'll be playing that in the famous rooms of St James's before the year is out. Fast-forward a century or so and you'll see, down by the docks, a couple of dagos holding the jolly jack-tars to ransom in a game of *Perudo* (or liar's dice). Further forward still in time, the renaissance wags are playing *Farkel*, the Guernsey fisherman bring *Canoga* and our returning WWII heroes pass the long hours *Passing the Pigs*. Ah, the noble dice game. Steeped in folk history and colourful, evocative chronicles from Ye Olde Albion.

So what did we get when our turn came to have a throw? What noble dice game defined the Cream era? Bloody *Yahtzee*, that's what. Bloody *Yahtzee*, the devil's own dice game. Bloody *Yahtzee*, invented by a cosy bloody Canadian family on their cosy bloody yacht (of all places!)[1] to play at cosy bloody dinner parties with their mates from the cosy bloody boating coterie.[2]

So goes the official story, anyway. History rewritten by the victors, we suspect, to ease the game into the fondue and Frascati homes of '50s America (and from thence to the rest of the world in less time than it takes to roll a full house – ooh, you've not got one of those! Quick, write it down!). A bit of bourgeois pandering never did a good game any harm. Who'd've picked up the damn dice cup if they thought it'd once been shaken by a Spanish-speaking street urchin? Not us, that's for sure.

Once Milton Bradley bought up the rights in the early '70s there was no stopping *Yahtzee*. It rolled into Yuletide living rooms with a fake baize box-liner, pads, pencils, and poker scores. Cut to the scene of Dad digging out his reading glasses to pore over the rules before the Queen's speech. They could be summed up thus: roll five dice, write down what you got, do it again. There were, of course, many variations – *Casino Yahtzee*, *Challenge Yahtzee*, *Word Yahtzee*, *Jackpot Yahtzee* – all intended to be played with a furrowed brow and a nice glass of sherry. What a way to ruin a nice glass of sherry.

---

1 Typical Canadians, mind, pointlessly updating a simple game into something louder and more annoying. If you want to play a dice game, you just need dice. You don't need some contrived scoring system and a catchword to yell out just to piss off everyone else. We Brits already invented bingo for that. Oh, and don't even get us started on what they did to hockey. **2** Try saying that sentence five times fast after a few beers. It took us three pints just to write it.

Zoids
Warring biomechanoids

Supposedly hailing from some far and distant planet, depending on who you believe,[1] *Zoids* were the part-insectoid, part-dinosaur-skeleton-like vehicles used for transport by small gold androids that resided in their cockpit (i.e. head). The average *Zoid* toy was clockwork-powered and utilised a snap-together self-assembly method, which – thanks to the sparse and wordless instructions – was a task that made even the construction of an elaborate *LEGO* play set seem like a relaxing bit of thumb-twiddling.

When eventually they were assembled to some degree of completion, *Zoids* had a frustrating habit of doing their 'walking' schtick for a few steps only before their peculiar centre of gravity caused them to topple over. Wind-up *Zoids* came in Bird, Elephant, Spider and Frog flavours at first and there was, it must be admitted, some creepy-crawly pleasure in setting them all off in 'battle' against one another. (Inter-species war decreed that loyalty to either red or blue *Zoid* factions be announced before hostilities broke out.) A far more impressive addition to the range, however, was the battery-powered overlord, Giant Zrk, a hefty and heavy brontosaurus-like contraption that thundered along in an imposing fashion. Later oppos, such as Redhorn the Terrible and Mighty Zoidzilla, were even more exciting, with flashing red lights for eyes and deadly looking weaponry.

For a time, *Zoids* enjoyed considerable popularity, even starring in their own Marvel UK comic. Even today, the *Zoid* diaspora proliferates across the Earth, dominating Japanese anime films, Internet role-playing games and further toy ranges, amassing ridiculous three-letter acronyms (TLAs) for each new generation.

So, if you're anything like the staff of TV Cream Towers, who can tell an OER from an OJR or an NBZ from a CBZ,[2] the chances are you are also a SWM ISO LTR IRL.[3] In which case, you may be interested in the following factoid: the *Zoids* comic was written by Grant Morrison, the millionaire wunderkind of the comics world (most famous for the biggest-ever-selling graphic novel and Batman caper, *Arkham Asylum*). It was one of his first professional commissions, and he made the whole thing into a hugely complicated allegory about the Cold War. Thanks, Grant. Any chance of a loan 'til we can cash this giro?

Born	1983
Batteries	
Players	
Breakage	
Ads	
Envy	
eBayability	
Overall satisfaction	

See also
Transformers,
Terrahawks Action
Zeroid,
Star Wars

---

1 Woah! We're going to leave that particular nest of vipers undisturbed, but it's no exaggeration to say there are as many different and fabulously complicated explanations for the *Zoids'* origins as there are actual *Zoids*. In the UK, the *Spiderman and Zoids* comic was about as close as we got to a definitive back-story.

2 Original European Release; Original Japanese Release; Neo-Blox *Zoids*; Custom Blox *Zoids*.

3 Single White Male; In Search Of; Long-Term Relationships; In Real Life.

ZX Spectrum
Programmable proto-Playstation

Born	1982
Batteries	Mains
Players	🧍
Breakage	🏆
Ads	▪️▪️▪️
Envy	🏆🏆🏆🏆🏆
eBayability	🖱️🖱️
Overall satisfaction	👍👍👍👍👍

See also *Commodore 64, Binatone TV Master, Stylophone*

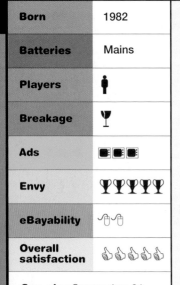

It is no exaggeration to say that the British home-computer market was created almost entirely by Sir Clive Sinclair. This bearded, bookish boffin brought the microchip to the masses, making a splash in the electronics industry by successfully marketing the first pocket calculator. By 1981, he'd sold several hundred thousand Sinclair computers that were nominally more sophisticated. With the introduction of the *Spectrum* 16K personal computer a year later, however, he finally hit paydirt.[1]

Inspiring the first generation of amateur programmers, the *ZX Spectrum* was quickly appropriated by teens as a glorified games console. Widespread ownership cracked open opportunities in the software, peripherals and specialist magazine industries and brought popular arcade classics into the living room. Enthusiasts and early adopters suffered from ropey British engineering and after-sales service, but for those of us who bought from the catalogues, the choice was astounding (just check out any of the million books and websites devoted to the history of home computers). The Kempston joystick, Prestel modem, Centronics RS-232 interface, ZX Printer and Microdrive, Cheetah SpecDrum and Currah Microspeech were just some of the hardware devices on offer.

The *Spectrum* was not without its detractors, though. Those lazy, comedy, shared-

---

1 The *Spectrum* name refers to the computer's ability to display colour, and that 16K refers to the total amount of on-board ('read access') memory available.

That's less than your average Web graphic requires. Even notionally more powerful machines such as the *Acorn Electron* and *Atari VCS* failed to dent the *Speccy*'s dominance

experience memory-joggers in full, then: waiting half an hour for a cassette game to load up, only to have the computer crash at the last second; typing in transcribed lines of BASIC from the back of *Your Sinclair*, only to have the computer crash at the last second; beating a high-score only to accidentally yank out the joystick/expansion port/power cable and cause the computer to crash at the last second.

But, oh, the games – there were some cast-iron masterpieces knocked out for our rubber-keyed friend: *Jetpac*, *Manic Miner*, *The Hobbit*, *Alchemist*, *Skool Daze*, *Chuckie Egg*, *Elite*, *Rommel's Revenge*, *Football Manager*, *Mugsy*, *Hyper Sports* – every single man jack of them tape-to-taped on to Memorex C90s and swapped in classrooms the nation over. Random acts of piracy in a battle for bigger and better games that ultimately bankrupted some of the software publishing 'houses' who'd dared to believe their own hype.[2]

The fiercely competitive American triumvirate of Apple/Microsoft/IBM killed off the inept British micro business, after which only dedicated 'consoles' appeared in the shops (the shrewder games companies had already spotted this niche market and jumped ship early). However, where the limited *ZX Spectrum* scored over your *Megadrives* and *Nintendos* is that they at least allowed the owner to learn something about computing – the layout of the QWERTY keyboard at the very least. All those late-night machine-code sessions laid the foundations for understanding the workings of PC operating systems, interfaces and networks, without which we would not have the Internet, the World Wide Web or, indeed, books based on blogs published on it.

And that, dear reader, is a very good thing.

ZX Spectrum games
Loads of fun

Sega Megadrive
'Sole trader

---

2 Particularly Liverpool-based Imagine, whose hubris-accelerated demise was filmed during the making of 1984 BBC TV documentary *Commercial Breaks*. Their budget-busting 'megagame' *Bandersnatch* was the ultimate prick-tease for addicts – heavily advertised yet never actually released.

About the author

Steve Berry was born in 1971 and was raised in Huyton, Liverpool (until 1976, when he moved to Lancashire, and then in 1978 to America for a bit). Still unsettled, he has yet to find his true vocation in the media, having been employed variously in television, radio, newspapers, magazines and the Web. He has also worked at a hospital, a Crown Court, an investment bank, a haulage company, a German university and Directory Enquiries. In 2005 he played the part of 'robot butler' in a Dr Who audio adventure.

Since 1998, he has been one of the contributors to TV Cream, www.tv.cream.org, Britain's favourite online nostalgia destination. Association with the site has led to his many appearances on 'remember when'-style programmes for TV and radio – some of which have lasted as long as ten seconds.

He currently lives in Hertfordshire with a wife (his own), a cat (rescued) and a spare room full of toys and games. This is his first book.